PRAISE FOR PROPHETIC WISDOM

Not many books I'm aware of deal in a constructive way with the issue of how the believer should respond to the prophetic word. Graham Cooke beautifully addresses the prophetic impact of the Scriptures themselves as they were received by the biblical authors and provides biblically sound instruction on how to receive and lay hold of the prophetic word spoken through prophetic people today. Even better, he reveals the incredible, unfathomable love of the Father while speaking into the nature of true discipleship. Prophetic words find fulfillment in the life of one who has become Christ-like! Destinies are made in this way and ministries are born and thrive. This book is filled with "zingers," bits of concentrated prophetic wisdom compressed into nourishing pills to be washed down with the water of the Spirit to enrich our lives.

R. Loren Sandford
Author of *Understanding Prophetic People, Purifying the Prophetic*, and *Renewal for the Wounded Warrior*

Graham has been part of The Mission's culture and development since 1998. Along with others that the Lord has brought to us, he has played a key role in us changing from a traditional church to a vibrant Kingdom community. We have developed from a church that loves prophecy to a prophetic community that makes decisions in the light of what the Lord has spoken to us and over us. Not only has he prophetically spoken the will of God over us, but he has actively worked with the leadership to cultivate our response and help to orchestrate our progress into a place of critical obedience. I heartily recommend *Prophetic Wisdom* to any individual, church or leadership team that seeks to understand the process of walking out their prophetic future in the here and now.

David Crone
Senior Team Leader
The Mission, Vacaville CA

Graham writes that our spirituality is not earthbound but heavenly, meaning that things of this realm can't define us — only God can truly tell us who we are. We are a prophetic people because we live out of His speaking. This book helps us to redefine the prophetic *from* a gift *to* a dimension or an operating system for life. He also ties the character of Christ to our prophetic operations. Every believer is called to the prophetic, and Graham Cooke does an outstanding job helping the body of Christ find out what that means and how it is applied in everyday life.

Scott Webster
Congress WBN

Prophetic Wisdom is classic Cooke at its best. As Graham provides the process of training you to be a mentor, in actuality you find you are being mentored yourself. As you sit and read *Prophetic Wisdom* you feel as though Graham is sitting across from you and mentoring you personally. Each page provides you with his years of experiential wisdom that become your teacher and a guide on your prophetic journey. This book becomes a valuable map in the hands of every believer who wishes to traverse the difficult questions and misconceptions concerning the prophetic. Graham provides his readers with practical inventory checklists that become a compass to point the way in their personal development for their prophetic journeys. Not only will Graham's book equip you; it will equip you to help others in realizing their prophetic destinies.

Dena McClure
Dena McClure Ministries
Leadership Team at The Mission

The concepts captured in *Prophetic Wisdom* have not only transformed how I view prophecy, but also served as a catalyst for closing the gap between my own prophetic words and their ultimate fulfillment. Graham has given us priceless wisdom keys that unlock prophetic potential and accelerate eternal outcomes.

Dan McCollam
Founder of *Sounds of the Nations* and the
Institute for Worship Arts Resources (iWAR)

Graham Cooke has learned the secret of walking in the promises and anointing of God's Word. By trusting in His nature, integrity and character, we can know God's guaranteed favor, enabling us to confidently respond well, no matter what confronts us. Graham pens, "Love God outrageously and we will discover what it means to be the Beloved." Herein lies the focus and anointing for our prophetic destiny. Embracing God's vision for our lives is the litmus test for intimacy with Him, and proves the accuracy of knowing His voice—allowing God alone to define our identity and calling. Graham's warm and compassionate insight will inspire you to courageously move forward and embrace God's prophetic call over your life!

Francis Anfuso
The Rock of Roseville, Roseville CA

For the last decade, Graham Cooke has been both a mentor and dear friend to me. His life, teaching and writing have had a profound impact on the way I think about God and His Kingdom. Graham's most recent book, *Prophetic Wisdom*, carries both insight and impartation that will empower you to realize the intended benefit of wisdom and prophecy in your life. I highly recommend it to those who are committed to partner with God in the process of transformation—both personal and corporate!

Bob Book
Worship and Arts
The Mission, Vacaville CA

In classic Graham Cooke style, the prophetic function is set forth with profound insight and on-line zingers that go to the heart like a sharp arrow from a well-strung bow. With Graham, you get words from a life chiseled by conversations spent with God that bring to life his Father-heart. In this new book, Graham explains how Scripture must become a prophetic "now" word and how to receive it as such. He calls for our responsibility in the prophetic process and the profound way God's promises create accelerated opportunity through the Holy Spirit. With Graham, I always receive breakthrough.

Bob L. Phillips
Senior Leader of Encourager Church
Father of In His Presence Network

"The chief service of a prophet is not to rebuke sin, nor instruct in virtue; it is to give the world a radiant idea of God."   *–John Watson*

When I read this quote from John Watson, I think of Graham Cooke. Between the lines of everything Graham has spoken or written is a radiant idea of God. My first encounters listening to Graham left me thinking, "This sounds too good to be true." I have now come to realize that if it sounds too good to be true, it must be God. Prepare yourself for a radiant encounter with God!

Curt Klein
Overseer, Potter's House School of the Supernatural
The Mission, Vacaville, CA

PROPHETIC WISDOM

BY GRAHAM COOKE

WALKING IN THE INTENTIONALITY OF GOD

THE PROMISES OF GOD AND OUR DEVELOPMENT

PROPHECY ELIMINATES NEGATIVITY

Brilliant
BOOK HOUSE

www.BrilliantBookHouse.com

Prophetic Wisdom is the third of six books in the *Prophetic Equipping Series*.

Brilliant Book House LLC
6391 Leisure Town Road
Vacaville, CA 95687
U.S.A.
www.BrilliantBookHouse.com

Unless otherwise indicated, Scripture quotations are taken from the NEW AMERICAN STANDARD BIBLE, © 1960, 1962, 1963, 1968, 1971, 1972, 1973, 1975, 1977, 1995 by The Lockman Foundation. Used by permission.

Requests for information should be addressed to:

Graham Cooke

E-mail: office@grahamcooke.com

ISBN: 978-1-934771-14-3

Printed in the United States of America

Cover by Natalie Phillips with the central image originally by Jeff Zumwalt

DEDICATION

I dedicate this book to Graham Perrins, one of my most profound mentors in the prophetic realm. For years I used to make a round-trip journey of 240 miles from my home to his, one evening a month, to sit in on a teaching/dialogue session on the prophetic.

He led a community of prophetic people in Cardiff, UK, who were all committed to prophecy in all its forms. I loved Graham's incredible teaching, his incisive comments and questions. He passed on to me his love of scripture. To this day, I read it aloud to the Lord just for the sheer pleasure.

He taught me to study the Word, to trace through the generations the footsteps of God's intention. He made me aware that I stood in a long line of prophets stretching back to Moses. He had a great sense of time and timing. He taught me how to become a son of Issachar, who understood times and seasons.

In terms of participation in those classes, I was definitely his worst student. Some would have excellent questions; others were full of their own observations. Dialogue time was usually lively and rambunctious… but not for me. I was always mesmerized by what I was learning. I don't think I ever spoke in those sessions, in five years.

Each month I kept my head down, wrote copious notes, and then studied them relentlessly. I still read those notes a quarter of a century later. I wove them into my messages and my books.

Apart from listening to Graham, I also watched him as he taught. I noted how he spoke, how he engaged people. I saw his patience to facilitate our development. Some teachers have no patience and can only create clones. Graham wanted real sons in the faith.

I observed his prophetic creativity in that community as they produced drama, musicals and songs. I'm doing the same in my own events: writing scripts, producing stage sets… creating an atmosphere and an environment for things to happen.

More than anything, I appreciated Graham's love of solitude, meditation and mystery, the need to spend time aside in the Presence of God, and the desire for reflection and deep thought. He never chased public ministry and the big platforms. He seemed to seek relevance in a different way.

Graham Perrins left an indelible mark on my heart. I hope that in some small way I can repay him by continuing in the prophetic legacy that was always his passion.

ACKNOWLEDGEMENTS

I assign brilliance to all my team at Brilliant Book House!

Matt, who creates the graphics for all our resources. I appreciate his passion and diligence and the way he sets his heart to learn new things.

Kellie, our customer contact beauty. Kind, generous, funny and a lover of people, she is brilliant as our front-of-house face for our loyal fan base. She talks to huge numbers of people and makes sure that our materials get to all the designated places.

Jenny types the manuscripts as well as being my assistant. A voracious worker with a ready smile—she is a bonnie lass!

Mark and Sophie, team leaders who oversee the whole shebang with unflagging commitment, brilliant sense of humor and a dedicated hunger for excellence.

They are all committed to the work of Reaching Christians for Christ.

Contents

INVOCATION

Father,

Thank you for teaching us to see everyone and everything through the eyes of your goodness. It is such a delightful discipline to learn. You make every day, every occasion, interesting and fascinating. Your joy and loving-kindness teach us how to run and not be weary; walk, and not faint.

To know you is to trust you. To trust is to rest in your great heart for us; to be still and content in where we are in you, knowing that when it is time to move forward, you will apply the gentle pressure of your heart to ours. You create longing and desire for more. When they show up, it's time to go. Until then, we can stay, enjoy and celebrate all that you are in our lives.

Wisdom knows when to abide and when to press in. Grant us wisdom.

Amen.

INTRODUCTION

"And it shall come to pass afterward that I will pour out My Spirit on all flesh; your sons and daughters shall prophesy, your old men will dream dreams, your young men will see visions. And also on My menservants and My maidservants I will pour out My Spirit in those days" (Joel 2:28-29)

THE WORLD CHANGED THE DAY the Holy Spirit fell on Jesus' remaining disciples in that upper room in Jerusalem. The Spirit of God, reserved in the Old Testament for a select few, was now placed on anyone who sought and loved Christ. With that outpouring came the gifts of the Spirit. While once only a few could prophesy, today everyone can.

I have been in prophetic ministry since 1974. I began prophesying the year before. That's more than thirty years of sharing the love God has placed in my heart. Amazingly, I'm still learning—and I never want to stop. Every year, I understand something new about God and His ways. He never ceases to intrigue me.

In 1994, my book *Developing Your Prophetic Gifting* was first published. It has been a greater success than I could have ever imagined. Almost half a million copies have been sold. But I've come a long way since then. For one thing, I have taught countless prophetic schools during that time. As I work with students and emerging prophetic voices, I have had my own gift shaped and honed. *"Iron sharpens iron, so one man sharpens another,"* as it says in Proverbs 27:17. The people I have met have pushed me further into the things of the prophetic. They have challenged me to find fresh ways of equipping, explaining, and encouraging.

In 2004, I felt the Lord prompt me to expand *Developing Your Prophetic Gifting*, adding the material I have taught in my schools over the past ten years. This book is the third of several manuals that will more fully equip people longing to speak the words of God to those around them.

Together, we will study the practical elements of hearing God, of moving in the Spirit, of knowing God's nature and of representing His heart to someone else. We will learn how to be grounded in the love, grace and rhythm of God. It's my prayer that these books will give you something fresh about who God wants to be for you. As you read the principles and illustrations within, I pray that you will be excited and inspired to venture further into what God has for you.

Prophecy comes when we have a burden to encourage and bless the people around us. There is no magic formula to prophesying; it all depends on our love for God. When we love Him fully, that love should spill over onto the people around us. Prophecy is simply encouraging, exhorting and comforting people by tuning them into what God has for them. In every church in the world, there are people who need that life-giving word from God. These aren't just the individuals who are obviously struggling; some appear to have everything together. But God knows what's really going on.

Everyone could benefit from a prophetic word, even those for whom everything is soaring. I love to prophesy over people who are doing really well. If we can target those people and increase their faith at a critical time, they can fly even higher in the things of the Spirit.

After the prophecy comes the process: a series of steps that take us from where we are now to where the Lord wants us to go next. God is present–future in the landscape of our lives, not present–past. He has wonderfully dealt with our past in Christ on the Cross.

Process is the journey of trust. Most people have developed situational trust. We trust God for things, events, situations, provisions and circumstances. Our language reflects that! However, everything that God does in our lives is for relational development and ongoing experiences of Him in our hearts. He is not specifically situational. He seeks to establish trust as a lifestyle, an affair of the heart.

He allows in His wisdom what He could easily prevent by His power. He is the author and the finisher of our faith.

Faith is relational; it works by love. It begins and ends in our relationship with Jesus. Our part is to pay attention to His nature. Prophetic ministry speaks of what God is authoring in each of us. We are the echo of God—we speak the same language from the same heart.

When you hear a New Testament prophet, you should not hear a pre-Calvary voice, but a post-resurrection anointing. It is a voice that both introduces you to your favor and inheritance in Christ and prepares you to overcome the personal obstacles to fullness and abundance.

I believe strongly that the more encouraging, exhorting and comforting prophecy we have — as opposed to the heavy-handed directive words that dispatch people to difficult mission fields and so on, the better our churches will be. Blessing and encouragement stir up anointing. The more of this kind of prophecy we can have in church, the less we will need intensive, time-consuming, pastoral care. People will actually be touched by God and come into the things of the Spirit themselves. Individuals will realize that, yes, they are loved personally by God. That kind of revelation will stoke up their faith in ways a counseling session never could.

I know I need that kind of encouragement every day from the Holy Spirit. I can't remember the last time I asked Him to encourage me and He didn't. He may not speak it out immediately, but He always meets me at the point of my greatest need. That's just who the Holy Spirit is and what He loves to do.

This book can help you go further in the prophetic than you may have ever dreamed. After all, *"Things which eye has not seen and ear has not heard, and which have not entered the heart of man, all that God has prepared for those who love Him."* (1 Corinthians 2:9)

Prophetic Wisdom is divided into three chapters, or modules: *Walking in the Intentionality of God, The Promises of God and Our Development,* and *Prophecy Eliminates Negativity.* These modules are not meant to be read in a day or a week; instead, I encourage you to take your time going through each, reading them until you understand the themes and thoughts they contain. Furthermore, don't neglect the exercises, case studies, and Bible readings included at the end of each chapter—they are valuable practice tools, which will take the lessons taught and put them into practice in your life. These exercises are meant to stretch and grow you to become more like Jesus.

Blessings on your journey into the prophetic!

Graham Cooke.

MODULE ONE

WALKING IN THE
INTENTIONALITY OF GOD

4

Walking in the Intentionality of God

I N MINISTRY, ONE GETS USED to being asked the same questions over and over. People all over the world have similar wonderings, dreams, fears and concerns when it comes to walking with God. But there is one question that I am asked more than any other. In fact, I hear it so often that I wish I had ten bucks for every time I've answered it: "What is the will of God?" If I had been paid every time someone asked me that question, I would be rich enough to never work again! "What is the will of God? What is God saying about this? I don't know what God wants me to do." These are questions that seem to roll around the minds of countless Christians.

The answer to that question is very simple: God always wants us to move forward. It's natural to pray and commit things to Him; this is an important part of our relationship with Him. Yet we must learn how He says yes, no, or wait.

These are relational issues. Guidance is the by-product of a right relationship with God, assuming that we are learning the lessons of abiding, which are: to stay, be still, and remain, consciously indwelling and being a partaker of Christ within. A simple turning and yielding of our hearts throughout the day. Remaining joyful, thankful. Seeing all of life through the eyes of God's goodness. Basking in His love, living every day under His smile. A much-loved child learning to become a confident, more mature son.

> Relationship is the key to knowing God's will

In the will of God, a right relationship is the key to moving forward. Everything in Christ is "yes and amen" (2 Corinthians 1:20). Therefore, the Lord does not have to speak all the time about everything. The will of God is first relational. As we abide, we become sensitive to His heart. He loves confidence.

As we move forward, we always have a green light — everything is yes! The Father takes responsibility for the light turning amber, wait; or red, meaning stop. Yes, no, and wait are the main directives. Yes is always priority.

Go until you hear no! There is no inertia in the Spirit. We are subjects of His great love; therefore, we make ourselves vulnerable to His goodness.

In relationship we become sensitized to the nature of God. It helps if we live in awe, wonder and astonishment. These are the beautiful attributes of beloved children. The nature of God is our most compelling adventure. His heart is a land worthy of exploration.

I love my story in God. In the hardest chapters I have seen beauty and extreme loving-kindness. I have been to hell and prospered because He held my hand. I have lost everything and thrived. I have been in the valley of shadow and lost all fear. I've been on the mountain, bathed in a light so strong I thought I would dissolve in happiness.

In the depths of humiliation and embarrassment, crushed by my own inadequacy and stupidity, He mined grace for me at a depth I hardly knew existed. Grace purified me by restoring me to holiness and leaving me awestruck with gratitude. In all those encounters, everything has been relational. It is the ongoing purpose of the Godhead. Relationships are the business of Heaven on earth: that we love one another as He has loved us.

The matter, therefore, of how much we are loved, is most vital. What if every day, every circumstance was cleverly designed to show us another glimpse of the Father's heart? Abiding empowers us to see. We always behold what we most look for in life.

Everything the Father does is relational first. Every application of His will and purpose is to make us in His image. We are learning how to grow up into all things in Christ.

Sometimes, God will say yes by not saying anything at all. He simply allows us to move forward. On other occasions, things are confirmed or witnessed by other people. Once in a while, we will get a prophetic word; we may not have been looking for one, but it confirms what we're doing. I've had many letters and phone calls from people who will tell me that they dreamed about me the night before and that I was doing something specific. Often, that dream will be God confirming His will for me. I wasn't seeking confirmation, but God was gracious enough to break in and let me know that I was doing okay.

God is a master at letting us know what His will is. We need to be aware of the times when He takes away our peace or allows us to be confused or uncertain. Perhaps we are sensing that this is not the right time to proceed. Maybe God wants something for us eventually, but not immediately. Maybe we need to be further prepared.

God absolutely loves us, and has ways of communicating these things to us. He will never let us walk in darkness. When we give ourselves to a full relationship with Him, His will becomes

> *There is no inertia in the Spirit*

crystal clear. We never have to ask for a word of guidance again. Instead, it will flow to us out of the largeness of His love for us.

"My people know My voice," God promised. We serve a God who is dedicated to seeing us get things right. In return, He wants us to be dedicated to seeking His face. He wants us to live in the sheer pleasure of waiting on Him. To ensure that we feel the delight of being in His presence, He has given us the Holy Spirit as an inheritance. We can be assured that God will always show up and talk to us. We can rely on Him, live in His rest and peace and adore His nature. We can be overwhelmed by our own insignificance and marvel at His greatness. We can be humbled by our weakness and captivated by His strength. We can live with an understanding of how weak and small we are, and be fascinated by the grace, sovereignty, power and majesty of the God we serve. Our present smallness cannot prevent us from entering the fullness of God — this is His will for us.

New Covenant, New Practice

In the Old Covenant, there was a prophetic concentration of the mind and will of the Lord upon a small number of people. The priests were allowed to wear the Ephod, a priestly breastplate that contained the Urim and Thummim which represented the lights and perfection of God. The Urim represented oracular brilliance and the Thummim was the emblem of complete truth. People could go to the priests to inquire of the Lord concerning a matter in which they needed prayer for direction. Alternatively, they could inquire in His temple in an act of worship and prayer.

Seeking the face of God was to present oneself before the priests, or personally in the temple, to make petition — literally, to desire a favorable audience with the Lord as Hannah did when praying for a child (1 Samuel 1:7-11) or David's experience in Psalm 27:4-8.

People could also inquire of the prophets. This was an acceptable practice in the Old Covenant. Prophets spoke from God to the people and also inquired of the Lord for the people. All prophets occupy a place of intercession and enjoy spending time in the presence of God not just for the sake of their ministry, but also as a personal place of relational adoration.

All of this activity comes to a place of closure in Christ. John the Baptist was the last of the Old Testament prophets who came to prepare a way for people to follow Jesus, who is the first of the New Covenant prophets. "He must increase, I must decrease," spoke John, signifying an end to Old Testament prophetic methodology.

Jesus came to do the Father's will — namely, to take away the first covenant in order to establish the second (Hebrews 10:9). The Holy Spirit also testifies to the New Covenant (10:15-18). The Old

| Abiding empowers our vision |

trust that He is with us. Now, we learn to believe that "God will never leave us or forsake us," and we establish a pattern of simple faith that "He is with us always."

God has not left us — just withdrawn from our feelings for the purpose of establishing trust and simple faith. It's a tough lesson initially, but also immensely rewarding.

Now I can enjoy my emotions in the Father but not be dependent on them as a way of life. My lifestyle is one of simple trust and joyful believing in a God of infinite goodness, grace, mercy and kindness. His love never fails.

Whether I am doing well or badly, He remains totally consistent in His nature toward me. In trust, I learn to be confident in who He is for me when all my attendant feelings are not working.

It is a key discipline to learn, and one that the Holy Spirit is so brilliant at teaching us.

Perhaps the simplest way to explain it is to say that manifestation is a time of *blessing*; hiddenness is a time of *building*. God desires to bring us through seasons of hiddenness because He wants us to learn the discipline of walking by the Spirit.

Manifestation takes place in our reality...

Developing an ongoing walk with God by the power of the Holy Spirit is a discipline. Practicing faith is a discipline, and hiddenness is God's way of establishing that discipline in our life. Once established, it prevents the enemy from invading our life and touching us, because regardless of our emotions, we know how to find the presence of God. We have a constant assurance of His presence and His commitment to us.

Understanding the fact that God is sometimes hidden and sometimes manifest grounds us in our faith and helps us to have a more consistent walk with Him. Whether it's a *good* day or a *bad* day, we will know how to live in the grace of God. Some days we will feel very close to God, and other days we won't, but it won't matter, because we will know that we can live, enjoying God's presence when we feel it, and enjoying living in our faith when we don't.

Hidden Wisdom

Hiddenness connects us with God's wisdom, and wisdom is the revelation of who God is and the internal recognition of how He likes to work in our lives. Faith depends upon one thing — our understanding of the nature of God. Faith which is grounded in a sure understanding of the nature of God and what He is like will never be short of things to believe for. We know what God is like, we know that He is faithful, that He'll never leave us or forsake us, that He's made provision for us and that God never changes.

...hiddenness takes place in His

Faith in the nature of God is what keeps us moving even when situations are against us. Because we know that God is faithful, when a situation seems bleak or even impossible, we know just enough to wait for Him to come to our aid: "I know You, Lord,

You're here somewhere. I'm just going to wait until You come or wait until You speak. I know You're doing something. I haven't figured out what it is yet, but I'm just going to wait because I *know* You."

Job's life was a textbook example of hiddenness and manifestation. It's no surprise, then, that the following statement can be found in the record of his life: *"Where then does wisdom come from? And where is the place of understanding? Thus it is hidden from the eyes of all living and concealed from the birds of the sky."* (Job 28:20-21)

Real wisdom is hidden from us until God reveals it. He often chooses to do that in His training ground of hiddenness. In hiddenness, God teaches us the wisdom of how to walk with Him, how to know Him, how to understand Him and how to live a life of reverent fear. David said, *"Behold, You desire truth in the innermost being, and in the hidden part You will make me know wisdom,"* (Psalm 51:6) because he understood that hiddenness and wisdom went together. Like-wise, Paul wrote, *"Yet we do speak wisdom among those who are mature; a wisdom, however, not of this age nor of the rulers of this age, who are passing away; but we speak God's wisdom in a mystery, the hidden wisdom which God predestined before the ages to our glory."* (1 Corinthians 2:6–7)

> *Manifestation is a time of blessing*

In times of manifestation, we cannot hear deep truth. If we do hear God speak while we are enjoying a season of His blessing, we often don't understand what He is saying. Times of manifestation are about experiencing God. They are about moving in a flow of body ministry — participating in the peace, joy and life of God.

Hiddenness is one of the most exciting disciplines that we can learn in the realm of the Spirit. When we learn how to access it and live in it, suddenly everything makes sense forever. Everything falls to us. All the things which come against us only enable us to go deeper into God, because we have learned the discipline of living in His presence. A man involved in hiddenness, looking for meaning, is a delight to the Lord. Isaiah understood God's ways, and all his attention was upon God and what He would do. Therefore, understanding hiddenness and manifestation will train us in how to determine the *windows of the soul* — those moments when we perceive what is happening in the spiritual realm.

I believe there is a wealth of revelation and understanding that God wants to pour into our spirit. Sometimes we become so weary of struggling through the Christian life because we don't know how to replenish ourselves in the Spirit. The discipline of hiddenness will enable you to recover, restore your soul, renew your mind, and refresh your spirit. For me, coming into that place of hid-

> *Hiddenness is a time of building*

denness has been one of my greatest joys and blessings, and one of the reasons why, to a degree, I've perfected the art of *bouncing back* in life. I know that I can defeat the devil by ignoring him, by retreating into my spirit and just doing business with God. Living in that place where God wants us to be, no matter what the enemy throws at us, will only makes us stronger. We come out of our hidden place with greater revelation than we had when we entered it. It is the key to the place of power and significance in the Spirit. You can learn more about this subject from the journal *"Hiddenness and Manifestation."*

Trusting and Being Trustworthy

"Trust in the LORD *with all your heart and do not lean on your own understanding. In all your ways acknowledge Him, and He will make your paths straight."* (Proverbs 3:5-6)

The Holy Spirit is teaching us two things in life: firstly, how to trust the Lord, and secondly, how to be trustworthy ourselves.

Firstly then, we are learning that every situation is about trust. Because we are in Jesus and filled with the Holy Spirit, it is our normal, instinctive, intuitive desire and response to want to trust the Lord.

It is vital that we take time to acknowledge the Lord in all of life's events, prior to making decisions. This cannot just be a cursory look at who He is for us. It must at least be in line with the severity of our circumstances. Acknowledgement is a key part of finding and living in the will of God for each set of circumstances. Any decision made without the due process of acknowledgement and thanksgiving, may well prove to be worthless. God must be acknowledged in every situation in a thorough manner before the Holy Spirit. Everything the Father does in our lives is for the purpose primarily of building a relationship with us. Heaven works on a relational paradigm into which the Lord introduces service, ministry, gift and function. His prime purpose is love, oneness and friendship.

> In manifestation, we have great experiences

The world works on a functional paradigm where the primary purpose is task oriented, purpose driven toward job completion. In the world, we primarily function together and have left over time for relationships. In the Kingdom, relationships are a key part of everything we do.

When we acknowledge the place that God has in our hearts, we are more able to hear His voice and know His mind. Time spent in waiting on the Lord will enable us to see His Presence and His hand on things. Having a passion for rejoicing and thanksgiving gives us access to a higher dimension of peace and rest where we are lifted up to recognize a different perspective. Trust is easier the higher up we go in the affections of the Father.

This is fellowship. Acknowledgement is a key part of our fellowship. We get to confess and declare who God is for us. We worship our testimony back to Him. We love, adore and give thanks for who He is! We rejoice in Him. It is so wonderful to rejoice, to speak out to Him of our pleasure in who He is. To rejoice is to be passionately outspoken in our praise. It is not casual, nor matter of fact. It is focused, intentional and highly personal. The more we get into the face of God in our worship, the more of Him is personally available to us when we come to ask, seek, and knock.

This type of rejoicing is standard worship for a life with the Spirit. Without it, our mind has no defense against anxiety. The situation overwhelms us unless we become consumed by who God is for us. Rejoicing produces such an amazing sense of well being that trust becomes the consequence of confidence.

Trust is a by-product of rejoicing. As we give thanks, we experience God's Presence. Trust comes with Him because He is eminently trustworthy. Trust is not something I have to call up in myself. It is massively provoked in me by God's Presence. As I rejoice, He fills all in all with Himself. He generates trust in me by His beauty, His integrity, His very nature.

> *In hiddenness we learn deep truth*

It is the nature of God to believe. Why do we make faith such an issue? God is a believer, and since we are in Him it is normal for us also. The practice of a lifestyle of rejoicing is an incredible aid to faith. The truth is that faith and worry cannot inhabit the same space at the same time. One of them has to go, and we get to choose. Likewise with trust and anxiety; they are mutually incompatible, and only one can be chosen. It is the same with power and being fearful; one robs the other of life and expression.

We can choose the negative option by default. Simply put, not choosing positively puts us in the category of a victim. We are overcome rather than being more than conquerors.

In all the circumstances of life, the Father is teaching us how to relate to Him by rejoicing, praying and giving thanks. These all lead to trust in the nature of God and faith in the operation of God on our behalf.

We trust Him by not being worried, anxious, or fearful. When we speak out our trust, our spirit pushes away the negative.

It is time for people to banish fear forever and learn to live in the love of God. When fear grips our hearts, negative faith (unbelief) rules our minds. Negative faith occurs when we believe that nothing is going to change. We are stuck with how things are now, or we believe that we will never be any good.

> *God withdraws from our emotions to teach us faith*

We can have more faith that we won't make it than in the love of God to enable us to succeed by the power of the Holy Spirit.

There are two ways to trust God, because we all have two relationships with Him. The first is **vertical,** in which we relate to God one-on-one. We access all that He is and can do, personally. The second is **horizontal,** in which we can access the Father through the relationships that he has strategically placed around us. One of my favorite comments to friends and family when we are talking about issues of faith is, "You can borrow mine," if they are expressing a

Trusting and Being Trustworthy

lack. We have a saying in England: "God redeems us eighty percent and then He gives us friends." The idea that we can be wholly redeemed without relational involvement with brothers and sisters in the Lord is quite bizarre.

Friends and family are a crucial part of our discipling and our development. There are times when God chooses to come to us through our friends as He did for David with Jonathan. The Father has chosen human friends in order to come to us in a different reality.

When God moves us into a high place in the Spirit, He uses friends to ground that spiritual growth in the natural, in the reality of living. If it works in the Spirit, it must be out-worked in life.

When God shows up in our weaknesses, it is our dear ones who get to be part of our training in discipleship. To stand with a friend when you are in dire need is a beautiful experience.

I can never understand how the Church can walk away from people when God is dealing with their sin, learned behavior and wrong thought processes. We need people the most when we are being adjusted. I thank God that I have people around me who love me enough to stand with me when God is dealing with issues in my life.

This is perhaps the main difference between leaders who are fathers and those who are merely pharisees. Fathers are essentially redemptive. They are not embarrassed by sin or the shortcomings of people. They see everyone through the lens of the Father looking at Jesus. They point people to their freedom.

Everything is Relational

When we understand how God interacts with us, we grow in confidence. We know what God is doing in us, and what He is doing through us. We no longer confuse the two. We spend time in His presence receiving revelation, guidance and love.

This is not usually an immediate experience. Waiting on God takes patience, because there is a perfect time for everything. *"To everything there is a season, a time for every purpose under heaven,"* as Ecclesiastes 3:1 reminds us. We have to resist the urge to doubt God when things take longer to happen than we want or expect. "Nothing's happening," we whine sometimes. "Am I even in the right place?" I've discovered that the more impatient I am, the more God slows things down. He's like a watched kettle — He never boils when we're in a hurry.

We live in Christ, not our circumstances. He is our rest and peace. We do not try to apply peace to our life situations. Peace comes from the heart, not the head. Peace is relational, not circumstantial.

Rejoicing and true thanksgiving produce peace and rest. Rejoicing and giving thanks from the heart will always over-power anything negative. Rejoicing from the mind gives only a temporary relief. Rejoicing from the heart changes our lifestyle. Thanksgiving

> *Peace is relational, not circumstantial*

is not casual; it's an experience of the Lord's joy that liberates us to rejoice. Joy is the abiding atmosphere of Heaven, and so it changes our internal atmosphere permanently. Joy is who God is; rejoicing is our response to who God is! We can abide in joy, simply because He does.

Confidence is a lifestyle that emanates out of our internal abiding atmosphere. Do not just visit the nature of God; live in Him. Abide in Him, and He will abide in you (John 15:1-11). Confidence is the consequence of Abiding. Confidence is part of our inheritance with the Father. He is our inheritance.

"But by His doing you are in Christ Jesus, who became to us wisdom from God, and righteousness and sanctification, and redemption" (1 Corinthians 1:30). Inheritance, like guidance, is relational. Jesus possesses everything we will ever need for life and godliness (2 Peter 1:2-4).

Our inheritance and our guidance are tied to our relationship with God. I want to run and not be weary; I want to walk and not faint. This boundless, sustained energy only comes from spending time with God. We can't receive it through the laying on of hands or some other form of ministry — it only flows from resting in the Lord. As mature Christians, we must stop asking people to pray for us to receive something that can only come through our own relationship with God.

Should we pray for people? Of course. But we shouldn't develop a culture that says a person needs that prayer to survive another week spiritually. Every Christian needs to learn how to wait on the Lord, how to bring themselves to rest in Him, and how to simply be still. We need to know how the Holy Spirit ministers in everyday life. We don't come to church for a spiritual top-up; we come to church to top someone else up. We live our lives out in the real world with a desire to encourage, bless and spiritually attract someone who has never experienced God.

Imagine a body of believers that came to church ready to give, not to receive. What a community that would be! I want to be very clear: I am not saying that people who are in spiritual need shouldn't come to church and receive prayer. I am saying that there is a more excellent way, however, and our mission must be to teach everyone how to interact with God for themselves. Sometimes, instead of praying for someone, we should be checking what they believe: "What are you not believing about God that is causing you to feel this way or do these things? Are you clinging to an old or incorrect idea about God?"

God wants us to be constantly moving forward in our faith. We are called to walk a path of spiritual maturity. We have to grow up in our understanding of waiting on Him. He has made more provision for us than we can possibly imagine, as we read in 1 Corinthians 2:9 *"Eye has not seen, nor ear heard, nor has it entered into the heart of man the things which God has prepared for those who love Him."* But to inherit this gift, we have to live in Him. We must enter the place He has set aside for us in Christ. The goal of all our gatherings is to

Everything is Relational

establish each of us in that relationship with Jesus. We have a personal responsibility to the Holy Spirit to learn how to abide and stay in Christ. Taking care of our relationship with Him is our top priority.

A Culture That Transforms

"Love the LORD *your God with all your heart, with all your soul, with all your mind, and with all your strength,"* the Greatest Commandment, found in Mark 12:30, instructs us. As we make honest attempts to live where God has placed us in Christ, the Holy Spirit's grace and mercy will overwhelm us, fill us up and enable us to become the people we are called to be.

In a way, we are like a barrel of God's Spirit. We are not called to leak; in fact, the mission of the Holy Spirit is to help us plug all of those holes. Instead, we are called to overflow with the goodness and grace of God. Most of our holes come out of the theology or doctrine of our skewed view of who God really is.

We face many choices of what we really believe, but by allowing the Holy Spirit to establish His truth in our hearts and lives, we can make the correct choice and take a step forward in our maturity. To do that, we must spend time with God and cooperate with the Holy Spirit in His transforming work.

I would love to be a part of a church where the majority of people arrive refreshed and leave more anointed. Mature people have a passion for the Presence of God which is greater than their zeal for ministry. People who are wonderfully anointed in ministry, but very average in intimacy, are not mature. At some point their lack of intimacy will betray their anointing. The enemy will draw them out beyond their sphere and isolate their gifting. Lack

> *Church can be a full-service, Christian cocoon*

of intimacy often means we have no protection against our own arrogance. The appreciation, approval and applause of others are seen as a right by these people, and their status in ministry cannot be challenged. Lack of humility makes us immune to personal correction.

I thank God for the counsel, sound advice and occasional butt-kicking I have had through the years when my own stupidity has been the biggest thing about me. I am more grateful than I can say for people who stood up to me and would not let me weasel out of anything that was not righteous. At times I have humiliated myself because of my own words and actions, but wonderful people stood by me and rescued me from my own folly. These are the people who have helped my ministry to become what it is today. Many of them talked to me about my level of intimacy with Jesus and helped me go to a new level. Humility is a by-product of real intimacy.

The enemy loves to accuse us of our shortcomings. Intimacy allows us to take that accusation and turn it into astonishment at the goodness of God. Humility lies in knowing what we are like in Jesus and what we can be like without Him. Humility keeps us camped out near the fear of the Lord.

Many people use meetings as a pick-me-up. I have no problem if those

> **Constraint without development is punishment**

people are new to faith or those going through major transformational dealings with the Lord. In those instances, meetings should be a lifeline because we need the support of others either to achieve a breakthrough or sustain the follow-through. We can't all get it together, but together, we can get it all.

The difficulty comes when people live this way indefinitely. Some churches establish a culture of dependency so that their people never seem to grow up. An industry has grown up around this culture that enables consumerism to be elevated to an art form. Everything is provided for people so that they don't have to go anywhere else. It's a full-service, Christian cocoon. We are shielded as much from the culture of Heaven as we are from the influence of the world. When we touch Heaven, the influence of the world decreases dramatically. As Heaven increases, other things are reduced.

When we say "yes" to Jesus we must learn to say "no" elsewhere. If our "yes" is not followed by a "no," then it will lose its power. *"He must increase, I must decrease"* (John 3:30) is our delight.

There is a cult of consumerism in the western church. When we constantly do things for people, we empower their disability. We enable their immaturity. I love the multiplicity of ministries that are available in the Kingdom to ensure that people are set free. We must keep a watching brief on pastoral ministry to ensure that it empowers people to stay free themselves.

Pastoral ministries, when not overseen by apostolic and prophetic leadership, can, on their best day, only take people so far in the purposes of God. Without the benefit of real apostles and prophets, churches become settlers with no heart to explore what else is out there. Pastoral and teaching ministries are brilliant at establishing the breakthrough. Prophets see far and have foresight; teachers dig deep and have insight. Teachers establish what prophets reveal. Pastors provide follow-through on what apostles create in breakthrough. They take that new ground, and they hold it. When people are set free, pastors ensure that they remain free. A release must evolve into a freedom, or it returns to captivity.

I loved listening to John and Carol Arnott in the very heart of renewal. I loved the fact that they were passionate about people maintaining their freedom. They know that there is no breakthrough without follow-through. They were concerned that people did not just have an encounter with God, but that they were empowered to turn that encounter into an ongoing experience.

Some churches did brilliantly at renewal because they enabled people to grow up in God as well as be refreshed. I had a marvelous time in renewal because the guys with whom I walked knew how to produce transformation out of what God was doing.

We did not want to see people touched, but not changed. We concentrated pastoral ministries on people who were being touched; we pressed their refreshing into a place of life transformation. We focused teaching gifts on the areas of breakthrough so that we could create follow-through and establish spiritual maturity.

Sadly, many churches only saw renewal as a time of refreshing. It was so much more than that. It was a place of encounter that would lead us into ongoing experience. People must be taught to fend for themselves. Maturity is receiving and establishing our own personal breakthrough from within the place of our own personal relationship with God. We can and do receive freedom, help, and breakthrough from other ministries and movements, but we are not dependent upon them as a lifestyle. There are too many conference junkies looking for the quick fix, the impartation that will catapult them into a meaningful place in the Spirit without the need to work out and walk out their salvation in Christ.

The Church is responsible for setting a corporate culture that produces personal freedom and responsibility at all levels of personal and corporate lifestyle: freedom to hear the Lord and obey, freedom to worship God and pursue Him, freedom to explore the Word of the Lord and seek its fulfillment — all our precious and vital freedoms that must be upheld. People need development that allows them to be responsible for their personal walk with God.

There must be freedom to worship creatively, freedom to be led by the Spirit, freedom to challenge inauthentic belief and lifestyle, freedom to pursue dreams, freedom to develop accountable relationships of mutual respect and integrity and freedom to resist overbearing, manipulative, coercive oversight that constrains people without facilitating their development.

Good shepherds do not treat people like sheep. They understand that shepherding is a metaphor, not an office. Shepherds are sheep also, and they need to lead people in the same manner as they themselves are led by the Lord.

Part of development in our corporate culture must be founded on the freedom of the individual. Constraint without development is punishment. All around us people are learning about God and about themselves. It is vital to respect that learning, and as much as possible, empower people to love the learning process. Of course, people are going to resist personal change, blame others, and not take responsibility for their own stuff.

Leaders create the culture that shapes people as they grow from petulant children to mature sons in Christ.

The goal of God is to bring us to a place where we abide in Christ, where we get our needs met by Him, and where we can help meet the needs of others. He wants us to be at the pinnacle of our giftings and callings, so that we can find Him in whatever is happening around us. It shouldn't matter how much the enemy spins us around; if our heart is fixed on God, we are immediately focused on Him. When this happens, the Church is going to grow up.

We'll live by the Book. We won't question the will of God because we will be in relationship with Him.

Tangible Reality

We can be so full of God's Presence that all things become possible through Him. We are an unstoppable force when we develop confidence in His goodness. The promise of Isaiah 40:28-31 becomes ours to possess:

> *Have you not known?*
> *Have you not heard?*
> *The everlasting God, the* LORD,
> *The Creator of the ends of the earth,*
> *Neither faints nor is weary.*
> *His understanding is unsearchable.*
> *He gives power to the weak,*
> *And to those who have no might He increases strength.*
> *Even the youths shall faint and be weary,*
> *And the young men shall utterly fall,*
> *But those who wait on the* LORD
> *Shall renew their strength;*
> *They shall mount up with wings like eagles,*
> *They shall run and not get tired*
> *They will walk and not become weary.*

> *Scripture is about encounters and experiences*

There is a tangible reality in our relationship with Scripture that must bring us into a physical manifestation of the Presence of God. If this is not the case, how can we say that we have a relationship with a personal Savior? The Word of God must have an impact upon us physically, mentally, emotionally, and spiritually.

The Word of God must affect us in a holistic manner, otherwise it makes no sense.

"He sent His word and healed." (Psalm 107:20)

"The Word is health to all their body." (Proverbs 4:22)

"The Word is living and active." (Hebrews 4:12)

"The Word became flesh and dwelt amongst us." (John 1:14)

"Christ in us is the hope (profound realization) of glory." (Colossians 1:27)

The very idea that God's word has only a partial effect upon His people is anathema to the true gospel of Jesus Christ. The concept that there could be a full gospel experience for the Early Church but not for today's believers would lead us to think that the Father loved that church more than the present one. What does it mean for us to be made in the image of God? What does Heaven on earth look like? What does being Christ-like mean? Is it only in character that we get to become like Him? *"As He is, so are we in this world"* (1 John

4:17). Surely this means as He is now, not as He was then. Now, He stands in the Presence of God as the exact representation of the Father. At some point, we must abandon our rational western-minded foolishness and accept that the Word of God is for the whole person, to enable us to have encounters and experiences that affect the sum total of all that we are in Jesus. Anything less is not a so great salvation. It is measure, not fullness. It is mediocre, not abundant. Such a salvation is not glorious because there is no possibility of God receiving great glory from it.

As the people of God, we are defined by our promises, prophecies and all the possibilities of life in the Spirit that exist in the heart of an all-powerful God. He does not get weary, and therefore neither should we! He gives power to the weak and increased strength to those who have no might. We expect that, and we pray for it as a matter of course.

> *The place of encounter supersedes any other*

However, when we enter the secret place of abiding in the Lord, we encounter a much different proposition. Those who practice waiting on the Lord have another place of encounter that supersedes the other.

Strength is renewed constantly. We can rise up and soar in the Spirit. We are weightless, like an eagle on the wind. Life becomes effortless when we are with Christ in Heavenly places. We can ride the thermals of the Holy Spirit. We get to increase our speed spiritually. We access a divine acceleration. We discover the ability to move faster and travel further in shorter periods of time. We encounter a quickening spirit in the form of Jesus (1 Corinthians 15:45) moving at a more pronounced speed in our conscious relationship with the Father. The second Adam is a quickening spirit. Jesus did not come to restore us to the Garden of Eden. That was the first Adam's relationship, which was with God on earth.

We are a new creation, all the old things are passed away, **everything** has become new, and all these things are of God (2 Corinthians 5:17-18). What does new creation mean? It means a new race of people that have never been seen in the earth before! In the Old Covenant, everyone had the Holy Spirit upon them. People served a God who lived **among** them, but He was never **in** them.

In Christ, the New Covenant produces a people who are vastly different. God lives in us! He abides and dwells within. We can hear His voice, know His will personally, and move in His power. We have access to His very throne in Jesus (Hebrews 4:16). We are seated with Him in Heavenly places in Christ (Ephesians 1:20 and 2:6). We are blessed with every spiritual blessing in Heavenly places (Ephesians 1:3). We bear the image of the Heavenly (1 Corinthians 15:49).

There has never been a people like us at any time of the world's existence. We are a brand new creation. David saw it coming when he wrote Psalm 102:18:

"This will be written for a generation to come, that a people **yet to be created** *may praise the Lord."*

We are a Chosen Race, a Royal Priesthood, a Holy Nation, a People for God's Own Possession, so that we may proclaim the excellencies of Him who has called us out of darkness into His Marvelous Light (1 Peter 2:9).

We are dead and our life is hidden with Christ in God (Colossians 3:3); even so, we consider ourselves to be dead to sin and alive to God in Christ Jesus (Romans 6:11).

All our favor is tied into the new creation and not the old. The Father, knowing that our old nature is dead only relates to our new nature in Christ. Therefore, when He looks at us He does not see what is wrong with us. He sees what is missing from our current experience in Christ, and He is deeply committed to our ongoing encounter. We are learning to grow up in all things in Christ (Ephesians 4:15).

Our relationship is to live in the second Adam who is occupied with the Father in Heavenly places. It is a completely different relational paradigm that gives us a stronger connection and access to the Heavenly places. We are not earthbound in our spiritual walk, but have a huge array of possible encounters with God available to us in the person of the Lord Jesus Christ. Like an eagle, we are free to fly, not just to explore earth from a Heavenly perspective, but also to encounter Heaven in the context of all that the Father has called us to establish on earth!

We see it constantly in the Old Testament, where people had encounters with God that empowered incredible victories against impossible odds, experiences of the Kingdom realm that overwhelmed the properties of our natural world: the sun standing still in the sky for twenty-four hours, waters parting to allow passage, raising of the dead, miraculous provisions, axe heads floating. All around also were amazing encounters with God, angels and the Heavenly realm. This was under the Old Covenant, supposedly lesser than the New. It is a type of the New, which would be fully revealed in the Lord Jesus. That is why He came saying *"you have heard it said, but now I say to you."*

The Stimulation of the Inner Man

We learn the disciplines of the Spirit through the circumstances of life. Every situation we encounter tells us something more about the Lord and ourselves. Our truth comes to us on the journey. Truth is a person (John 14:6) who sets us free by indwelling (John 8:32). As we walk with God, we have our own inbuilt stimulus package that empowers us to know a life of abundance.

We become people of the Spirit when we discover the nature of God in the situations we encounter. What if every circumstance was primarily about us discovering who God wanted to be for us?

Firstly, God causes everything to work together for good to those who are intent on loving God in their situations (Romans 8:28). That is, finding and resting in that relational place of worship and affection. Rejoicing is the response we use to express our appreciation and attachment to God's nature. Joy is who God is; rejoicing is our response to who God is!

> *There is discovery of God in every situation*

Secondly, for things to work together for good, we must have a sense of calling to the relational purpose of God within the situation we face. Everything God does is relational. It is vital that we are empowered to see the fullness of love which the Father wants to commit into our lives.

We are called the children of God, and our destiny is to be made in His image, on earth as it is in Heaven. He deals with us as with sons because His purpose is to bring many sons into glory. Every circumstance is about following the relational purpose of God so that situations do not get resolved without us being transformed into being Christ-like.

There is a process that will totally engage us in a faith-filled encounter with God that overcomes the enemy and brings us into a place of enlargement. In this relational process, our inner man becomes aroused to the point where a new strength rises up within.

Unless we put the relational transformation before our desire for situational change, we will not develop our inner man beyond the simple yearnings of the soul. We are learning to be people after God's own heart. It is therefore only what we know by experience of the nature of God that can sustain us in this life.

We must see who God is for us. We must have an understanding of the particular aspect of God's nature that He purposes for us to discover. Relational purpose empowers us to be still in our present difficulty. It is His will that we become like Him in the situation that we are presently encountering. It is possible to go through some circumstance, achieve a reasonable outcome, but not discover the nature of God or be changed in Him. Thus, we guarantee that we must undergo the same relational training at a later date. We must not squander these important circumstances.

What is it that God wants to be for us now that He could not be at any other time? The will of God is always relational. When we miss the main purpose, we must repeat the training. Every situation provides us with an opportunity to discover God in a new and a deeper way.

If the Lord wants to kill off our capacity to worry and be anxious, in favor of us learning rest and peace, then He will come to us relationally as the Prince of Peace. He will want to take our current experience to a deeper level of intention and favor. We have encountered an opportunity for God to come into our life in a way that he has been planning to do for some time.

When we renew our mind, it is to bring it into alignment with His heart. We are heart people first. Our mind comes under the weight of God's love in our heart. If our mind fails this most basic of tests, then we are downgraded in our thinking to a place of reasonable, rational and sensible thinking as our first response to the majesty of God.

A rational mind always settles for less. Doubt is too often easily accessible from a place of reason. Wisdom, trust and faith are intuitive. They come to us from the place of perception where the eyes of our heart have been enlightened. We can only practice our heart relationship when we give ourselves to praise, rejoicing, thanksgiving, and worship. Rational people often do not allow themselves to become abandoned in intimacy.

> We can squander our circumstances

In the will of God, He seeks people to worship Him. Such people enjoy faith, abound in trust, and know how to punish doubt. Worship stimulates our inner man and refreshes our thinking. Our mindset will take us down unless our inner man has been refreshed. The first barrier to overcome is always within us. I love thinking, reasoning and comprehension, but not at the expense of faith and the Presence of God. A sound mind is one that has lined up behind our heart experience.

When we do not allow this simple discipline to upgrade our mindset in line with the Spirit, then we lay ourselves open to disillusion and despair. *"Why are you in despair o my soul? Why have you become disturbed within me? Hope in God! For I shall again praise Him for the help of His Presence."* (Psalm 42:5)

Despair can be a usual experience of the soul, but not the inner man of the Spirit. For a more full version of this vital truth experience see *Toward a Powerful Inner Life* at www.BrilliantBookHouse.com.

The mind set on the flesh (natural world) is death; it leaves faith undeveloped and contributes to our lack of encounter and experience. A mind set on the Spirit is life and peace. It has purpose.

We can only replace a mindset with another mindset! A mindset that is hostile to God's will and purpose is one that fails to apprehend faith, promise or provision. A hostile mind does not have to be antagonistic toward God, just unwelcoming. When our mindset is hostile, it often means we are held hostage in our own circumstances.

It is imperative that we fulfill the will of God in terms of how we perceive Him so that we gladly submit to His ongoing purpose. All prophets are concerned with the issue of how to think with the mind of Christ. God is not asking us to kiss our brains goodbye. He is requesting that we elevate our thinking to the correct level. Our heart is the elevator that lifts us up into an experience of Presence. When our thinking comes from a heart perception, we are opened up to see what God has prepared for those who love Him.

> *"As it is written, 'A FATHER OF MANY NATIONS I HAVE MADE YOU' in the presence of Him whom he believed, even God, who gives life to the dead*

The Stimulation of the Inner Man

and calls into being that which does not exist. In hope against hope he believed, so that he might become a father of many nations according to that which had been spoken, 'SO SHALL YOUR DESCENDANTS BE.' Without becoming weak in faith he contemplated his own body, now as good as dead since he was about a hundred years old, and the deadness of Sarah's womb; yet, with respect to the promise of God, he did not waver in unbelief but grew strong in faith, giving glory to God, and being fully assured that what God had promised, He was able also to perform. Therefore 'IT WAS ALSO CREDITED TO HIM AS RIGHTEOUSNESS.'"(Romans 4:17-22)

Abraham has a promise that he will become the father of many nations. Every promise is tested so that our faith can increase! We have to consider everything with God. He knew that neither his nor Sarah's physical ability to reproduce was the issue.

Promises are relational. They depend upon how we view the people making them. We do not look at the situation containing the problem. We look at the heart of the One who has spoken the promise. When everything goes black, the heart that made the promise is our only light source.

Worship allows us to think through the implications of our circumstances without becoming weak in faith. Without that relational stimulus, our thinking may destroy our opportunity to discover the Father. Abraham looked at his own body and Sarah's womb, and then he looked at the promise of God and the nature of the One who gave that guarantee, and he gave glory to God.

> All promises are relational

A mind set on the flesh would have brought reason that produced doubt that led to unbelief. A mind set on the Spirit brought assurance and faith.

Never ask questions until your heart and mind are in a good place. Worship releases fresh perspective. When we encounter the nature of God, we can stand in His personality and have a better conversation.

What aspect of His nature are you learning? The will of God is that you become that! God loves to promise. It's the language of love. Rejoicing brings us to a place where revelation of God gives way to a revelation of His will for our situation.

Pursuing God's purpose in our situation is where we learn the business end of faith and walking with the Father. We simply must get moving in faith. We have no idea how it's going to turn out, and we are not called to speculate—only believe. The outcome is God's part; the process is ours.

Simply follow the path. Continue in worship and trusting. Go with God as He goes after your circumstances. Pursue what you know to be true of God. He goes before us and travels with us. We do not chase the outcome; we pursue the heart of God. He guarantees the outcome as we follow His goodness. It is always relational.

Sign Seeking

The word "sign" in the Hebrew is '*ôwth* and is used sixty times in the Old Testament. It has numerous meanings:

- It represents something by which a person or a group is characteristically marked, as in Genesis 4:15. God put a mark on Cain so that no one could kill him.
- A sign was the evidence that God had put a division between His people and others in Egypt. Swarms of insects were prohibited from settling on Goshen (Exodus 8:22-23).
- Rahab asked for a sign as a pledge of truth that when the Israelites sacked Jericho, her family would be safe. The scarlet rope with which she allowed the men to escape became the sign (Joshua 2:12-18).
- The rainbow was a sign, a reminder to God and people that a covenant existed that would prevent another flood from occurring (Genesis 9:12-15).
- The Feast of Unleavened Bread was a sign of all that God worked in Israel's deliverance from Egypt (Exodus 13).
- In Exodus 3:12 and 4:8, signs were tokens enabling people to see and believe something particular.
- Signs attested the validity of a prophetic message (Deuteronomy 13:1-5).

In the New Testament, the word "signs" is used fifty times. The Greek word *Semeion* denotes a sign, mark, or token; a distinguishing of one thing or person from another. Signs and wonders were tokens of divine authority and power.

The Jews often confronted Jesus looking for signs (Mark 8:11-12). They wanted signs of an outward Messianic Kingdom, of temporal triumph over the Romans, and material greatness for them as a chosen people. The idea of a crucified Messiah was anathema to them.

> Signs must be about pursuing the Lord

Jesus came to His own, and they did not perceive who He was. He was a stumbling block to them. The culture of sign-seeking only really works when we are wholehearted about loving and pursuing the Lord for His glory.

Jesus was often faced with the religious system in the form of pharisaical aggression and an argumentative spirit. Religious people always listen with prejudice. They are set on defending a system that supports their authority and attacking anyone they feel might be in opposition to their way of doing things. A religious system never dies; it just morphs into the next thing. Both old and new wineskins can have the same pharisaical feel. Traditional and newer church models can also be remarkably free from "churchianity."

Seeking signs is legitimate as long as it is part of our wholehearted spiritual journey and not an excuse for not moving out of our comfort zone. The problem that Jesus faced was religious people seeking a sign that gave them an opportunity to discredit or disclaim the words of Jesus. In Matthew 12:38-41 and 16:1-4, we see that religious spirit in operation.

Generally, there are three types of people seeking God's will today. There are the super spiritual believers who see signs in everything and often have little discernment. There are also genuine sign seekers who are pursuing the Father passionately and who appreciate that signs and wonders are a viable part of our training in a supernatural lifestyle. Finally, there are people who are constantly putting out a fleece to determine the will of God.

The wheat always grows up with the weeds. Farmers do not consider a crop to be spoiled because weeds are present. Our enjoyment of color and fragrance in flowers should not be ruined by the presence of weeds in the garden. Similarly, we don't allow the enemy to ruin what God is doing in our midst. The presence of sin proves that the Holy Spirit is in residence, since the flesh and the spirit are hostile to one another (Romans 8:6-7). When there is a fresh move of the Spirit in a place, sin is always a casualty, simply because the Spirit is holy! Normally, the enemy likes sin to be hidden, not exposed. It can cause more damage that way. Sin does not reveal itself; it is exposed by the Holy Spirit. So we can only see sin because of the light. Sin is revealed so that it can leave.

Immaturity and maturity walk together for a while, thus enabling us to choose one over the other, as do childishness and childlikeness. Never allow the presence of a negative to prevent you from choosing and enjoying its opposite.

I love mystery, and I love the fact that God is a mystical (not mythical) being. He is both knowable and unknowable in our finite, time-space world. In Heaven, it will probably be a different story. Super spiritual people like to jazz things up, to make them appear more grand and powerful than they really are. Often this can be a poor self-image at work. We are not yet fully secure in the greatness of God's love for us, so we look for a measure of esteem from celebrity, not reality. It's the Wizard of Oz syndrome at work.

The supernatural realm is often quite ordinary. I prayed for a guy on the street in Los Angeles. He was blind in one eye, the result of

> *The wheat always grows up with the weeds*

a street fight. He would not let me pray for him to come off drugs, but he felt that having another eye would not go amiss. I prayed; his eye opened. "Thanks, dude," he said and walked off, no big deal. I laughed. People think that the truly supernatural must be awesome and other-worldly. Sometimes it is; mostly though it's so normal we could miss it.

Our challenge in the supernatural is to be real, normal and real normal. God is the most normal person I have ever met, except when He wants to be majestic, outrageous and glorious. Funnily enough, he doesn't need me to be His press agent, though I would love to do it. He pays well and the benefits are simply out of this world.

When I began in ministry eons ago, I learned from a bunch of guys who did dress things up. I walked as I was taught until one day the Father told me that He always felt sorry for me, that I did not really know Him well enough to behave differently. As put-downs go, it was gentle, beautiful, and broke my heart. My journey since has been from celebrity to reality. As a result, I have seen more and experienced a greater Presence than I could ever have imagined.

Sign-seeking for the hyper-spiritual is a mix of fact and fantasy. It's what we call in England, felt-led poisoning. "I felt led to do this, say that, go there." Often, it's an excuse for weird behavior; mostly its window dressing that creates a specific image. It's the walnut veneer that covers an inferior grade of material.

Several years ago I attended a conference incognito. I sat in the back because I wanted to hear a couple of guys speak. I enjoyed the event and learned some things that were helpful on my journey. A few months later, I had dinner with one of those men who testified to me in glowing terms about the event I had attended. "Presence of God was awesome. We had everything going on, man. Angels in the room, gold dust on people, gold teeth appearing in people's mouths, wind of the Spirit. It was amazing!" Must have been a different conference. My heart went out to him in his insecurity. I asked the Father if I should say something. He smiled gently in my heart. "No need, son. He's a good man; he'll come to his senses and will need a friend."

We are all a work in process and in need of being cleaned up by the Holy Spirit. I have been in meetings many times when supernatural things were happening. The Holy Spirit never draws attention to the act, only to Jesus. He adores glorifying the Son. When the act is glorified, people talk about the ministry of the individual. There is a cult of personality abroad in the church, and we must watch it closely. Appreciation is justified, acclaim is not. We reserve that for the Lord Jesus.

> *Maturity is having integrity in the usual*

I have seen the Lord do astonishing things in both a spectacular and deeply unspectacular way — same results, different methodology. If we want God to be real, we must start first.

On tour in Ireland, I spoke at a Sunday morning meeting and had lunch with a family in the congregation. They had a five year old child who had never spoken. They were having tests to determine if he was mute. He was sitting on the floor watching television. I sat next to him, put my arm on his shoulder, and prayed quietly in tongues. Nothing spectacular. I ate lunch and departed for the next town. That same day he spoke. The result was amazing; the process was routinely normal.

Some hyper-spiritual people have a martyr complex. They believe that God wants them to do the opposite of what they want. Whatever makes them happy, fulfilled, or financially secure seems wrong and even dangerous. They want to live a life of incredible sacrifice. Often the root of this type of thinking is that circumstances have made us suspicious of ourselves and other people. God doesn't just pour words through us; we're not drain pipes. He uses our personality and our individuality. Look at the four gospels — each one carries the personality of its writer. John's gospel focuses on intimacy — not surprising for the "disciple Jesus loved." Matthew's gospel includes Jesus' genealogy. As a tax collector, he was well aware of Jewish custom and family ties. Luke, a doctor, was amazed by the healings Jesus performed. Mark, an evangelist, kept his account the shortest, no doubt to draw new listeners in. These Scriptures were inspired by God but carry their own individuality. Today, we are richer for that diversity.

Because God uses our uniqueness, we need to be open to Him purifying us. We need to allow Him to filter out the things that hinder His ability to communicate to, and through us.

The second type of Christian seeking God's will is a legitimate sign seeker. They know that signs and wonders are a viable expression of spirituality for all of us.

The Bible outlines three different types of signs and wonders: *allegorical signs, natural signs, and fleeces.* Signs and wonders are demonstrations of God's power to believers. Scripture teaches us to expect such manifestations as a natural consequence of walking in the Spirit, and of being in the corporate Body of Christ on earth. The miracle in John 5:1-17 was just such a sign, mainly for religious people. A man, defeated by an illness for thirty-eight years, is lying by the pool of Bethesda. He has an encounter with Jesus on the Sabbath where, contrary to religious law, he is healed. It's a sign that the rules are changing. There is a fresh move of God, and permission is granted to do things differently in the Kingdom.

"You have heard it said, but now I say to you," was a familiar comment by Jesus.

Five thousand people were fed in a supernatural picnic that was a sign to everyone that we could live from a completely different power source in the natural world.

> Signs are a wonderful part of our spiritual journey

Jesus walking on water and then speaking peace to the storm were two signs to His disciples that the power of Heaven had been restored to the earth.

Jesus waited longer than seemed necessary to demonstrate supernatural power over death. Lazarus had been buried in a tomb four days before Jesus arrived on the scene. He was met with anguished complaints: *"If you had been here, he would not have died."*

Essentially, people were saying, "You're too late." Jesus, however, had never had an intention to heal Lazarus, but to raise him from the dead. Funnily enough, he wasn't too late for that! He was demonstrating that He in Himself was the resurrection and the life (John 11:25).

Raising the dead is not a spiritual gift in itself. It comes under the general heading of "the effecting of miracles" (1 Corinthians 12:10). It is however, a strong part of the Great Commission as we see in Matthew 10:7-8.

When He prayed at the tomb of Lazarus, He did so in a manner that would be a sign for the people gathered (John 11:40-44).

The lame man at the gate Beautiful was healed as a sign that the Kingdom had come upon ordinary people, like fishermen (Acts 3:1-10)!

Their anointing to bring healing and miracles testified as a sign concerning the resurrection of Jesus (Acts 4:33; 5:12-16).

Jesus' life was attested by miracles, wonders, and signs (Acts 2:22), as was the Apostles' ministry (Acts 2:43; 4:29-30).

Philip's ministry was a sign to these people steeped in the occult (Acts 8:9-13). Signs are evidence of the full Gospel of mankind (Romans 15:18-19). Signs were the evidence of true apostolic anointing (2 Corinthians 12:12).

Signs are a true part of our *"so great salvation"* (Hebrews 2:1-4).

Allegorical signs foretell the nature of a coming event or judgment. For example, Isaiah walked naked and barefoot for three years to show Egypt and Ethiopia how they would be led away naked and barefoot (Isaiah 20). How would you like to have him in your home group? Then there was Ezekiel, who laid on his side for more than a year as a prophetic symbol of what God wanted to do (Ezekiel 4). Imagine being called to that!

There are also *natural signs*, like the star over Bethlehem in Luke 2. That star represented a promise and fulfilled prophecy. The shepherds were told by angels that the star would be a sign for them to find a baby wrapped in swaddling clothes. Noah's rainbow, centuries earlier in Genesis 9, was a promise from God that He would never again flood the entire earth. These signs were a way for God to convey what was on His heart. He chose a different way of breaking into our time and space in order to reveal something to us.

Finally, there are *fleeces* like Gideon's famous one in Judges 6. When God called Gideon to deliver the Israelites from their enemies, he reacted the same way Moses reacted years earlier. He tried everything to convince God to send someone else. Both men carried such a low self-image that they couldn't possibly envision themselves doing what God wanted them to do. Gideon used a fleece, a miraculous test, to ensure that he was, in fact, the man to lead Israel.

Before we get into the specifics of that initial conversation and the subsequent reason for Gideon bringing a fleece before the Lord, let us examine the vital sign of how the Father loves to engage in process with His people.

The Dynamics of Spiritual Development

Spiritual development is at all times relational, positional, material, and exponential.

It is good for us to recognize that the Lord usually has a number of objectives in mind in our life circumstances. We tend to focus on the one that is causing the most anguish or difficulty. We want freedom or release from something. The Lord has that in mind also, but mostly as a consequence. We see it as a major objective; He sees it as a by-product. He has other things that He also wants to achieve. There are times when our circumstances can be prolonged because we are not seeing or are not complying with other objectives that the Lord has in mind.

Remember, all spiritual development is primarily relational. Firstly, the Father wants us to know Him as He is in His own glory; so a revelation is available about an aspect of His nature that He wants us to see and worship. Secondly, His intention is that we become partakers of that particular divine nature, so that we are filled and energized by it. Thirdly, we are to put on Christ and be made in God's image within the context of what we are learning in our situation. An encounter always creates ongoing experience.

> *Freedom is a consequence, not an objective*

When the Father gave me a revelation of His loving-kindness to me, my heart swelled with rejoicing. I got it! I understood who He is in terms of kindness! Then He began to be that for me, day after day. I began to see that whatever God is, He is relentlessly. He never changes. His love never ceases. His mercy is never-ending. He is extravagant, overwhelming in His goodness. His love covers a multitude of sins. His grace is enough and much more than enough!

His kindness ran riot all over my life. Every single day He would do something or say something that would be hugely generous and kind. There is no season with the nature of God. It is ongoing and relentless. I was overwhelmed pretty quickly. He poured out His kindness like a baptismal encounter, full immersion. I drowned in it. I was filled up, immersed, overwhelmed. The blessing of God kills the darkness in each of us. I felt my sarcasm, cynicism and unkindness tear loose and float away.

My heart became enlarged by His kindness. I wept for joy. I could feel His heart; really feel His nature of loving-kindness. My eyes filled up. I could feel His heart moving into my eyes. I began to see people differently. I was seeing them through the lens of His loving-kindness. When my mouth opened, different words came out — words of affirmation, release, empowerment, affection. I could see people's sadness, self-loathing and fear. I began to learn how to speak to negatives and turn them around.

I could see the negativity that covered some people like a shroud. I began to learn the art of reframing: empowering people to see the provision that was present with every problem. As the Lord drew what He was doing in my life into a place of ministry to others, more changes became apparent in my experiences. I became a partaker with Him, conscious of His Presence and deliberately acting in partnership with Him. Then, He withdrew from the majesty of my experiences and I stayed the same! I no longer had the same physical intensity, but the results were the same. He had made me like Him, and now I was learning to abide. He lives in me, and I do those things unconsciously. He gives me occasional upgrades and sometimes rises up and inhabits me — I think just for the sheer pleasure that He has in involvement with His sons!

The relational element in our development produces a place in us where we are positioned before the Lord in a very specific manner. All growth is positional, and therefore, must include the confidence required to occupy a particular place with strength and passion.

This place is called intentionality. The Father is very focused and deliberate in all that He does. He has an incredible resolve which, when coupled with His astonishing patience, makes Him formidable in His passionate pursuit of His people.

Life in the Spirit is not about measure. That comes from an inferior way of thinking. Abundance is the norm for people living a life of faith. It is important that we commit our intentionality to a higher way of seeing, thinking and believing. It is called being renewed in the spirit of our mind (Ephesians 4:23). When our heart is free to live from the place of intentionality with God, the alignment it creates in our spirit causes faith to rise. Confidence toward God is the goal of all the Holy Spirit's interactions with us.

> All growth is positional

When we move with the Father in His intention, we cannot be disappointed. In intentionality, God welcomes us to flow with Him in divine purpose. When we confess His intention back to Him, we welcome God to be at work in us! We learn how to call out to God to simply be what He has promised. Intentionality empowers us to combine faith and patience so that we inherit all that the Father loves to promise us (Hebrews 6:12).

Intentionality must be embraced fully because a double-minded person cannot inherit (James 5:1-8). It is the Father's plan that His intention and the confidence it engenders in us should be the bedrock on which we stand before Him.

We are not yet the finished article. We are a work in progress. We must, therefore, be fully persuaded about the Father's intention toward us and His ability to see it through. *"For I know whom I have believed and I am convinced that He is able to guard what I have entrusted to Him until that day."* (2 Timothy 1:12)

The enemy would love us to live in the present–past. That occurs when we allow past situations to dominate our thinking, perceiving and living in the present. Old wounds, hurts, betrayals and disappointments are still given power by us to affect us in the here and now. The Cross is an end to the old nature. The old nature is dead in Christ, and we must learn to walk in newness of life (Romans 6:4).

The Dynamics of Spiritual Development

If the enemy cannot overcome us through our past, he wants us to have little or no confidence about the future. Often, he wants us to be overwhelmed by all the things which we are not and by the changes that still need to be made. He is a liar and a thief who must destroy everything the Father is doing.

Salvation is the necessary process of celebration. Therefore, with joy shall we draw water from the wells of salvation (Isaiah 12). He has turned our mourning about ourselves into joy. We live present–future with the Lord. That is, we celebrate who we are now, and we look forward to who we will become in the Lord Jesus. In the present, we do not only look at what still needs to be done in us. Salvation is the celebration of process! We must enjoy where we are now and rejoice in what the Lord has become for us. Then we can turn our attention joyfully to the next area of our renewal and upgrade. Development should be delightful. God loves transformation and wants us to enjoy the process of change and becoming more.

We see this in communion (1 Corinthians 11:26-30). Communion is built on proclamation, not introspection. It is an act of rejoicing in all that Jesus has done for us by His death and sacrifice. We proclaim what that means to us in the present, and we declare what it will mean in terms of our future development. We have been changed to date, and we will continue to be changed by His faithful application of freedom in Christ. *"It is for freedom that Christ has set us free."* (Galatians 5:1)

When the Scripture (1 Corinthians 11:28) encourages us to examine ourselves, it uses the word "dokimazo," which means to "look at with a view to approval." We examine ourselves so we can be encouraged by what the Lord has done in our life, and we proclaim Him by celebrating that!

We live a life of celebration in Jesus, for both the present and the future. I love what God has done in me, and I joyfully look forward to what He wants to do next. Let me quote Paul again: *"For I know whom I have believed and I am fully persuaded that He is able to keep/guard what I have entrusted to Him, against that day."* (2 Timothy 1:12)

Confidence before God is a marvelous way to live and undergo continuing transformation. When we look forward, we bask in the intentionality of God to make us like Christ in all things. We enjoy the process of learning to become fully formed in Christ (Galatians 4:19). It will take years and years of joyful discovery, surrender and release.

The process must be enjoyable, delightful, and lead us into constant gratitude. Rejoicing is positional. It postures us in joyful celebration before the throne of grace. That position must result in our understanding and experience of favor. Intentionality provokes favor.

God's intentionality is fixed to His own excellence. It is partnered with fullness and abundance. This is our inheritance in Christ. We inherit God. We are heirs of God and

> *Salvation must involve celebration*

joint-heirs with Christ. The Holy Spirit is given as a down payment on our total inheritance. "Here is a down payment!" says the Lord, "and there is more to come." God inherits us in Christ! Salvation is about enjoying what we have now and looking forward to more coming.

Favor involves our discovering that the Father has an intentional bias toward us because of Jesus. In His personal identity statement (Isaiah 61:1-7), Jesus proclaimed that He had favor. His favor is to train and equip us to live from a place of confident expectancy in the goodness of God. The Holy Spirit will empower us to become positioned so we stand in that favor, no matter what circumstances are present.

The way the Holy Spirit does that is to teach us about divine displacement. The key word in the Isaiah 61:1-7 passage is the word "instead." It means in place of or an alternative to. He gives us beauty instead of ashes. When we feel burned out, and our life has turned to dust and ashes, He turns it around and grows something beautiful instead.

When we are surrounded by sorrow, and our hearts weep with the hardness and bitterness of life, He pours out the oil of joy. When our hearts are heavy, and we feel the crushing weight of depression, lethargy, passivity and indifference — He comes to us with His own innate happiness and empowers us to put on a garment of praise; literally, a covering of joy and rejoicing. He restores us to gratitude and worship as a way of life.

"Instead" means that the Father intends for something else to occur in place of the negative. It means that He has created an alternative occurrence for us to step into, instead.

What shall we say instead, to those things? Romans 8:31-39 is about learning an alternative mindset and heart disposition. Instead of being overwhelmed by things against us, we can become astonished at who He is for us! We are in the business of learning an overcoming lifestyle. Therefore, we are not consumed by the negative; we are overjoyed at the opposite. Whatever the enemy has planned, God has provided an alternative instead. It is our heritage to move in the opposite spirit to what is coming against us.

Favor is God's intentional bias toward us

"No weapon that is formed against us will prosper. And every tongue that accuses us in judgment will be condemned. This is the heritage of the servants of the Lord" (Isaiah 54:17). A heritage is a value that is passed down to all succeeding generations. Favor always comes in the context of vengeance (61:2). God has made provision for us against the enemy. Vengeance is the anointing to extract favor when we are under attack. It comes from an ancient promise that God gave Israel in the Exodus from Egypt. *"I will make all your enemies turn their backs on you"* (Exodus 23:27). Everything about the Christ life is concerned with turning the tables on the enemy. When he attacks, something

else is supposed to happen instead. Therefore, at the moment of attack, we can focus on what God is giving us permission to overcome.

Think the opposite. Move toward it. Reposition yourself for a blessing. The ultimate revenge on the enemy is that everything he tries against us only makes us bigger, better and stronger. Permission is granted for us to prosper when under attack. For a more detailed understanding of this truth, go to www. BrilliantBookHouse.com. There is a free MP3 download called *Recession Buster* with our compliments.

As God develops us in Him, we come into a realm of experiencing the tangible blessings of God in the material sense. As Israel was being delivered from bondage, they received these tangible, material prophecies about inheriting great and splendid cities they did not build, houses full of all good things which they did not fill, hewn cisterns which they did not dig, vineyards and olive trees which they did not plant so they could eat and be satisfied (Deuteronomy 6:10-12). That we may prosper and be in health even as our soul prospers (3 John 1:2).

Our development is exponential

All throughout Scripture we see that God is concerned to meet not only the immediate, basic needs of His people, but also to establish them in their inheritance. We see Jesus in the Gospels continuously looking after people's material needs — whether feeding thousands of people (Mark 6), helping Peter pay the tax (Matthew 17:24-27), or blessing business people (Luke 5:1-11) who eventually become disciples.

Into this earthly domain and material world the Kingdom comes with power (Mark 9:1). All power is given to Jesus in Heaven and earth (Matthew 28:18). Greater things will His people do (John 14:12) because Jesus will intercede for us before the Father (Hebrews 7:25). He gives us authority to tread on serpents and scorpions, and over all the power of the enemy, and nothing will injure you (Luke 10:19-20).

And He said to them, "Go into all the world and preach the gospel to all creation. He who has believed and has been baptized shall be saved; but he who has disbelieved shall be condemned. These signs will accompany those who have believed: in My name they will cast out demons, they will speak with new tongues; they will pick up serpents, and if they drink any deadly poison, it will not hurt them; they will lay hands on the sick, and they will recover." (Mark 16:15-18)

Finally, all that the Father bestows upon us has the capacity for exponential growth. As we give out, it will be given back to us, pressed down, shaken together, and running over (Luke 6:38; Mark 4:24-25). There is a standard principle connected with giving that works across the whole of life. Life in the Spirit is concerned with abundance (Ephesians 3:20) and God's people learning to abound in everything (2 Corinthians 8:7). Living an exponential lifestyle is a hallmark of our place and capacity in Jesus (2 Corinthians 9:6-15).

Walking in the Intentionality of God

Only God has abundance; the enemy has a budget. In a time of recession it is hell that is running out of cash. God does not change, and Heaven is always full. Life in Christ cannot cease to be abundant simply because the world is having a hard time. "On earth as it is in heaven," is not only the Lord's Prayer, but also our testimony.

> *God is always present–future, not present–past*

Assurance, Not Guidance

One man who benefited from understanding the will of God was Gideon. At the time, Israel was not being faithful to God. In fact, the nation had done such evil in His sight that He had given them into the hands of the Midianites. Things were so bad in Israel that the people were hiding in caves and fortresses. The Midianites were absolutely brutal: every harvest time, they would sweep through the nation and steal everything that wasn't nailed down. Again and again, the Israelites lost their sheep, donkeys, food supplies, and everything else.

In Judges 6:11-16, God decided to change all that. His intervention would have huge implications for Israel and one man in particular.

> *Then the angel of the LORD came and sat under the oak that was in Ophrah, which belonged to Joash the Abiezrite as his son Gideon was beating out wheat in the wine press in order to save it from the Midianites.*
>
> *The angel of the LORD appeared to him and said to him, "The LORD is with you, o valiant warrior."*
>
> *Then Gideon said to him, "o my lord, if the LORD is with us, why then has all this happened to us? And where are all His miracles which our fathers told us about, saying, 'Did not the LORD bring us up from Egypt?' But now the LORD has abandoned us and given us into the hand of Midian."*
>
> *The LORD looked at him and said, "Go in this your strength and deliver Israel from the hand of Midian. Have I not sent you?"*
>
> *He said to Him, "o Lord, how shall I deliver Israel? Behold, my family is the least in Manasseh, and I am the youngest in my father's house."*
>
> *But the LORD said to him, "Surely I will be with you, and you shall defeat Midian as one man."*

> *God elevates His persona above our personality*

We see two things taking place with Gideon: firstly, the initial conversation that He has with the angel of the Lord, and secondly, we note the careful nature of his eventual response.

Gideon has issues of a personal and national nature. He is worried about the nation, is concerned that their capacity to flow with God is diminished, and is angry enough to feel abandoned by the Lord. On a personal level he feels inadequate, insecure and lacking in confidence. We can learn much from his initial conversation with the Angel of the Lord.

Angel: *"The Lord is with you, o valiant warrior."*

Gideon: *"Really? Where's the evidence? Why is all this happening? Where are all the miracles? God has abandoned us into the hands of Midian!"*

Gideon has not picked up at all on the fact that this is a personal calling. *"I am with you!"* is always the very essence of our ministry call. It is highly personal. I have experienced many times when God has not been with the people where He sent me to speak. However, He is with me, and therefore I must position myself in His favor so that His purpose can be achieved through my obedience. Gideon missed that initial point.

God is not interested in answering our questions about the past; He is focused on what is coming next. It was His will that Gideon deliver the Israelites into freedom, despite the young man's protests.

Instead of responding to Gideon's questions, the Lord looked at him. There is usually a moment when we are not getting the message when the Lord is silent. The look speaks a thousand words. It brings us into line with purpose.

Sometimes the look reminds us of who we should be and how we should live in our present situation. When Peter denied the Lord for the third time, a rooster crowed. Jesus turned and looked at Peter, and he remembered (Luke 22:59-61).

Notice that Heaven ignores our negativity. The Lord just continued as though Gideon had not spoken.

Angel: *"Go in this your strength and deliver Israel from the hand of Midian. Have I not sent you?"*

The calling of God always elevates His persona above our own personality. He comes to give us Himself. I AM is with us. Our destiny is always transformed by His identity at work within us. When the Lord declares His intentionality within our call, it causes our inadequacies and insecurities to surface. They must rise up so that He can empower us to deal with them as part of our training.

Gideon: *"o Lord, how shall I deliver Israel? Behold, my family is the least in Manasseh, and I am the youngest in my father's house."*

In other words, there are surely better people than myself for you to choose. My household has no seniority or authority in our tribe, and I am the low man in my family's hierarchy. I am the youngest of the worst.

> *The antidote to our past is our future*

If we are going to be successful in serving the Lord then, our I AM statement must become the same as God's I AM statement to us. Double-minded people are unstable and have poor expectations of God. Part of our training is to learn to receive under pressure. Knowing God's intentionality is vital. Again, notice that God ignores the response we make when it is incompatible with His perception. The Lord ignores excuses and stays focused on what He is doing.

Angel: *"Surely I will be with you, and you shall defeat Midian as one man."*

Our weakness, when turned over to God, can become a place of strength as He inhabits our lives with His intention. All our initial conversations with the Lord will go in the same direction. He chooses us because of what He wants to be for us. His appointment and anointing become our commission and authority. His power shows up best in weak people (2 Corinthians 12:9-10) so that no one will confuse our victory with our ability. The very thing that we think disqualifies us from serving God is, in fact, exactly why He chooses us.

Gideon perceives the intention of God and comprehends that it will revolve around God's favor.

> *So Gideon said to Him, "If now I have found favor in Your sight, then show me a sign that it is You who speak with me. Please do not depart from here, until I come back to You, and bring out my offering and lay it before You." And He said, "I will remain until you return."*

> *Then Gideon went in and prepared a young goat and unleavened bread from an ephah of flour; he put the meat in a basket and the broth in a pot, and brought them out to him under the oak and presented them (Judges 6:17-19).*

This action cost Gideon a lot. We tend to forget that his family was poor: killing a goat cost them dearly. With the Midianites stealing everything again and again, this goat was an important part of their family wealth. Gideon's sacrifice reveals something about his faith: he believed this was God. When someone is destitute, they don't give away their food unless they're very sure. Gideon seemed certain that this was God. He wanted to make an offering as a part of his response to the call. The meal would have taken a considerable time to prepare and serve. All this time his heart is beating to the call he had received.

When God speaks, an action is required from us to demonstrate that we have heard and received the call. That response must initially cost us something. David said, "I will not offer to the Lord, that which cost me nothing" (1 Chronicles 21:24). In a time of famine and despair we must sacrifice toward our deliverance. We are required to take actions in line with our future, not our present.

> *The angel of God said to him, "Take the meat and the unleavened bread and lay them on this rock, and pour out the broth." And he did so.*

Then the Angel of the LORD put out the end of the staff that was in his hand and touched the meat and the unleavened bread; and fire sprang up from the rock and consumed the meat and the unleavened bread. Then the angel of the LORD vanished from his sight.

When Gideon saw that he was the angel of the LORD, he said, "Alas, o Lord GOD! For now I have seen the angel of the LORD face to face."

The LORD said to him, "Peace to you, do not fear; you shall not die."

Then Gideon built an altar there to the LORD and named it The LORD is Peace. To this day it is still in Ophrah of the Abiezrites.

Fire burst from the rock and consumed the offering, prompting Gideon to experience the fear of the Lord and be concerned about his own mortality. This should be a critical part of mentoring anyone into the ministry. The fear of the Lord must be passed down from generation to generation. If people learn the fear of the Lord at the beginning, they'll be less arrogant and more teachable in their own development.

Gideon needs reassurance and receives it. He builds an altar of remembrance to this, his first encounter with the Angel of the Lord. Altar building is hard work. No one seeing fire come out of a rock is in doubt that they have just encountered the Almighty and been called by Him. Gideon knew the will of God.

On the same day, he heard God's voice again giving him further directions:

Now on the same night the LORD said to him, "Take your father's bull and a second bull seven years old, and pull down the altar of Baal which belongs to your father, and cut down the Asherah that is beside it; and build an altar to the LORD your God on the top of this stronghold in an orderly manner, and take a second bull and offer a burnt offering with the wood of the Asherah which you shall cut down."

Gideon knew the will of God

Then Gideon took ten men of his servants and did as the LORD had spoken to him; and because he was too afraid of his father's household and the men of the city to do it by day, he did it by night.

When the men of the city arose early in the morning, behold, the altar of Baal was torn down, and the Asherah which was beside it was cut down, and the second bull was offered on the altar which had been built. They said to one another, "Who did this thing?" And when they searched about and inquired, they said, "Gideon the son of Joash did this thing."

Then the men of the city said to Joash, "Bring out your son, that he may die, for he has torn down the altar of Baal, and indeed, he has cut down the Asherah which was beside it."

But Joash said to all who stood against him, "Will you contend for Baal, or will you deliver him? Whoever will plead for him shall be put to death by morning. If he is a god, let him contend for himself, because someone has torn down his altar." Therefore on that day he named him Jerubbaal, that is to say, "Let Baal contend against him," because he had torn down his altar (Judges 6:25-32).

Again, no one would go and pull down the local demonic stronghold without knowing it was God who had told them to do so. Furthermore, Gideon wouldn't have killed his father's two best bulls unless he was very confident that he was walking in the will of God. Gideon even convinced a group of men to help him; this is more proof that he completely trusted God.

When we are called to extra local ministry we must ensure that our home base is securely in the hands and will of God. Overcoming what is against us at home is a sure sign that our anointing will increase as we go to battle elsewhere. Consistency is drawn from our militancy on the battlefield and our intimacy at home. Gideon obeyed the voice of God because he knew it was the will of God.

The whole neighborhood was angered by Gideon's actions. The townspeople had awakened that morning and gone to the high place to say their morning prayers. Imagine your surprise if, this Sunday morning, your church was gone! Instead, there was a pile of ashes, blood, skin, and bone. The smell must have been horrendous. After some quick investigating, it became apparent that Gideon was to blame, and off the mob went to kill the man who had overthrown Baal. Only his father, Joash, saved Gideon from being torn to pieces.

Still, Gideon was convinced that he was in the will of God. After surviving the mob's anger, he blew a trumpet and sent messengers across Israel.

Then all the Midianites and the Amalekites and the sons of the east assembled themselves; and they crossed over and camped in the valley of Jezreel. So the Spirit of the LORD came upon Gideon; and he blew a trumpet, and the Abiezrites were called together to follow him. He sent messengers throughout Manasseh, and they also were called together to follow him; and he sent messengers to Asher, Zebulun, and Naphtali, and they came up to meet them (Judges 6: 33-35).

At every encounter, Gideon shows himself to be a man of integrity and obedience to the will of the Lord.

Gideon blew that trumpet because he was totally convinced of the will of God. If he hadn't known, he would have never acted. He was utterly confident in what God wanted to do. When we don't know what the will of God is, we don't do anything. Inertia sets in as we wait for something to come to us. Gideon, on the other hand, was focused and moving ahead. He wouldn't have sent people across Israel if he didn't know the will of God.

So, therefore, the fleece he laid out before God had nothing to do with guidance. When we do not know the will of God we don't make large gestures for fear of being embarrassed. He sent messengers out to gather the tribes for a fight. The Spirit of God had come upon him, and he had made proclamations to other tribes.

The fleece was not about Gideon seeking guidance from God. He needed reassurance that he was the man to lead the fight.

> *Then Gideon said to God, "If You will deliver Israel through me, as You have spoken, behold, I will put a fleece of wool on the threshing floor. If there is dew on the fleece only, and it is dry on all the ground, then I will know that You will deliver Israel through me, as You have spoken." And it was so. When he arose early the next morning and squeezed the fleece, he drained the dew from the fleece, a bowl full of water. Then Gideon said to God, "Do not let Your anger burn against me that I may speak once more; please let me make a test once more with the fleece, let it now be dry only on the fleece, and let there be dew on all the ground." God did so that night; for it was dry only on the fleece and dew was on all the ground (Judges 6:36-40).*

> **The fleece is not concerned with guidance**

Why would someone who had acted so confidently in the will of God need a fleece to double-check? The fleece had nothing to do with finding God's will and everything to do with his own poor self-image. Gideon wasn't seeking guidance; he was asking for reassurance. He knew the war had to be fought, but he wanted to be sure that he was the one to lead it. "Is it really me?" he asked God. Reassurance is a key part of God's intention for us. When He commits us to impossible situations He knows that it will throw us into a crisis of self-confidence. The Lord had to ensure that Gideon was not only in the center of His will but that he was also strengthened and encouraged to fight the way God intended. One person walking with God is always in the majority. That person will require reassurance from the Lord.

Gideon wanted to be sure that he was the one to carry out God's will. He was convinced and determined to do God's will, but he wanted reassurance that God was with him. What did God do? He accommodated Gideon's weakness and insecurity. God knows who we are; He has no illusions about our nature or abilities.

The fleece was a one-time event, and we shouldn't be crafting entire theologies around it. Putting out a fleece isn't a divinely ordained way to get guidance;

it was simply God's reassurance to one man who needed it. Sometimes, I think we use fleeces to rationalize away the requirements of obeying God. We shouldn't use them as a spiritual-sounding excuse for laziness or ignorance.

Gideon's issue wasn't about knowing the will of God; it was about being reassured that he was the one to fulfill it. God continued to stretch Gideon in this regard. In Judges 7, He sent away ninety-nine percent of the army Gideon had gathered. In verses 9-15, we read of how God again reinforced Gideon's self-confidence:

> Now the same night it came about that the LORD said to him, "Arise, go down against the camp, for I have given it into your hands. But if you are afraid to go down, go with Purah your servant down to the camp, and you will hear what they say; and afterward your hands will be strengthened that you may go down against the camp." So he went with Purah his servant down to the outposts of the army that was in the camp.

> Now the Midianites and the Amalekites and all the sons of the east were lying in the valley as numerous as locusts; and their camels were without number, as numerous as the sand on the seashore. When Gideon came, behold, a man was relating a dream to his friend. And he said, "Behold, I had a dream; a loaf of barley bread was tumbling into the camp of Midian, and it came to the tent and struck it so that it fell, and turned it upside down so that the tent lay flat."

> His friend replied, "This is nothing less than the sword of Gideon the son of Joash, a man of Israel; God has given Midian and all the camp into his hand."

> When Gideon heard the account of the dream and its interpretation, he bowed in worship. He returned to the camp of Israel and said, "Arise, for the LORD has given the camp of Midian into your hands."

Tens of thousands of Midianite soldiers were camped over several miles, and Gideon miraculously ended up next to the one tent where one of those soldiers had a strange dream. Only God could be so confident that He would send a vastly outnumbered general into the enemy's camp for prophetic reassurance. The man's dream of a barley loaf smashing them to pieces was interpreted by another enemy soldier as being a sign that Gideon's sword was going to destroy all of them. Gideon was so staggered, so encouraged by the dream and its interpretation, that he started shouting worship to God in the middle of the enemy's base. I'd be running away as fast as I could; Gideon was kneeling in praise.

It is this abundant confidence in the will of God that we are called to possess.

Waiting On the Lord

We generate that type of radical faith by waiting on God. Waiting on the Lord means exactly that — waiting for Him. It's not about waiting for guidance or waiting for a sign; it's waiting on Him. Guidance will often flow from that right relationship with God, but it is not the primary goal. What we must seek is relationship, not direction. Waiting is relational activity.

David, as a shepherd, psalmist, and king, understood this dynamic better than anyone throughout Scripture. He loved to wait on the Lord, as we see in Psalm 25:3-5:

Indeed, none of those who wait for You will be ashamed;

Those who deal treacherously without cause will be ashamed. Make me know Your ways, O LORD;

Teach me Your paths. Lead me in Your truth and teach me, For You are the God of my salvation; For You I wait all the day.

David wanted to know how to walk before God. He wanted to know how God's mind worked so that he could think like Him. He wanted to know how God wanted him to act on days of adversity and trouble. David was a lot like Gideon — so confident in God's ability that it didn't matter if it were 32,000 or three hundred men in his army. *"If God is for us, who is against us?"* as Paul phrased it in Romans 8:31. That is outrageous confidence in the will of God.

Waiting on the Lord is purely relational. We just sit in His presence, improving the quality of our worship and adoration. We get filled up with the things of Heaven. Imagine just reclining in God's arms, not bothering Him with dozens of questions, but simply loving who He is. Waiting is about breathing in His presence and becoming saturated with who He is. We are called to be completely preoccupied with God.

> *Waiting on God is purely relational*

"One thing I have asked from the LORD, that I shall seek: That I may dwell in the house of the LORD all the days of my life, to behold the beauty of the LORD and to meditate in His temple," David sang in Psalm 27:4. Joshua lived the same way while in the desert all of those years: *"Thus the LORD used to speak to Moses face to face, just as a man speaks to his friend. When Moses returned to the camp, his servant Joshua, the son of Nun, a young man, would not depart from the tent,"* Exodus 33:11 records. Joshua's priority was to live where the presence of the Lord was.

How many of us are making plans this year to improve our worship? How much time are we putting aside to simply adore Jesus? When do we just let Him be God and bask in the presence of His magnificence?

None of us have a desire to be the worst Christian who ever lived, but few of us have a plan to become the best one. If we don't plan to worship, we won't do it. If we don't set time aside to sit in the presence of God, we'll never get around to it. We're so busy working through the issues of everyday life that we have completely forgotten how to interact with the very Source of it all. This is the currency that our lives run on. Time is precious. To spend time with someone proves that you love them.

Time is our most valuable commodity. Determining how we use it can lead us to success or failure. Insignificant people waste time. Good people find time. Great people make time!

"When You said, 'Seek My face,' my heart said to You, 'Your face, LORD, I shall seek,'" David wrote in Psalm 27:8. This command is simple: seek Me for who I am. If you seek Me, I'll make sure you find Me. David's ability to wait on God became the very foundation of his confidence in God's will, as we see in Psalm 27:11-14:

> *Teach me Your way, O LORD,*
> *and lead me in a level path because of my foes.*
> *Do not deliver me over to the desire of my adversaries,*
> *for false witnesses have risen against me,*
> *and such as breathe out violence.*
> *I would have despaired unless I had believed that I would see*
> *the goodness of the LORD in the land of the living.*
> *Wait for the LORD; be strong and let your heart take courage;*
> *Yes, wait for the LORD.*

> Waiting is the cultivation of anticipation

David's ability to wait on God is truly remarkable. In the worst seasons of distress, with hostile troops surrounding him, and an angry king out to kill him, he waited on God. His followers must have been worried, but David wasn't: he knew that worshipping God on the day of trouble was the very thing that would ensure his victory. Again and again in his psalms, David sang of the beauty of waiting on the Lord.

"Rest in the LORD and wait patiently for Him; Do not fret because of him who prospers in his way, because of the man who carries out wicked schemes," he said in Psalm 37:7. It is an absolute delight to wait on the Lord. It creates such a natural relationship with Him that we begin to carve out more and more opportunities to simply dialogue with Him. Suddenly, we begin to talk to the Lord about everything. Our cars become charismatic chat rooms where we talk to God. We look around and are reminded constantly of His beauty and grace.

Building a relationship with God secures our inheritance: *"Wait for the LORD and keep His way, and He will exalt you to inherit the land; When the wicked are cut off, you will see it"* (Psalm 37:34). We don't have to worry about our future, destiny, or identity because God has got all of that covered. All of these things are simply added to us while we bask in His presence. The plans He has for us unfold in His heart. Once we ensure that we are in His presence and ready to receive them, they will surely flow to us. *"The steps of a man are established by the LORD, and He delights in his way,"* says Psalm 37:23-24. *"When he falls, he will not be hurled headlong, because the LORD is the One who holds his hand."* We may stumble, but God holds our hand. Relationship belongs to us, but guidance is His alone.

It is not our job to seek God's will. It's our joy to seek His face. Relationship is the key to all things spiritual. I choose to spend time in worship, adoration, and meditation. Seeking the Lord's face is a pleasure. The Lord knows what is coming, and I am confident that He will show me if I cannot work it out for myself (John 16:13).

At the moment, I turn down around seventy percent of all speaking engagements I am offered. I could spend hours and hours lying on my face asking the Lord where He wants me to go. There are some invitations that are not in line with my calling and present anointing. They are the easiest to decline. Others are from places where I have an involvement already; they are the easiest to accept. Occasionally the dates do not work, but with over half the invitations, I need some input from the Father.

God speaks in many different ways. Sometimes, it is clear from the start that this is the will of God, because His fingerprints are all over the situation. His hand is unmistakable, like the Macedonian vision, and we cannot deny it. Other times, God outright forbids us from doing something. Either way, I'm happy for His intervention because I know I'm in His will. It's not an agonizing process. It's actually very peaceful and occasionally quite humorous. Many years ago the Father was talking to me about some people that He wanted me to meet, develop a friendship with, and work alongside. My question was: "How will I know if this invitation is a relational connection rather than a ministry opportunity?" The answer startled me. "You will hear a click," said the Lord, and I heard an audible click, like the snapping of a middle finger and thumb.

> Seeking God's face is a pleasure

A few weeks later I was sorting through some invitations. My ministry often goes in cycles in terms of current anointing, particular assignments, and defined breakthroughs. I tend to immediately discard those that are not in line with how the Holy Spirit is using me at that particular time. I had a number of invitations in my *not at this time* pile. Reading through the remainder, I heard a click. I immediately wrote to that person, and we have been friends ever since.

I came into my UK office one day as our fax machine was printing out something. As I drew level with it, I heard a click. Putting my briefcase down, I read the fax. It was from Randy Clark. I wrote my reply on his message and faxed him back! He has been a very good friend for me, and we have both been there for one another at significant times.

While we do not see the word *click* specifically mentioned in Scripture, there is a general heading called "a sound from heaven," in Acts 2:2. It was fun; every time I heard the sound, my spirit would leap in excitement, knowing that a divine connection had been made. The sound has now been replaced with something else. The Father likes variety. He is still creating. He loves the interaction of His heart with ours and the relationship that it provokes.

We wait on God at certain times and for certain seasons. The Lord loves to be specific on particular occasions. There is a lovely sense of drama about putting time aside to cultivate a special word, thought or invitation. Often these times are characteristic of Heaven's interaction in our lives. Doors open, new permissions are granted, fresh anointings are released. We move to a different level in the Spirit.

We also wait on God within the sensitivity of our heart to His. Waiting on God is a relational activity that runs throughout each busy day as a lifestyle experience — a turning and a lifting of the heart in praise and thanksgiving, a rest of mind and heart, a unity of peace within that enables us to be still. It's a simple delight in listening, the cultivation of anticipation, knowing that if God does not speak initially, He will speak eventually. Waiting on God is part of our abiding in Christ, learning to dwell and remain in an attentive manner. It's a joy to hang out in the Holy Spirit.

It's the simple, beautiful demonstration of the fact that my life is no longer my own. I share all of it with the One who knows me best and loves me the most.

Guidance and Direction

It is important to note that all of our steps are ordered by the Lord and He delights in seeing us led by the Spirit (Psalm 37:23). He takes great pleasure in planning our lives *"for I know the plans that I have toward you, says the Lord, plans for your welfare not for your calamity, to give you a future and a hope."* (Jeremiah 29:11)

> God loves the initiative

The revealing of those plans can be relational through guidance or ministered through prophetic direction. It is important for a prophet to not only know the difference between guidance and direction, but also to empower people in the appropriate manner.

Guidance comes from the Lord through our ongoing relationship with Him. The goal of the Holy Spirit is to teach everyone how to hear the voice of God for themselves. It is to teach people devotionally how to worship, pray, be still, meditate on the Word, and wait on the Lord. In the joyful practice of these simple disciplines, we learn real sensitivity to the Holy Spirit. He is our indwelling Presence that guides us into all truth and discloses to us what is to come (John 16:13). Guidance is the by-product of a right relationship with God. Guidance is an internal process; direction is an external revelation.

Direction comes from God through a third party. He takes initiative. It is a sovereign action by the Holy Spirit — not in response to our seeking out a prophet, but in reply to our prayers.

The Old Testament prophetic anointing made no distinction between guidance and direction. They were one and the same. This is because people did not have the indwelling nature of Christ and were not capable of being led by the Spirit. Their spirituality was ordained through the office of prophet and priest who represented God to man and man to God. They stood in the gap between humanity and the Almighty. People went to them for sacrificial absolution and prophetic input.

> *The world changed on the day of Pentecost*

The world changed on the Day of Pentecost. The Holy Spirit is now in people, not on them. In the Old Testament, the prophetic gift was concentrated on a few people. In the New Testament, thanks to Pentecost, the ability to hear God and to move in the gift of prophecy is now available to every Christian (1 Corinthians 14:1, 5).

In the Old Covenant it was okay to go to a prophet to inquire of the Lord. In a New Covenant, that would be deemed illegal behavior. We have the indwelling Presence of God and therefore are capable of hearing His voice ourselves (John 10:27).

The role of a New Testament prophet has now dramatically changed. The chief role of a prophet is primarily to teach people how to hear God themselves. They train people in how to discern and obey the will of God. They instruct, train, equip and release people in the prophetic gift, ministry and office of a prophet. In the process of that training directive, they also bring prophetic words to individuals and people groups.

In the Old Testament, the prophets gave *now* words and *new* words. Now words are about guidance. New words are concerned with direction.

Examples of those words are seen in 1 Samuel 9 when Saul asks the prophet the location of his donkeys (and got more than he imagined!). He wanted a *now* word (guide me to the livestock) and received a *new* word, about becoming king (1 Samuel 9:3-10:1). New words come out of nowhere. They are a complete surprise to us. It is the Lord charting our course and revealing His plans and purposes.

Many years ago I was overseeing a prophetic conference at my home church base in Southampton, UK. My good friend, John Paul Jackson, was one of the speakers. The Lord showed me that there were several people in the church who needed some prophetic input. I invited them to a brief meeting with myself and John Paul. Some of the group I knew just needed some meaningful encouragement regarding life and what they were facing. I brought a couple of friends, David and Leyna Clarke, who I thought were in that category.

Imagine our surprise when John Paul gave them a *new* word that was extremely directional to the effect that "David would be headhunted for a job in the Middle East and would be working for royalty." We came out of that meeting bug-eyed with astonishment. Sure enough, within months David was working for the Saudi royal family representing their business interests in Dubai.

The role of the New Testament (NT) prophet is different than their Old Testament (OT) counterpart because another element is dropped into the mix. Now that people are set free to hear God themselves, the NT prophet not only gives now and new words, but also brings confirmation to people; that is, we confirm through prophecy that what the Lord has said to an individual or group is true and accurate.

When I first connected with David and Deborah Crone, Senior Team leaders of The Mission in Vacaville, CA, it was in that type of situation. I was taking a leaders meeting in Sacramento. At the end the Lord gave me some words for people. It was an odd moment. I had just given a significant word over Bill and Beni Johnson, and then the Lord pointed out Dave and Deb. We had never met, and I knew nothing about them. All I had was one sentence which was in stark contrast to the previous prophecy! It was: "The Lord is putting precious stones into your foundations."

That was it! Kind of boring, cryptic and nonsensical, to me anyway. David's face went white and Deborah burst into tears. Sometimes what actually makes a word prophetic is the situation we are speaking into. Context often determines what God has to say.

In this context, David and Deborah were building a new sanctuary. They felt the Lord was telling them to do it prophetically by placing objects in the walls and foundations — swords, shields, flagons of oil, Bibles wrapped in oil-skin, that sort of thing. However the Lord had also asked them to put diamonds, sapphires and opals (precious stones) into the foundation of the building as the concrete was being poured. That very day they had picked up thousands of dollars worth of gems in Sacramento. David was new to the prophetic at that level and both were very nervous. Was it the Lord? How can we be sure? They prayed, asking for a confirmation. Here I am, almost embarrassed because I only have one sentence that feels a little weird!

In the modern church, many people go to prophetic conferences because they want a prophetic word, not because they want to learn to prophesy or hear God's voice themselves.

Prophets are put under incredible pressure to prophesy. I have been given marks out of ten by leaders, most of whom had never prophesied but were comparing me to other prophets they knew.

Guidance and Direction

At every meeting people line up wanting to hear a prophetic word over their lives One woman in Singapore looked me straight in the eye and said, "The Lord told me that you have a prophetic word for me."

"Really?" I said. "When the Lord said that to you was His voice really strong or quite faint?"

"I heard it very clearly," she said.

"Sister, if you can hear God that clearly, you don't need me to prophesy over you. Have a nice day!"

> *Context can determine what God wants to say*

There are a number of issues to address when people come seeking prophecy, guidance and direction. My personal primary response is to only do what the Father is doing and only say what He is saying. There are times when I am asked to prophesy, but I sense the Holy Spirit immediately saying "no." I'm happy then to move into prayer and perhaps some advice.

The gift of discerning of spirits enables us to discern what is God, what is man, and what is an evil spirit. If I hear the Lord saying no to prophesying, I will often move into prayer for people. A lot of times I ask questions to enable them to perceive the next step for their life.

- What did you do with the last word you received?

- Why do you want another one?

- Are you fulfilling the conditions for that particular word to come to pass?

Guidance is a relational issue, not a prophetic one. If people are not walking with God properly, prophecy will not solve that problem. Prophets cannot come between people and God. We point the way back to God. We equip and empower people to have a spirit of wisdom and revelation in the knowledge of Jesus (Ephesians 1:17). When asked for guidance, a true prophet will first question the current status of people's relationships with God.

If people are passive in their prayer life, lethargic in their worship, or apathetic in their morality, those issues need to be addressed. If we prophesy over these people, then we reinforce their poor behavior. Obviously there are times when we receive grace and mercy to speak into such situations to bring a prophetic release. It is an exception, not the rule.

Some people are lazy. They do not seek the Lord themselves. They don't ask in prayer. They do not knock on the door of relationship (Matthew 7:7-8). There are some amazing relational guarantees that the Father provides for us in our fellowship with Him. The Father gives us those assurances so that we will keep on seeking, asking and knocking until fulfillment arrives! Some people would rather seek a prophet than seek the Lord.

If their problem is caused by lack of fellowship in their relationship with God, we want to ensure that they do not remain in a backslidden state. Sometimes prophecy can jolt them out of it and move them back into fellowship by giving them a *now* word. Mostly I have found that asking questions, instead of moving in the gift, is more productive.

If we do not stay in fellowship, life can get ahead of our intimacy, and we come under pressure through events, circumstances, and people. We all need Jesus much more than we need prophecy. Failure to upgrade our relationship with God is ultimately what makes us tired, weary, and open to oppression. When life increases, our fellowship must increase also. Prophesying over people in this context may bring temporary relief, but it may also establish a mindset that is out of order. Prophecy is not a shortcut into something; only a proper response to God is a sure thing.

The principle is this: we take care of the relationship and God takes care of the guidance. In itself, guidance is the by-product of a right relationship with God.

Everything a New Testament prophet does should push people back into their own relationship with God. Direction is God's responsibility, not ours.

When we accepted Christ, God took us out of the kingdom of darkness and put us in His Kingdom of light. Scripture promises us that we will have the light for our whole lives. While there are many verses telling us to seek God, none tell us to seek guidance. God will communicate His will as we develop our relationship with Him. Throughout Scripture we read many examples of the direction that comes when we seek first God's face:

- *"In Your loving-kindness You have led the people whom You have redeemed; In Your strength You have guided them to Your holy habitation." (Exodus 15:13)*
- *"For such is God, our God forever and ever; He will guide us until death." (Psalm 48:14)*
- *"Nevertheless I am continually with You; You have taken hold of my right hand. With Your counsel You will guide me, and afterward receive me to glory." (Psalm 73:23-24)*
- *"I will instruct you and teach you in the way which you should go; I will counsel you with My eye upon you." (Psalm 32:8)*
- *"But He led forth His own people like sheep and guided them in the wilderness like a flock." (Psalm 78:52)*
- *"So he shepherded them according to the integrity of his heart, and guided with his skillful hands." (Psalm 78:72)*
- *"Trust in the LORD with all your heart and do not lean on your own understanding. In all your ways acknowledge Him, and He will make your paths straight." (Proverbs 3:5-6)*
- *"Your ears will hear a word behind you, 'This is the way, walk in it,' whenever you turn to the right or to the left." (Isaiah 30:21)*

When I am asked for a personal prophetic word, I steer the conversation back to the individual's own relationship with God. "How are you doing with the Lord?" I might ask. "What's the state of your relationship with Him?" Guidance, after all, is the fruit of a good relationship with God. Those who follow Him have light to guide their way. For me to prophesy into their circumstances isn't going to be helpful for them, long-term, because the message they will receive is that their problem is a product of their lack of direction. My job as a prophetic minister is not to prophesy, but to instead pray for their relationship with God. Is there anything in their lives that they shouldn't be doing? That's the starting point to get back on track with the Lord. When they deal with the hindrances to relationship with Him, they will receive His guidance. To prophesy in the Old Testament manner is to intermediate between God and man, and the New Testament forbids that by anyone except Christ Himself.

In New Testament prophecy, we have to resist the urge to over-prophesy, otherwise we will infringe on the deeper issue of their one-on-one relationship with God. That relationship is built on the revealed truth in Scripture, not on outside prophetic revelation.

People come seeking prophecy because they don't know God's will and they want a shortcut to help find it. A prophecy cannot accomplish that; instead we need to work to reestablish and restore the dignity of their relationship with God. Christians must learn to wait on God for relationship, not guidance. If we seek His face first, everything else will fall into place.

What If We Get It Wrong?

Firstly, it's important to note that when we do anything spiritual for the first time, we cannot make a mistake. We can only learn. There is always an abundance of grace available to us as we grow up in all things in Christ. If we do not learn and change our methodologies, then we are making mistakes and heading into error.

The fundamental difference between mistake and error is that the first is an internal disorder that leads to an external disobedience. Any action, good or bad, is usually preceded by a thought. Even in an apparent thoughtless act, there is usually a moment when we ignore consequences, or we do something that stems from a wrong belief.

A mistake is concerned with our inward territory. We think inappropriately, we understand poorly and we believe wrongly.

The assumptions we make become the actions we produce. We are acting out of a belief system that, at best, is undeveloped.

An error is a fundamental defection from the right path. It means to miss the mark continuously — to go astray by wrongdoing. It means to be affected more by external circumstances or influenced by the wrong people. This produces an internal fault that creates a breakdown. The conclusions that we make become the resolutions that we follow.

When we hold to a particular line of thought, we create a belief system, good or bad, that drives all our actions. Our belief system empowers us to see the world in a particular way. In our perception, we adopt a position that enables us to walk through this world in a distinctive manner. It is where we develop attitudes and perceptions that are a blessing, or we develop prejudice and distortions of mind and heart.

> The assumptions we make become the actions we produce

When our mind is renewed it is because we have accepted that God has all the best thoughts, and we want them too. Repentance is to *think again* literally. Restoration is the external consequence of an internal renovation. In Christ we get to change our mind for His. We can learn to perceive differently and believe something that will empower us to be Christ-like in the way we act.

When our mind is renewed, our spirit is refreshed, and our walk with the Lord is unrestrained. When I see people behaving oddly my first question is: "What is it that they believe about themselves that makes them behave in this manner?" My next question usually is: "How are they seeing and thinking about this other person that makes them speak and act toward them in this improper way?"

It seems that most discipling involves putting constraints around people so that they do not do things that are inappropriate. We terminate people. We pull them out of their function, but we do not empower them to change. Restriction without development is punishment. Loving people enough to enable them to think again is a powerful part of the Kingdom.

In the prophetic realm, it is all too easy to have our input toward someone colored by how we view them or by our understanding of them both positively and otherwise. Eli thought Hannah was drunk and became indignant because he was watching her mouth (1 Samuel 1:12-14) and not listening to the Lord. She was crying out to the Lord in distress, desperately wanting a child. Moses completely misunderstood the heart of two of the tribes, Reuben and Gad, in the time of the Exodus (Numbers 32). Actually, they were the first to see their inheritance and receive it. Moses accused them of being a sinful brood of men like their fathers, who were discouraging Israel from entering the land of promise.

It is always too easy to get caught up relationally with people around us and prophesy out of what we see and know about someone. David and Nathan had a good friendship. Nathan saw David's passion for worship. He probably read some of David's psalms. No doubt these two good men, serving the Lord together, had many conversations about the health, wealth, and wellbeing of the nation.

Seeing David's desire to build a temple for the Lord touched Nathan's heart. When in conversation David expresses his intention to build a temple, Nathan steps into the place of ministry because of what he thinks and believes about David (2 Samuel 7:1-17). He spoke prophetically: *"Go and do all that is in your mind, for the Lord is with you."*

How could such a passion be wrong? David is a man after God's own heart. Surely, everything fits together. A mindset about David, a lack of understanding about God and a belief that everything fits together — these all led Nathan to give permission to something that the Lord had not spoken.

When Nathan and David got it wrong, the Lord took responsibility for putting it right.

That same night, God made it clear to Nathan that He wanted a man of peace to build His house. David could collect materials, but his son was to build the temple. A man of blood couldn't do it, only a man who knew the peace and rest of God. The next morning, Nathan went to his friend and king and gave him the word. "Sorry, my friend, I was wrong," he probably said.

God made His will known when both the king and prophet had missed it. If we stay in relationship with Him, constantly seeking His face, He will guide us in the same manner.

Boundaries Around the Will of God

God guides us through our relationship with Him. He fulfills that responsibility by giving us incredible freedom within a few boundaries. Peace is one of those boundaries. *"And let the peace (soul harmony which comes) from Christ rule (act as umpire continually) in your hearts,"* says Colossians 3:15 (The Amplified Bible). Peace is our umpire in the game of life. Peace lets us know when we're in danger of striking out, or when we've hit a home run.

> *Peace empowers our sensitivity*

Using peace as an umpire in our life makes perfect sense when we consider that the foundation of our relationship with God is peace and rest. Christians should be the most peaceful people on the planet because we're intimately connected to the Prince of Peace. Peace, therefore, should be a by-product of our lives. Peace empowers our sensitivity. It enables us to wait patiently and listen.

We can mature to a place in God where it is impossible to worry. When we rest in Him completely, we frustrate the enemy. The kingdom of darkness cannot find us when we are in our secret place of rest in God. In the Psalms, David referred to God as his hiding place, his fortress, and his strong tower. We can access that same place of protection. When we are wrapped up in Christ, the enemy's ability to influence us is seriously diminished. The secret place is where we overcome — firstly ourselves; secondly our circumstances and finally, any opponent that is against us.

Each one of us, including those called to the prophetic ministry and office, is called to a high level of relationship with God. Out of that friendship comes our ministry and significance. It doesn't work the other way around; our relationship with Him must take precedence over any work we do for Him. How we see and live with God transcends what we can do for Him.

We need to learn how to allow peace to be our umpire. A referee only stops a game when things get out of hand or when a rule is broken. Great referees let the rest of the game proceed naturally. When we discover that living in peace is God's absolute design for our life, we can trust Him to shake us up when we move out of His will. As long as we are fulfilling the conditions for a right relationship with Him, we are at peace. If we begin to move away from God's purposes, He will blow the whistle on us by lifting our peace.

God gave us peace as an umpire for one simple reason: He doesn't want us to spend our lives searching out His will; He wants us to spend that time seeking His face. Our goal is to get as deep into the presence of God as we possibly can. "Further up and further in," as C. S. Lewis put it in *The Last Battle*. God is responsible for guiding us, and we are responsible for our relationship with Him.

There is no rigid, God-ordained blueprint for our lives. The will of God is not a tightrope; it's a broad, green pasture. The pasture has some boundaries to it, but the space between them is immense and unimaginable.

> *The will of God is not a tightrope; it's a broad green pasture*

Sin, of course, is a boundary to the will of God. If we move so far to the side that we know our next step will take us into sin, we don't need a prophecy to tell us to stop — we will be walking out of God's will. Ethics is another boundary; we have to live in a way that doesn't cheat or hurt anyone.

Truth and integrity are also boundaries. Scripture is another boundary, especially as we interpret God's instruction for our lives. We cannot do anything that transgresses the written Word of God. Peace is the final boundary. The boundaries give us great freedom to explore the values of Heaven in a sin-sick world. When we make mistakes ourselves, our true friends surround us with a love and grace that pulls us back inside the circle of redemptive living. Unbounded love emanating from a place of bounded integrity — what a marvelous paradox!

The Apostle Paul knew these boundaries well. *"All things are lawful, but not all things are profitable. All things are lawful, but not all things edify,"* he wrote in 1 Corinthians 10:23.

The apostles modeled this idea of knowing God's will perfectly. Paul and Barnabas, for example, traveled extensively throughout the Mediterranean region. The Bible doesn't record a single instance of them asking God where to go next. In Acts 13, the pair were commissioned and sent out for the first time. They went to Cyprus, Pamphylia, Pisidia, and Lycaonia, establishing churches in Antioch, Iconium, Lystra, and Derbe.

Paul only asked two questions when he entered a town: He wanted to know where the local synagogue was, and where the local prison could be found. He knew that his appearance in one may lead to an appearance in the other! Paul and Barnabas caused a stir in many of these towns, to the point that Paul was stoned in one city. The two didn't interpret that attempt on Paul's life as a sign that they had stepped out of God's will. They didn't spend forty days fasting and asking God to reveal where they should go next. They just went, knowing that they would be persecuted everywhere because of the message they carried.

In Acts 16, Paul went on another missionary journey, this time visiting Phrygia and Galatia, preparing to continue on. Suddenly, in Acts 16:6, God made His will known: *"They passed through the Phrygian and Galatian region, having been forbidden by the Holy Spirit to speak the word in Asia."* God kept them on track by telling them what He didn't want them to do. It's like that with God; sometimes, He tells us where not to go. They went on to Mysia with the intention of going to Bithynia, and again, the Lord stopped them: *"and the Spirit of Jesus did not permit them"* (Acts 16:7). Instead, they went to Troas where Paul had an incredible vision of a Macedonian man asking him to come and help them. Paul concluded that the vision was God's guidance, and he went to Macedonia.

God intervened whenever it looked like Paul was about to make a wrong choice. Otherwise, He just let them go and preach. He invited them to Macedonia while they were preparing to spend a lot of time in Troas. He protected them from straying out of His will.

Paul had a deep, intimate relationship with God. He continually submitted his heart and life to the Lord and trusted God's nature. Paul took care of the relationship, and God took care of the direction.

We see this pattern again and again in Scripture. In Acts 1:23-26, the disciples cast lots to see who would replace Judas Iscariot in their ranks. There was no fasting and prayer, just trust that God would ensure the correct outcome.

Abraham was so secure in God's provision that he let his nephew Lot choose the territory he wanted first. Abraham took the leftovers, even though custom dictated that Lot should have deferred to his uncle (Genesis 13).

God is silent a lot of the time in regard to His will. He knows that if He is too vocal we will not make the slightest move without His permission. It is His way of teaching us sensitivity and maturity. He wants us to make right choices.

> *Trust the nature of God*

In the natural, we adopt different processes for contrasting situations. For small children, we keep them from stumbling by holding their hand. A good father stays close and personal. So, in the Spirit, we are learning to be much loved children developing confidence and security in the Father's permission.

For teenagers, such attention would be deemed overbearing. We develop maturity through counsel, dialogue, and wise advice. We coach them into a place of maturity by teaching them to make wise choices and to take responsibility. In the Spirit, we teach them to be led by God through an interactive process.

When they become adults, we facilitate them into new growth and opportunities. We empower them to "do what is in your heart to do." We have instilled in them the capacity to make wise decisions. Momentum is the key to this stage. They have a green light until it turns red. At this stage in the Spirit, God mostly intervenes when we look like we're going off track. *"Your ears will hear a word behind you, 'This is the way, walk in it,' whenever you turn to the right or the left"* (Isaiah 30:21). It is not until we turn off track that we hear the Lord speak.

God's silence does not imply disapproval. He is letting us learn how to walk and flow with Him. We can reach out knowing that He is there and that He is faithful. We can practice our trust until it becomes instinctive and intuitive. The Holy Spirit teaches us about waiting on God, developing stillness, practicing the art of meditation and contemplative prayer. As we cultivate our sensitivity by active listening, we learn how to anticipate His heart of goodness.

The normal way of guidance in the New Covenant is to be led by the Spirit from within. In relationship, we allow the Spirit to cultivate our fellowship with God so that we think and speak as He does.

The normal way of guidance is therefore more concerned with having a renewed mind than possessing a prophetic word.

God's silence also does not imply His approval. He does not continually remonstrate with us about sin. We have the Scriptures, our conscience, the indwelling Holy Spirit and of course, people in our lives who love us. We learn to develop the sensitivity of the Holy Spirit as well as becoming accustomed to His holiness. We do not grieve Him. We learn to live in the revealed word of Scripture. In our passion, we become God-conscious. We want God in all of our thoughts.

A Process of Peaceful Elimination

In the 1970s, when I was first entering prophetic ministry, everyone seemed to stress the importance of discovering the will of God for every area of our lives. I mimicked a lot of what I saw during those times. For example, friends of mine had fasted and prayed for weeks on end, asking God who they were supposed to marry. When I came to the Lord I assumed I had to do the same thing. I fasted and prayed, for a whole day.

On the second day, I felt the Lord tap me on the shoulder and ask me what I was doing.

"I really want to marry the right woman," I said.

"Have you got anyone in mind?" He asked me.

"Well, yeah," I replied.

"Do you like her?" He continued.

"A lot," I said.

"Okay," He said with a chuckle.

> We choose,
> God confirms

Confused, I went to talk with one of my mentors: "I'm really praying about Heather and me getting married," I said.

"Do you love her?" he asked me.

"I do," I said.

"Well," he said, "ask the Lord if He has any objections, and if He doesn't say anything, marry the girl."

So I did. I had learned an important lesson. God wants us to choose what we do with our lives. If He doesn't like our choice, He'll make that clear. God is in the business of producing mature sons and daughters who can think with the mind of Christ, not a bunch of spiritual babies who need a word just to brush their teeth in the morning.

Soon after, I was interviewed by three different companies for a job. As the businesses mulled over the candidates, I asked God which one He preferred. The best case scenario would be that all three would offer me a job, and I wanted to be sure I took the one God ordained for me. What did God say during that intense time? Nothing.

When the largest of the three companies called me and offered me the best salary package I could expect, I gave God another chance. If He didn't say anything to me that night, I would take the job. After all, I wanted to be paid well.

The next morning I woke up and my first conscious thought was an uneasy feeling about the job. My peace was gone. I picked up the phone, called the company, and turned down their offer. It hadn't felt right, and God had lifted my peace to show me the way He wanted me to go. My friends, of course, thought I was crazy.

A few days later, the second best job was offered to me. Again, I told the Lord that I would accept the position the next day if He didn't say anything to me that night. Again, I woke up feeling uneasy and turned it down.

I took the job with the smallest company. God could have just told me from the start to take that position, but He didn't. Instead, He wanted me to learn how to discern the boundaries He had placed around His will for my life. He used a lack of peace to eliminate the jobs that weren't for me.

It was the right decision. Within six months the first company had gone bankrupt, and everyone had lost their job. Three months after that, the second company was bought out, and the division I would have been working in was dissolved. But at the job I took, I was promoted several times. I started as a training professional and ended up as business development manager.

God knew the place that He wanted for me but didn't feel that He needed to say anything to me up front. He had given me peace as a guide, and I used it.

Jesus came to bring peace to the world. He gives us peace in a world full of tribulation and antagonism. Life can contain hostile people. It is loud, noisy, restless, and disturbed. Peace is the ability to not let our heart be troubled

(John 14:27) because we know that it is peace that enables us to overcome in circumstances (John 16:33).

The path of peace (Romans 3:17) is to become spiritually minded (Romans 8:6) and to pursue peace as a way of life. Peaceful people are always the most edifying and encouraging (Romans 14:19).

I am diligent about entering and enjoying my peace every day (Hebrews 4:11). Rest is a state of promise for all God's people (Hebrews 4:1). We should rightly be concerned about inhabiting this most beautiful place. Initially we have to work hard at practicing rest, so that eventually we become it. We practice rest and peace by pushing away the opposites. I will not allow anxiety, fear, unbelief, worry, panic, or any other negative to settle in my heart or mind.

> Pursue peace as
> a way of life

I push them away while at the same time rejoicing that Jesus is my Prince of Peace. I will not allow myself to get flustered by circumstances. I want peace, therefore I must pursue it. The God of great expectations loves to fill our hearts with joy and peace in believing (Romans 15:13) so that we are super-confident in who the Holy Spirit is for us.

God is not the author of confusion, but peace. In my experience, many people say they are confused when actually they are recalcitrant. Their confusion is a mask; they really want to control the conversation and steer it away from the requirements of obedience. When I release my peace, it has no effect on them because they are not really seeking the Lord.

The Lord Himself continually grants us peace in every situation (2 Thessalonians 3:16). We cannot discuss our way into peace. Peace does not come because we have settled an issue and answered all the questions. Peace is not the result of what we do or talk about. It is a precursor. It's a forerunner of His Presence. It exists in advance of our circumstances being resolved. We have peace. Now let's talk. We always live from peace, not toward it. I do not push negatives away in order to obtain peace; I have peace. I am refusing to allow it to be disturbed.

In the matter of the will of God, therefore, peace is the arbiter, the umpire that decides a way forward.

> "Let the peace of Christ rule in your hearts, to which indeed you were called in one body; and be thankful." (Colossians 3:15)

The peace of God that passes all understanding (Philippians 4:7) is what guards our hearts and minds. Peace does not come because we understand something. It is present before our awareness is complete. Peace upgrades our perception, not vice versa.

In decision making, God does not have to tell us everything. He has given us peace. When we have peace, we keep moving forward. When our peace is disturbed, we stop and ask questions. In some cases, our lack of peace indicates a *no* solution. Other times it may signal a *wait/not yet* resolution that needs clarifying. Peace is designed to teach us sensitivity so that we listen differently. We develop maturity more quickly through peace than through training. The way of peace is like higher education. It takes us to another level so we can process life in a different way. I love the lessons of peace, but it really is the road less travelled.

If the Father is not talking verbally, He will speak through the process of peaceful elimination. Our options are first reduced until the chosen path lights up. It's just one of His ways to make us people of His Presence. *"My peace will go with you."*

God of Paradox

When one starts walking with God, we quickly learn two things about Him. First, He is utterly consistent. Second, He is completely unpredictable. He is consistent because His nature never changes: *"For I, the LORD, do not change,"* as was prophesied in Malachi 3:6. *"Jesus Christ is the same yesterday and today and forever,"* adds Hebrews 13:8. God will never change the way He sees us or feels about us because it is impossible for Him to do so. He acts the same way toward us on our best day as He does on our worst. He does not and cannot change. This is one of the great things about the nature of God: He never shifts the way He acts, thinks, speaks or sees. He is utterly consistent and faithful to His nature.

> God is consistent and unpredictable

But beyond that, God is totally unpredictable. This paradox – two seemingly conflicting ideas contained in the same truth, is at the core of who God is. There are many paradoxical facets to God: for example, He is a righteous judge who demands the death penalty for sin, and He is a loving Father who paid that price Himself. In God's Kingdom, everything is a paradox. We give in order to receive. We die in order to live.

God loves to do things unpredictably. Instead of sending in a huge army to liberate Israel from Egypt, the most pagan, evil empire on earth, he sent an old man with a stick and a stutter. Not only that, He hardened Pharaoh's heart so that he wouldn't listen! He's the same God who reduced Gideon's already badly outnumbered army from 32,000 to 300.

Only God would think of defeating the most fortified city on earth by getting people to walk around it silently for a few days and then to shout in expectation of God's direct action. Jericho was taken with no ladders, no siege towers, no battering rams, no earthen ramps — just the shouts of people who had been wandering around a desert for forty years. If I gave your church a similar prophecy, you would have me committed!

God's unpredictability means we have no security in what God is doing. We can only be secure in who He is. Our mission as Christians is to learn how to live in Christ and let that be the bedrock for our life. God will ask each of us, both individually and as part of a corporate Body, to do things that are outrageous, impossible and unpredictable. Unless we live in the consistent nature of God, we will never take that step of faith.

It seems to me that much of the Church is completely opposite to God. The Church is inconsistent in its relationships, but boring and predictable in the way we go about things. We must turn that model around and become rock-solid relationally and actively innovative. The world doesn't like what we have to offer at the moment because we're too inconsistent in friendship — we don't do what we say we will do, and we don't mean what we say. On the other hand, our church services are numbingly dull. No wonder God wants to bring us back into the place of being an enigma on the earth; it's His nature He wants to see reflected in us.

When Does God Speak?

One of the parts of God's nature that a mature Christian understands is that He is usually silent. This silence doesn't mean disapproval; in fact, when God is quiet, it is generally an indication that He is happy with us. He doesn't need to constantly reassure His mature sons and daughters when they are doing well; He just lets us be until we look like we're heading off track (Isaiah 30:21).

It is incorrect to think that God is continuously revealing His will to us. However, He does carry the responsibility of putting us back on the rails when we slip off. We can trust Him to steer us back if we are headed in the wrong direction.

Because God has placed the Holy Spirit in us, we can feel safe that we are within the will of God, even when we don't hear from Him every day. *"I am the Light of the world; he who follows Me will not walk in the darkness, but have the Light of life,"* Jesus said in John 8:12. This verse means exactly what it says: Jesus gives us enough light to see and know the direction we're headed. *"But when He, the Spirit of truth, comes, He will guide you into all the truth; for He will not speak on His own initiative, but whatever He hears, He will speak; and He will disclose to you what is to come,"* Jesus added in John 16:13-14. *"He will glorify Me, for He will take of Mine and will disclose it to you."* The Holy Spirit will disclose to us what is coming in our own life, and in our role within the Kingdom. We can trust Him completely. Our very relationship with Him is prophetic. On the day of Pentecost Peter emphasized that the Outpouring of the Holy Spirit was in line with an ancient prophecy given by Joel. *"I will pour out my Spirit on all flesh. And your sons and daughters will prophesy, your old men will dream dreams, your young men will see visions."* (Joel 2:28)

The very first emphasis for Pentecost was that now people are free to hear the voice of God, speak out of His heart, and have prophetic insight, vision and the capacity to hear and see what God is doing.

That was God's priority when He poured out His Spirit. It's interesting that initially the Outpouring was not for the preaching of the Gospel, but for prophetic relationship. Indeed, when God's people are walking in right relationship, the Gospel becomes more personal to those who hear it.

The Gospel being preached effectively depends upon ordinary people hearing God's voice for themselves! According to Joel, therefore, one of the credible signs of the end times is that all of God's people hear His voice and have a relational ability to prophesy.

Jesus is our Prophet, Priest and King. It is poor theology to only accept two out of three of those characteristics. The Holy Spirit discloses to us what is to come (John 16:13). Jesus is our internal prophetic relationship with the Father, and we are empowered to hear His voice by the Holy Spirit. Our very relationship is prophetic.

It is perfectly normal and healthy to ask the Lord about things we are facing in our life. This is part of our relationship with Him, part of learning how to commit things to His care. But we shouldn't live in fear if He is silent; we should trust Him to answer if and when it is necessary.

In 1 John 5:14-15, we are told exactly what to expect from God: *"This is the confidence which we have before Him that, if we ask anything according to His will, He hears us. And if we know that He hears us in whatever we ask, we know that we have the requests which we have asked from Him."*

The Father loves to reveal His will to us. He wants us to have the mind of Christ. All His ways are concerned with bringing us into maturity and confidence in His Name and His Nature.

When we ask in line with who He is for us then prayer becomes a certainty and His response, a fixed guarantee. That type of assurance sets us apart as the real people of God in a world of wannabes. Our testimony becomes our verbal confession of His relationship with us. Our confidence in all that He is in Himself becomes the bedrock of our lives. Anything built on it will last, regardless of the changing seasons and the gathering storms.

Confidence Through Abiding

The key element in determining the will of God is always confidence. The Father does what is right always, and He is amazing in His consistency and faithfulness. He always finishes what He starts (Hebrews 12:2), and we can absolutely trust that He will complete His purpose in us (Philippians 1:6).

Holding on to our confidence is the major part of being mentored by the Holy Spirit. Good coaches always impart personal conviction that a goal can be achieved. Mentors provide assurance. Our personal security is built upon our own understanding of who God is for us (Hebrews 3:6, 14). Assurance allows us to become. The Holy Spirit stimulates our inner man to stand up on the inside

> Good coaches impart personal conviction

of us with a smile and a confident assurance of the love of the Father. Abiding in Christ is a major source for confidence (1 John 2:28). It guarantees that we won't step back into a place of doubt or mistrust. No condemnation means that we are free to move about the Kingdom in confidence (1 John 3:21).

The will of God is never about doubt; it's always about discovery. Everything about God is potentially open to exploration. The will of God is not a mystery. It is relational. It is true that there are times when situations do not work out as we have prayed or purposed. We often cannot see the end from the beginning. We may only have enough light to take the next step. If God's will is relational, then our confidence lies in becoming like Him, not just in our own version of a successful outcome.

We must trust. As we abide, our confidence continues. We are certain of God's will being done even if the outcome is not what we would prefer. He sees more. He knows more. When we allow His will to be relational, we are saying that to become like Him through our present circumstances is a higher priority than just receiving a successful result.

When we make that a priority, confidence is always the outcome — full assurance of salvation. To be made in the image of God is everything to us. All our circumstances carry that relational priority. We are becoming partakers of Christ, we discover God's will more readily when we share His priority.

As we face all of life relationally in Christ, we can receive peace, rest, and joy. The love of God is ever-present. We are learning to become like Jesus. *"As He is, so are we in the world"* (1 John 4:17).The will of God then becomes something that we don't have to look for because confidence is a part of the relationship (1 John 5:14-15).

Sonship is our priority. All true sons are confident in the Father's character. There is a godly routine that the Holy Spirit employs consistently in His relationship with us. He encourages our heart. He renews our mind. We enter into a dialogue with Him so that we can learn to ask properly. He teaches us to pursue and go after God in all our circumstances. We learn to discover provision and power. We get to call ourselves up to a new relational level. We fight from victory, not toward it.

We develop confidence and cease from striving. The will of God is a settled issue when our relationship with the Lord is our first priority. Whenever people ask me for a prophetic word about the will of God, I know that prophecy

> *The will of God is not a mystery... it's a relationship*

will not help them. The problem is that their relationship is off track and must be restored. I'm very happy to pray for their relationship to be upgraded and for them to learn the lessons of dwelling in God. Worshippers abide. It's what we do best. All ministries should have a context that empowers them to release people to abide. It's the key discipline of the New Testament.

Conclusion

We all want to know and experience what it is to be swamped by God's majesty on any given day. To do that, we must be willing to expose and enjoy our weakness; for it is there that we are made strong. I encourage you to put yourself in God's way, and just relax there. Allow your relationship with Him to be the top priority in your life. Guidance will naturally flow out of that intimacy with Him.

I want to live simply before God. Prophecy is a bonus for me; I trust His nature enough to get along without a prophetic word for my life. I don't tend to get intimidated by things because I'm too busy being fascinated by Jesus. When things go wrong in my life, I watch Jesus and wonder how He's going to get me through this time.

God is bigger than my sin, my stupidity, my ignorance, and my personality. I'm just a normal man putting himself in the way of something divine and majestic. Life doesn't need to be any more complicated than that.

When we let God be God, we can walk with Him in joy, peace, safety and wisdom.

Conclusion

<u>Walking in the Intentionality of God</u>

Reflections, Exercises and Assignments

The following exercises are designed with this particular chapter in mind. Please work through them carefully before going on to the next chapter. Take time to reflect on your life journey as well as your prophetic development. Learn to work well with the Holy Spirit and people that God has put around you so that you will grow in grace, humility and wisdom in the ways of God.

Graham Cooke.

What Constitutes Maturity?

Knowing God's intentionality and faithfulness is a major part of developing prophetic utterance. New Testament prophets need to know how guidance works so that they can assist people in breaking out of any inertia.

- Maturity is knowing what God is doing in and through us as an individual and not confusing the two in our prophetic development.

- Cultivating a life of celebration is most vital if we are to avoid negativity in the ministry. Rejoicing plays a major part in developing trust and becoming trustworthy.

- When we do not know how to receive from our own devotional relationship with God, we become vulnerable in our contribution to others. Negativity is always at the door of our heart trying to get in. Praise neutralizes negativity.

- True prophets have a passion for the Presence of God, which empowers them to take responsibility for their own blessing, which in turn enables them to bring release and freedom to others. There is a progression of freedom from our own walk with God that commissions release for people around us.

- We must know the relational difference between moving in the power of the love of God instead of just having a love for the power of God.

- Central to our prophetic development is that we personally cultivate a present–future mindset and lifestyle. It allows us to experience favor as a prophetic expression which elevates our persona in Christ above our personality. It is this context that establishes obedience as a key to sustained growth.

- When we know by experience that guidance is the by-product of a right relationship with God then waiting on Him becomes a matter of delight, not duty. The difference between guidance and direction guides our actions into the true place of fellowship.

What Constitutes Immaturity?

Failure to comprehend that Jesus in Himself brings a whole new type of prophet and prophetic ministry into the earth — one that reflects the nature of God within the believer rather than the external legal structure that surrounded people in the Old Covenant. Law gives way to grace, mercy replaces judgment, goodness and kindness lead to repentance, the Truth becomes a Person within, and favor displaces performance. Prophecy that does not reflect the Good News will not pass the test of authenticity.

- When we are not sensitized to the nature of God in Christ, we are more likely to become super spiritual, overly intense and religious in life. There is a disconnect between God's heart and the prophet's mouth.

- Failure to develop a lifestyle of celebration means that we become casual about rejoicing and thanksgiving. It often leads people into living in their circumstances rather than in relationship with Christ. Such people live off the anointing of other people.

- People become poor in the prophetic because they do not develop the space that God has set aside for them. They have a greater passion for ministry than they do for intimacy. The end result is that we do things for the applause of man rather than the approval of God.

- The biggest failing of most poor prophets is that they have been touched by God but not changed. They have settled for knowing truths about God without developing an ongoing experience of Truth into a place of freedom and power. We fail to discover God in every circumstance and our prophesying is less significant as a result.

- Undeveloped intention is a sign of childish behavior. It leads us into settling for measure and reveals a poverty spirit. Prophecy not founded on intimacy cannot produce confidence.

- The thinking that prophecy is more important for guidance than a renewed mind often leads to low-level expression of the gift. Part of prophetic utterance is the realigning of people's belief systems with the internal Christ.

- When we cannot transform our own poor self-image, then we have no impartation to release. Being too restless to learn waiting on God means that our devotional relationship will hit a ceiling and level off. True prophets make plans and set aside time and resources to upgrade their worship and intimacy.

Reflections, Exercises and Assignments

ASSIGNMENT ONE

Read and meditate on Psalm 84.

Think of a person in your life at this time particularly, someone who is ready for an upgrade not only in their relationship with God but also in the way that they present themselves for ministry.

First, ask the Lord to touch your own heart with these words so that you may have an encounter with the Holy Spirit. Your own heart needs refreshing. Your devotional life needs to go to a higher place of inheritance and habitation.

Be filled with the Spirit. Go to a new place of joy and rejoicing. The Father is making your heart a place of celebration. This is no small blessing and requires a heart that is fixed and focused. God is not available to the casual seeker but will reveal Himself to one who is learning to become wholehearted.

With yourself and your friend in mind, prepare your heart to receive encouragement by answering the following questions:

1. What specific desires is the Father upgrading in the life of your friend?

2. What gifts and graces are being made available to this person?

3. How would you encourage this person to rise up and occupy a new place in the Spirit?

4. Make a list of every type of blessing available in this scripture. What is the Lord releasing in fullness and abundance?

Write out the word as a letter from the Lord to this person. Read it to them as you feel the Lord would read it in your place. Make a recording of your reading. Give the letter and recording to them.

Walking in the Intentionality of God

ASSIGNMENT TWO

Patience – Fruit Of The Spirit

The enemy is a crafty foe. Sometimes, he will forgo an overt attack and use simple, everyday ways to keep us from progressing in the spirit. Hurry and pressure are two such devices. Many people get out of sync with God because they are hurrying. They are too busy to pray, too busy to worship, too busy to meditate, too busy to enjoy intimacy with God. Humans can become so hung up with the destination of where they want to go that they completely forget to enjoy the journey.

I do not see this pattern in Jesus' life. If ever there was a man who was busy and had the right to rush, it was Him. He was trying to change an entire religious system and free the world from bondage in three short years. And yet Jesus was busy, but never hurried. Sometimes, He probably had no time to even eat, with the number of people coming and going and the traveling He did. But He knew He could not go any faster than the One, the Father, who was leading Him.

These days, people learn to read faster, talk faster, play faster, work faster. We have created generations of impatient people. It takes patience to build the important, lasting things, but our hurried nature wants an instant download from Heaven instead. We must learn that some things in God do not come quickly or in a big package. Sometimes they come in a series of small things to be enjoyed in the moment. Only when we look back at all of those small things will we realize the big thing God has done.

Patience is now completely counter-cultural. While the world may be more complicated than ever before, God has not lifted the spiritual quest for the fruit of patience from us. In fact, He wants us to focus on it more than ever before.

Take stock of your life right now. If a lack of patience is an issue for you, it should be very obvious. If God wants to grow your patience, you will face delays, traffic, slow line-ups, slowed prophetic action and the rest. He tests us on these issues because He wants to refine our character.

Patience is a virtue we need to develop, especially when we are about to birth something new spiritually. It takes time to grow as we sort through all of the things that are thrown at us and discover what exactly God is calling us to. We have to wade through everything and wait. My suggestion for people in a season of birth or upgrade is to write out a prayer for patience and pray it every day. In the midst of crisis, it is difficult to pray spontaneously because our requests of God shift with the pressure we feel in the heat of the moment. But if we have written out a prayer that asks God for a specific thing, we can be faithful to what God wants to do.

In my greatest season of breakthrough, I have written out a patience prayer, laminated it and put it in my wallet so I could access it anytime, anywhere. I would pray that prayer fifteen times a day and found myself becoming more patient every time I did it. The Holy Spirit calls patience up in us when we ask for it.

Take a piece of paper and write a prayer of patience on it. Put it up somewhere you will see it several times a day, and pray it whenever you notice it.

CASE STUDY

The delivery of a prophetic word must match its content.

The objective of the prophecy must affect your delivery. If the plan is to encourage or inspire someone, then your words and how you say them must be uplifting to that person.

If the objective is to empower them to make a stand and resist the enemy then your delivery must give them the necessary strength to rise up.

The context (i.e. the way that you speak the prophecy) must match the content (i.e. the actual word being released). Study the following prophecy and answer the questions following it:

Alexandra, this is your season for riding on the shoulders of your Heavenly Father. He has picked you up, out of your old ways and circumstances, and is carrying you into a new place in His love and affection for you.

The old has passed away and a new woman is coming forward. She has a new heart and a renewed mind. The Father will cause you to see life from a new perspective. You will learn the joyful discipline of seeing things the way that He sees them.

This is a time of joy and laughter. It is a time of redefining who you are and what you want to become. There is a new person emerging who is strong, vibrant, healthy and beautiful. The Father knows what kind of person you need to be in order to attract what you most want to receive in life.

He is carrying you. He has lifted you onto His shoulders. He is bearing the weight of this transformation. His strength is your energy. His joy is your sense of wonder. His love for you is your inner motivation and desire.

You are learning to be loved and upgraded, to be joyful and to persist with a smile on your face. You are learning to trust by depending upon His goodness.

As you move forward, His power will fill you. His pleasure in you empowers you to break through every obstacle. You belong to Him and your heart will resonate with His. No longer a victim, simply the Beloved.

Reflections, Exercises and Assignments

Answer the following questions:

1. What is the focus of this word?

2. What is the emotion and plan God has for Alexandra?

3. What will she need to allow in order for this word to be fulfilled?

4. How would you speak this word to her? What would you pray to seal the word in her heart?

LECTIO DIVINA

Lectio Divina (Latin for *divine reading*) is an ancient way of reading the Bible — allowing a quiet and contemplative way of coming to God's Word. *Lectio Divina* opens the pulse of the Scripture, helping readers dig far deeper into the Word than normally happens in a quick glance-over.

In this exercise, we will look at a portion of Scripture and use a modified *Lectio Divina* technique to engage it. This technique can be used on any piece of Scripture; I highly recommend using it for key Bible passages that the Lord has highlighted for you, and for anything you think might be an inheritance word for your life (see the Crafted Prayer interactive journal for more on inheritance words).

Read the Scripture:

The LORD is my light and my salvation;
Whom shall I fear?
The LORD is the defense of my life;
Whom shall I dread?
When evildoers came upon me to devour my flesh,
My adversaries and my enemies, they stumbled and fell.
Though a host encamp against me,
My heart will not fear;
Though war arise against me,
In spite of this I shall be confident.

One thing I have asked from the LORD, that I shall seek:
That I may dwell in the house of the LORD all the days of my life,
To behold the beauty of the LORD
And to meditate in His temple.
For in the day of trouble He will conceal me in His tabernacle;
In the secret place of His tent He will hide me;
He will lift me up on a rock.

And now my head will be lifted up above my enemies around me,
And I will offer in His tent sacrifices with shouts of joy;
I will sing, yes, I will sing praises to the LORD.

Hear, O LORD, when I cry with my voice,
And be gracious to me and answer me.
When You said, "Seek My face," my heart said to You,
"Your face, O LORD, I shall seek."
Do not hide Your face from me,
Do not turn Your servant away in anger;

Reflections, Exercises and Assignments

You have been my help;
Do not abandon me nor forsake me,
o God of my salvation!
For my father and my mother have forsaken me,
But the LORD *will take me up.*

Teach me Your way, o LORD,
And lead me in a level path
Because of my foes.
Do not deliver me over to the desire of my adversaries,
For false witnesses have risen against me,
And such as breathe out violence.
I would have despaired unless I had believed that I would
see the goodness of the LORD *in the land of the living.*

Wait for the LORD;
Be strong and let your heart take courage;
Yes, wait for the LORD *(Psalm 27).*

1. Find a place of stillness before God. Embrace His peace. Chase the nagging thoughts out of your mind. Calm your body. Breathe slowly. Inhale. Exhale. Inhale. Exhale. Clear yourself of the distractions of life. Whisper the word, "Stillness." Take your time. When you find that rest in the Lord, enjoy it. Worship Him in it. Be with Him there.

2. Reread the passage twice. Allow its words to become familiar to you. Investigate David's words and emotions. What images does it bring to your spirit? What do you see? Become a part of it. What phrases or words especially resonate with you? Meditate especially on those shreds of revelation. Write those pieces down in your journal.

3. Read the passage twice again. Like waves crashing onto a shore, let the words of Scripture crash onto your spirit. What excites you? What scares you? What exhilarates you about this revelation of the nature of God? What are you discerning? What are you feeling? What are you hearing? Again, write it all down in your journal.

Walking in the Intentionality of God

4. Write the theme of this passage in your journal.

5. Does this passage rekindle any memories or experiences? Does it remind you of any prophetic words you have given or received? Write those down as well.

6. What is the Holy Spirit saying to you through this Scripture? Investigate it with Him — picture the two of you walking through it together. Write those words in your journal.

7. Read the passage two final times. Meditate on it. Is there something God wants you to do? Is there something He is calling you to? Write it down.

8. Pray silently. Tell God what this passage is saying to you. Tell Him what you are thinking about. Write down your conversation together. Picture yourself and the Holy Spirit as two old friends in a coffee shop, chatting about what God is doing.

9. Finally, pray and thank God for His relationship with you. Come back to the passage once a week for the next three months. Read it and let more revelation flow into you. If you feel compelled to, craft a prayer based on this passage for yourself, your family, your friends or your church. Pray that prayer until you feel God has birthed it in you.

Notes

Notes

MODULE TWO

THE PROMISES OF GOD
AND OUR DEVELOPMENT

MODULE TWO

The Promises of God and Our Development

WHAT YOU WILL LEARN IN THIS SEGMENT:

- Knowledge always involves an encounter with God
- All promises elevate our relationship with the Lord
- The Law began as a prophecy
- All prophecy involves a process
- Every response is tested so it can be established
- Partnering with newness of life
- Take responsibility for your blessing
- There is no breakthrough without follow-through
- The difference between personal prophecy and the prophecy of Scripture
- Know the blessings of obedience and the pitfalls of disobedience
- Freedom must also bring restraint
- After the calling comes the training
- How to become present–future in lifestyle
- Developing an internal perception aligned with God's viewpoint
- God relates to us in the present through the destiny He beholds
- It is the process that makes us rich, not the outcome
- Exploring your territory in the Spirit
- Develop a pattern of behavior in faith
- How to attract destiny
- Receiving under pressure
- Favor is attached to the image of Jesus, not our behavior
- Encounters and experience are the norm for spiritual practice
- Challenge your circumstances with the prophetic
- A mindset can only be changed by a mindset
- The enthusiasm and encouragement of the Holy Spirit!
- Patience is critical to development
- Being open hearted when under extreme provocation
- Everything is given to us by the Father; our joy is to receive
- Living in the fullness of God's faithfulness
- All prophecy contains a moral imperative
- In prophecy, we must impart Presence
- The Father must destroy all resistance to His nature
- We pay a price to walk with God in the high places
- Prophecy comes to completion through partnership

MODULE TWO

The Promises of God and Our Development

WHAT YOU WILL LEARN IN THIS SEGMENT:

- Confrontation is intended to bring renewal and refreshing
- Prophecy is a significant discipling tool
- Blessing, not judgment, opens people up to God
- Moving from a paradigm to a paradox
- Character recognition involves compassion
- Speaking the truth in love and kindness
- Developing a culture of honor
- Integrity is concerned with internal consistency
- Self-control is the key to negativity
- Holiness is the only forceful deterrent to carnality
- Meekness is not weakness; it is strength under control
- Devotion to God is our prime ministry
- Start from a place of truth and work back to a point of need
- Know the difference between positive and negative anger
- How to be ordinarily inspirational in the course of life
- A lifestyle approach to spirituality is more powerful than a situational attitude
- The art of ministry is encouragement
- Knowing the intentional bias of God toward you
- Learn your Assignment in the Spirit
- Claiming your upgrades in the Spirit
- Intimacy as the source for all power in ministry
- The affection of God is the beginning of ministry
- Faithfulness guarantees the outcome in God's heart
- Authority gives us territorial jurisdiction
- Accountability is only concerned with imposing freedom
- Accountability is not a contest, it's a cooperation
- Prophecy gives us an outcome beyond the testing
- God speaks from the outcome to the outworking
- There is a difference between what is true and the Truth
- Faith combined with patience enables us to inherit

The Promises of God and Our Development

WHENEVER ANYONE MAKES US A promise, we are entitled to call it in, depend upon it, and trade on our trust in the one who made it. When we receive a promise from someone, we qualify it according to the character and integrity of the one who spoke it.

When we believe in the word spoken, when we trust in the integrity of the speaker, all fear and nervousness are banished from our heart. Peace is elevated above all worry and anxiety in our minds. We are settled. Our hearts are fixed.

What is true in the natural is much truer in the Spirit. When the Father speaks into our lives with a promise, all that He is becomes enshrined in our response. He is righteous. He can only do what is right. He is truth. He can never lie, flatter or deceive. He is holy, pure and innocent, without sin and with no guile.

The promise, therefore, is guaranteed by the quality of His Nature. When we know what God is like it is easy to believe Him.

What we believe about God, how we think about Him, what we trust about Him — these are the most important issues we will ever face in life. Indeed all of life, all our spirituality, is derived from this foundation. On this Rock, He builds His Church and hell has no hope of prevailing against the Beloved of His heart.

A promise from Him is a cast-iron guarantee. When a promise is given, the Holy Spirit is given with it. He becomes our tutor to school us in response and faith. A promise must be fully received before it can be entered into and realized in full.

Firstly, the promise must be studied and fully understood. What is God saying? Are there any obvious conditions that need to be fulfilled? The Holy Spirit is given to us to establish us in God's grace. Grace is the empowering Presence of God to enable us to enjoy the process of development and ensure that necessary conditions are met. All personal promises are conditional, whether those conditions are implied or stated. We are all in Christ, learning to be Christ-like, and loving the learning!

Promises are given in order to increase Presence. Promises are relational. They enhance our fellowship with the Godhead. They create opportunities for advancement. There is a quickening spirit attached to them; a righteous shortcut to transformation, an accelerated but somewhat irregular way of doing something profound. We have our normal lifestyle routines of walking in the Spirit: thanksgiving, rejoicing, prayer, daily devotion, trust and the delightful influence of righteousness — empowered in the holiness of the Holy Spirit, the joy and peace in believing, and the beauty of unceasing, unfailing love that consistently elevates us to the status of being the Beloved of God.

Into that delicious mix the Father drops a promise, a declaration of upgraded intention. A promise is like rolling a six in a board game. It increases momentum by creating a fresh opportunity for advancement.

When a promise comes, our normal routine is given a major boost. Something tangible and explicit has been placed before us. Favor has been specifically expressed.

Now, the Holy Spirit, our indwelling resident genius, can school us into a response that propels us into the new place that has been set aside — irregular, profound, and quite brilliant.

We are learning that when a promise comes, all our immediate possibilities are wonderfully increased. Stop right here! Go and check out your promises. It's important.

Grace and peace are never measured but always multiplied to us. The Father is lavish toward us in His pursuit of our fullness in Christ. Grace and peace bring us into dynamic encounter with who Jesus really is for us. The Father is absolutely delighted with the sacrifice of Jesus and all the possibilities that are opened up for us to know Him fully.

He put us into Christ so that our learning to relate to Him would always be joyful, wonderful and peaceful. When we have seen Jesus, we have seen the Father. They are fully One. When we know Jesus, we know the Father. In Scripture, knowledge does not just come by study but also by an experience of what we have discovered. If our study has not led us to practical encounter, then our head will always overrule our heart in matters of faith.

Our knowing about Jesus only becomes relational transformation when He is made real in our experience. The Father has put us into Christ so that His divine power — the Holy Spirit — could accelerate our growth into fullness. Everything that we will ever need to become Christ-like has already been given.

We are learning the difference between knowledge and true knowledge (2 Peter 1:3). Knowledge without experience maintains our immaturity in the things that matter. Bible skill is the poor relation to a new person in Christ. Theological understanding will always come second to a close walk with God (Acts

> *Promises increase*
> *Presence*

4:5-14). Obedience to the will of God will always trump academic theology (John 7:14-17).

Theology without experience can never be Truth. It can be right. It can be accurate. However if it does not release people into personal freedom and transformation, it is not the Truth. It is merely true. The Truth sets us free. It unlocks our prison, unshackles our chains, overcomes our oppression and removes all accusations of the enemy.

The Book points to the One. Scripture is true because Jesus is the Truth (John 14:6). The Truth is a Person, not a bound volume. Knowing Jesus by experiencing an encounter will set us free to become like Him. Any other form of knowing is just a memory verse.

It is for freedom that Christ has set us free (Galatians 5:1). In that freedom we are put into the one place that guarantees that everything pertaining to life and godliness will be made available to us. We are put into Christ!

The true knowledge of that position will lead us into practical experiences of the glory and excellence of the Lord Jesus Christ. Man has fallen short of that glory and it has been restored in the Messiah. As He is, so are we in this world (1 John 4:17).

Into this context, all promises are released and fulfilled (2 Peter 1:4). All promises are given to empower us to become Christ-like. It is vital that we see promises as being both precious and magnificent. Unless we understand that promises are much more than assurances, we will not realize their true value.

A promise is a particular part of a whole covenant come to life. It carries all the weight of the Father's commitment to the Lord Jesus Christ. By putting us into Christ, the promise is made as much to Jesus as it is to us. That is why when Jesus (who ever lives to make intercession for us) prays before the throne, he is petitioning the Father for the promise on our behalf. He is joyfully reminding His Father that: "You said" and "You promised."

As we join with Him in prayer, our hearts become aligned in obedience and cooperation. "By these promises we become partakers of the Divine Nature." Adherence to the promise makes us like Jesus. Becoming like Jesus triggers the fulfillment of the promise.

Promises are God's way of elevating our relationship with Him. Being in Jesus is a state of exalted spirituality that makes our life become of inestimable value in the Kingdom. We are priceless. We are cherished. We are His Beloved. There is a bond between the Father and the Son that is glorious. We are included in that place and relationship. The bond between us and the Father is made glorious by the Holy Spirit who makes us in the image of Christ.

Our spirituality is not earthbound but heavenly. Promises exalt us to the place that God has set aside for us in Christ. They are guarantees of God's intent. They release us to all the possibilities of becoming the men and women that God sees when he looks at us in Christ.

The Promises of God and Our Development

We respond to prophecy in the same way that we would to promise. We must become doers of the word, whether it is written or spoken. We live by every word that proceeds out of the mouth of God (Matthew 4:4).

Jesus came to elevate the prophetic word back to its rightful place in the relationship between God and man. He came saying, *"You have heard it said, but now I say"* (Matthew 5:21, 27, 31, 33, 38, 43). The spoken word became the written word. The law began as a prophecy (Exodus 20-23)! It was given as a direct word of God.

The commandments of Jesus are prophetic; they are spoken as a direct word of God. John the Baptist was the last of the Old Testament prophets bowing the knee to Jesus, who is the first of a new line of New Testament prophets. Jesus came as a Prophet, Priest and King.

Israel severed the law from its prophetic origin and roots and it became a system of rules and regulations as men tried to establish their own righteousness. Instead of a prophetic word, they created a ritualistic sacramental word that they used to establish their own performance as a means of righteousness. That is why in the same chapter, Jesus makes this telling statement: *"For I say to you, that unless your righteousness surpasses that of the scribes and Pharisees, you shall not enter the Kingdom of Heaven"* (Matthew 5:20).

The same thing that happened to Moses also happened to Jesus. His prophetic words have now been "evangelicalized" into the system. The Sermon on the Mount, instead of being prophetic, is now a code of conduct.

All prophets in the Old Testament continuously called people back to their prophetic origin: to obey prophetic commands and return to loving God and walking in His ways. We see the same in Paul's teachings. *"The law has become our tutor to lead us to Christ"* (Galatians 3:24). The law is not an end in itself; it is given to prophetically restore us to Christ. The "foolish Galatians" (Galatians 3:1) were off track. The law speaks of righteousness embedded in Jesus, not in us.

> *The law began as a prophecy*

The law is therefore dynamic because it leads us to the sufficiency of God.

The prophet's task is to establish relationship with God through a living response to a living word. The law began as a specific *now* word to that generation. The tragedy is that it was downgraded to a general word of God for every succeeding generation.

Separated from its prophetic source, it became highlighted and elevated to become a conventional word when it was a defining and distinguishing *now* word to that generation. It so blinded the generation around Christ that it prevented them from hearing the *now* word spoken by Jesus.

We see the same today when Scripture is elevated in some circles to the point where prophecy is outlawed and deemed satanic. A conservative approach to Scripture has robbed it of its prophetic power to renew, refresh and restore people to God's ongoing Kingdom power and purpose.

The Promises of God and Our Development

Scripture must be read prophetically as a *now* word. We must recapture the true essence of Scripture. It is not a conventional word spoken to a conservative people to help them maintain a standard on earth that does not exist in Heaven. It is not present to provide endless material for self-help teachings. Four steps to happy marriage. Six steps to a better prayer life. How to walk with integrity. How to witness to people at work. Five ways to restore the key of David.

The standard in Heaven is glory. People are measured by how much of God's glory is present in their life. When Moses prophetically spoke the law into being, his face shone. When the Pharisees interrogated Peter and John (Acts 3), they observed their confidence; they knew they were uneducated and untrained, but they took note they had been with Jesus (Acts 3:13). What did they see?

Jesus restores us to glory, awe and wonder. When we read Scripture prophetically, as a *now* word, our sense of majesty increases. In Scripture we must hear the voice of God speaking *now* to His people. We must respond to God's voice and live by every proceeding word. Prophecy is much more than inspired preaching. It is a dynamic that creates breakthrough, transformation, and the restoration of majesty that overcomes all obstacles and opponents.

Our response to the *now* word is crucial. Do we let the word live or do we allow it to die? Our response to the prophetic is so vitally important that the Apostle James gave us this injunction:

> *"But be doers of the word, and not hearers only, deceiving yourselves. For if anyone is a hearer of the word and not a doer, he is like a man observing his natural face in a mirror; for he observes himself, goes away, and immediately forgets what kind of man he was." (James 1:22-24)*

Those who hear without doing are prone to delusion because they continually forget what God has said. It is very easy to forfeit some sense of the power and the glory, the marvel and the miracle of hearing God speak into our lives and situations. Almighty God, the absolute Creator, has a heart so huge that he can be personally acquainted with hundreds of millions of people. He finds time to hear, speak, and respond to countless millions of prayers daily. He speaks countless messages of love, peace, truth and blessing on an hourly basis.

When God speaks, He does so with purpose, to create life, hope, faith and an awareness of Himself in the lives of His people. He wants to bring change, adjustment, correction, direction, renewal, restoration, redemption and encouragement. His words are always strategic and contain real purpose. They reveal His heart and plans for us. All He asks, in return, is for us to respond to Him.

Scripture should lead us to the place of encounter and experience. In the same way, our response to prophecy creates opportunities for us to receive God's promise and to become what He intends.

Linear and Cyclical

As human beings, we are very linear in the way that we think. This is part of the natural mind that thinks in straight lines and fixed points. We want the shortest route between here and there. When we receive a prophetic word, we want the outcome above all else. This is a perfectly normal, absolutely natural way of thinking.

God however, is a Spirit who lives on a different plane of perception. In our thinking, prophecy is mostly functional and therefore only about the end result. In His thinking, a prophetic word is primarily relational and mostly about the journey we undertake on the road to fulfillment.

Both are concerned about becoming what God intends. Our linear thinking will not reach the outcome because it cannot commit our heart to the process of how we should journey toward it. Our focus is destination. The goal of the Holy Spirit is transformation.

The Holy Spirit doesn't think in straight lines or fixed points because He has so many things He wants to accomplish in our lives. He wants to meander along the trail with us for a while, not race to the next stop. God has work He wants to accomplish in us before releasing us into any fulfilled prophecy; the only way He can do that is by spending time with us.

The Father controls the pace that we walk with Him. He will not allow us to gloss over issues of integrity or the development of faith, intimacy and faithfulness.

When we are learning about faith and patience for example, our circumstances will slow down our forward progression for a season. We simply cannot learn patience through acceleration. It can only be learned by persistence. Our perseverance must also be joyful (Colossians 1:11), otherwise we will not learn true endurance. Persistence cannot be properly achieved if we are downcast or melancholic. Persistence is waiting on the Lord with joyful expectation. It is not engaged with timing, but with Presence. It is not linear in its objectivity.

When we are focused on Presence we will cooperate with God's current assignment in our lives. Prophecy is relational because as we concentrate on becoming the people that God sees in the prophecy, then the outcome is drawn toward us.

If we receive a prophetic word that we are going to become a warrior but currently we are a wimp, some changes have to occur. What is the difference between a warrior and a wimp? That is our journey of exploration and discovery. Prophecy takes us on a journey of transformation by guaranteeing us the outcome as we travel the road.

The Holy Spirit will bring us to a place where we can trust God for everything, and to where God can trust us with what He wants to give us. Look at Isaiah 30:18-21:

Therefore the LORD will wait, that He may be gracious to you;
And therefore He will be exalted, that He may have mercy on you.
For the LORD is a God of justice;
Blessed are those who wait for Him.
For the people shall dwell in Zion at Jerusalem;
You shall weep no more.
He will be very gracious to you at the sound of your cry;
When He hears it, He will answer you.
And though the LORD gives you the bread of adversity and the water of affliction,
Yet your teachers will not be moved into a corner anymore,
But your eyes shall see your teachers.
Your ears shall hear a word behind you, saying,
"This is the way, walk in it,"
Whenever you turn to the right hand
Or whenever you turn to the left.

God works cyclically and seasonally in our lives because of the things He wants to accomplish. When we begin to stray from His path, He speaks to us: *"This is the way, walk in it."* He promises us that we will know where He wants to go. Our choice is to respond willingly to that guidance and choose to stay on the journey with Him. Wisdom comes when we learn how God thinks and how He likes to work.

The Holy Spirit wants to give us a desire to press into our prophetic journey with God. All prophecy starts a process to take us from what we are now to who God wants us to be. On every step of that journey, we are supposed to discover who God wants to be for us. Isaiah understood the grace that God has for those people who choose to walk the path that He has outlined.

Cyclical thinking involves times and seasons. When the Lord commits a prophetic word to us, He also provides a time of change as part of His intention. Mostly these times of change need only last as long as it takes for us to make the upgrade.

If we are unresponsive, the season can become extended until we make the adjustment. Every response is tested so that it can be established. It is one thing to get free and another to stay free. The test is designed to establish the freedom. If we fail to respond, our life goes on but turns in a circle (hence cyclical) to present us with another opportunity. If we respond but do not pass the test, it too, will come around again. God is always faithful.

> *Discover God's pleasure in you in the present!*

I have seen the lives of many, many people go through numerous cycles (some of which were repeats of cycles because of failure to adjust) and still not understand the ways of God in development.

Linear and Cyclical

When you are in the cycle, enjoy it. Love the learning. Enjoy your discovery of Jesus. Enjoy losing things you did not want to keep concerning your sin habit or old nature. Enjoy the process of putting off the old and putting on the new. It is usually only painful if you resist it.

Do not think in straight lines and fixed points. Enjoy the season you are in with Jesus. Make sure that you get the most out of your transformation. If you are locked in a season where you have not changed, it is likely that the cycle can become a spiral. The only way out is to practice full-on repentance. Humble yourself and be restored to the learning and change.

The opportunity to repent is a gift that must not be ignored. With joy, draw water from the well of salvation (Isaiah 12:3). Response is everything.

Cycles are about times and seasons — the necessary ebb and flow of life. There is the primary season where God cuts back our ministry to increase our intimacy in relationship. The planting season where prophetic promise opens us up to new life and possibilities. The hiddenness season where nothing seems to be happening but the seed is growing out of sight. The manifestation time where new growth suddenly appears and life takes a different form.

When we adjust our thinking and timing to Heaven's routine we are less likely to be caught out by life and events. Our perceptions can therefore be more in line with ultimate purpose.

Pregnant With Promise

Prophecy is mostly an act of conception. The word enters our spirit and grows in the secret place of our heart.

Promises are designed to possess us for the purpose of God. When we study the word and pray over it, we become charged with a reality from another dimension. Prophecy connects us with the next stage of our identity and intention. We must make the necessary adjustment in lifestyle in order to accommodate the new life that is present. Prophecy makes us pregnant.

Prophecy introduces us to the next upgrade on God's agenda. Renewing our mind means we must learn the Holy Spirit's pleasure and enthusiasm in cancelling out our old belief about ourselves.

When Samuel prophesied over David about becoming king, outwardly his circumstances did not change. He still looked after sheep and ran errands for his father. In his heart however, everything was different. David's ascent to the throne began with that prophecy (1 Samuel 16:12-13).

Throughout all the cycles of development that he endured in the wilderness and at the hands of Saul, David never forgot that moment with Samuel — the memory of oil on his head and Samuel's words over him, the conversations with his family afterwards, the Presence of God being upon him and going with him.

David pursued his destiny to its place of fulfillment. He behaved like a king before he was crowned. We develop our true identity in the secret place of our heart before God. Later, what is hidden becomes manifested. What is established in the secret place can never be disturbed by circumstances, people, or events. The external must always succumb to the internal place of God's Presence.

Mediocre people are always disturbed by the exterior world. An undeveloped inner life leaves us at the mercy of doubt, fear and anxiety. We lack drive, passion and initiative. Maturity is derived from the inner man of the spirit, never the outer man of the soul.

We must unlock the potential of the promise. To do that effectively, we must release our God-given imagination. This is not a time for earthbound logic. Reason cannot call up faith in its fullness. We can talk our way into responding but still not set foot outside of the boat.

We must internalize the place of promise in the same way that a woman would rejoice over the news that she had conceived. In the process that follows, she begins to make decisions and adjustments that are in line with her new found condition. She works in partnership with the new life that is forming.

It is possible for us to abort the word before it has really taken hold. Not responding to God's word will always kill life. Unbelief is easier than faith because it only demands denial. When we believe a word, we must do something about it. We have to act in line with its purpose. We have to take that internal development full term and see something birthed in actuality.

There are many similarities between childbirth and seeing prophecy fulfilled. Prophecy establishes the burden of the Lord for our life and destiny. We must carry it all the way to fulfillment. We labor to bring forth our calling, anointing, and ministry. It is necessarily hard. Life under the anointing is not for the faint of heart. We will be plunged directly into the conflict between two kingdoms. We become targets for the enemy, difficult people, wicked people and those who are supposed to be on the same side! Read Hebrews chapter 11, 1 Corinthians 4:9-13, and 2 Corinthians 11:23-33.

We need a powerful inner life if we are to walk as heroes of faith. I have known people to begin well in the Spirit, but relinquish their inner life to the flesh. Their ministry becomes stillborn before it has a chance to be fulfilled. All our preparations for ministry occur in the busyness of life.

At least let us distinguish our training in faith, maturity and character. Let us learn the partnership of faith and proclamation. Let us develop our persona in Christ above our normal personality traits.

Being pregnant with promise allows us to enter the dynamic place of alignment with purpose. Take responsibility for your prophecy — now!

Taking Personal Responsibility

Too many believers have an incorrect view of how prophecy is fulfilled. Firstly, there is a mentality that says, "If God said it, then it is bound to happen." This is the birthplace of Christian fatalism, and seems to absolve us of any personal responsibility in partnering with the Holy Spirit.

Secondly, the other school of thought declares that: "God will do it all; man does not have to do anything." Often, over the years, I have had significant opposition from these people. In particular they love to quote three specific verses of Scripture (1 Kings 8:56; Ezekiel 12:25; and Isaiah 55:11) to prove their point that God alone is responsible for prophecy coming to pass. It is important to deconstruct this myth.

"*Blessed be the* LORD, *who has given rest to His people Israel, according to all that He promised. There has not failed one word of all His good promise, which He promised through His servant Moses*" (1 Kings 8:56). I wholeheartedly agree that the promises of God referred to in this Scripture came to pass. None of them failed; they were wonderfully fulfilled. However, they were fulfilled by

> Never relinquish your inner life

the second generation of Israelites, not the first who had received the prophecy while still living in Egypt. These prophetic words, spoken first by Moses in Exodus 6:6-8, were cancelled in Numbers 14:20-23 on behalf of that first generation of liberated Israelites.

The issue here is not whether or not God's words were fulfilled, but whether they were fulfilled by the people who received the promise. It is also interesting to read the five verses following 1 Kings 8:56:

> *May the* LORD *our God be with us, as He was with our fathers. May He not leave us nor forsake us, that He may incline our hearts to Himself, to walk in all His ways, and to keep His commandments and His statutes and His judgments, which He commanded our fathers. And may these words of mine, with which I have made supplication before the* LORD, *be near the* LORD *our God day and night, that He may maintain the cause of His servant and the cause of His people Israel as each day may require, that all the peoples of the earth may now that the* LORD *is God; there is no other. Let your heart therefore be loyal to the* LORD *our God, to walk in His statutes and keep His commandments, as at this day* (1 Kings 8:57-61).

After saying that God's words will not fail, Solomon, the wisest man of his time, declared that there are four requests and responses that had to be at the forefront of the hearts of God's people:

1. For God's presence to be with us.

2. For our hearts to be turned to Him, that we may obey Him in all things.

3. For our prayers to be heard and our needs met.

4. For God's glory to be seen by all the earth.

On top of that, Solomon issued this command: *"Let your heart therefore be loyal to the LORD our God."* These requests, responses, and commands indicate that we cannot take a "wait and see" attitude with prophecy.

The second passage that has often been thrown at me is Ezekiel 12:25: *"For I am the LORD. I speak, and the word which I speak will come to pass; it will not more be postponed; for in your days, o rebellious house, I will say the word and perform it."* But Ezekiel 12 is a rebuke given to a rebellious nation. They had eyes, but could not see, Ezekiel prophesied. They had ears, but could not hear, because they were too rebellious. In the first part of the chapter, Ezekiel is commanded to put on a prophetic drama as a sign to Israel that they were going to exile because of their rebellion (Ezekiel 12: 1-10).

In this case the word that was going to come to pass was a prophecy about the future exile of the Israelites, when they would be held in captivity in Babylon. The people's response was exactly the same as the "wait and see" people counsel today: *"Son of man, look, the house of Israel is saying, 'The vision that he sees is for many days from now, and he prophesies of times far off'"* (Ezekiel 12:27). In other words, we do not need to respond right now. This word will not be fulfilled too soon, it can wait. The Israelites lack of remorse and repentance ensured that the prophetic word of exile would come to pass.

The final passage used is Isaiah 55:11: *"So shall My word be that goes forth from My mouth; it shall not return to Me void, but it shall accomplish what I please, and it shall prosper in the thing for which I sent it."* When we examine this passage, we must remember that there is a difference between the prophecy of Scripture and personal prophecy. Second, we must not confuse the difference between a human being's free will and the sovereignty of God.

The prophecy of Scripture relates to God's ultimate purposes for the earth and His people. He declares the end (Revelation) from the beginning (Genesis) and through all ancient and modern times. His purpose will be established and His good pleasure accomplished (Isaiah 46:10).

Those words relate to God's eternal covenant with His people. Having given us His Spirit, He declares that His word will never depart out of our mouths, nor our descendants for now and forever (Isaiah 59:21). In that context, Jesus declared that, *"Heaven and earth will pass away, but My words will by no means pass away"* (Matthew 24:35).

> All personal prophecy relates to the possible, not the inevitable

The prophecy of Scripture, like the piece contained in Isaiah 55:11, always points to an unchanging God who is the same yesterday, today, and forever. He has a fixed purpose and thus gives fixed prophecies that will undoubtedly be fulfilled — though not necessarily by the generation that first received the word.

We cannot put prophecy to individuals in that same category. Isaiah 55:11 refers to the prophecy of Scripture, the ultimate desire of God for the earth and humankind. God's word will come to pass; His purpose will be achieved.

However, I believe it also contains the element of God's ideal for the individual. If we were to ask God's intention for every personal prophecy given to an individual, I believe He would point to this verse as the evidence of His desire for us. Yet we also know that God's intention and desire will never override our free will. He does not impose personal words on us by His sovereignty. He graciously speaks out the possible, not the inevitable.

The verses leading up to Isaiah 55:11 are also interesting to consider:

> *"For My thoughts are not your thoughts,*
> *Nor are your ways My ways," says the* LORD.
> *"For as the heavens are higher than the earth,*
> *So are My ways higher than your ways,*
> *And My thoughts than your thoughts.*
> *For as the rain comes down, and the snow from heaven,*
> *And do not return there, but water the earth,*
> *And make it bring forth and bud,*
> *That it may give seed to the sower and bread to the eater,*
> *So shall My word be that goes forth from My mouth;*
> *It shall not return to Me void,*
> *But it shall accomplish what I please,*
> *And it shall prosper in the thing for which I sent it." (Isaiah 55:8-11)*

God describes a cycle of how He works. Rain comes down from Heaven and waters the earth before returning to the sky in the process of evaporation. Likewise, spiritual things come from Him, touch the earth and return back to Him. His word comes out of His heart, accomplishes what He wants and then returns to Him in a different form through confession, worship, prayer, proclamation and declaration. Yet we are an integral part of this process.

In Numbers 14, a prophecy was cancelled for two million adults and reactivated for their teenagers and children. Saul had his personal word cancelled in 1 Samuel 13. In fact, the Lord told Samuel that, *"I greatly regret that I have set up Saul as king, for he has turned back from following Me, and has not performed My commandments"* (1 Samuel 15:11). At that point, God expressed His sorrow, not a mistake. His intention was that Saul would receive the full promise; the reality was a source of grief to Him.

For twenty-three years, Jeremiah prophesied continually to Israel, proclaiming the message found in Jeremiah 25:5-6:

"Repent now every one of his evil way and his evil doings, and dwell in the land that the LORD has given to you and your fathers forever and ever. Do not go after other gods to serve them and worship them, and do not provoke Me to anger with the works of your hands; and I will not harm you."

Numerous prophets had spoken the same message, over and over, to the nation. God's intention and desire was to see Israel turn around, repent, and return to their first love, Him. For twenty-three years, the word of the Lord was spoken with no response from the people.

Reaching further into Israel's history, we discover some foundational principles that undergird every prophetic utterance given to that nation. Leviticus 26:14-33 expresses, in excruciating detail, the penalty for not obeying God's words, rejecting His statutes, and breaking a covenant with Him. These include ill health, destruction by their enemies, a hard land, a cast-iron sky, plagues, wild animal attacks, pestilence, rationed food, cannibalism and desolation. Disobedience would culminate in exile and banishment. In its Biblical history, Israel suffered all of these things.

Deuteronomy 28 is built on this theme, starting with the blessings of obedience to God's Word, followed by the curses of disobedience. The instruction was clear, as we see in Deuteronomy 28:14: *"So you shall not turn aside from any of the words which I commanded you this day, to the right or the left."*

When God desires to speak prophetically to us personally, it is His intent and desire that these things should happen. However, there can never be any room for fatalism or apathy in the heart of a Christian. We can't wander around singing, like Doris Day or Ned Flanders, "Que sera, sera, whatever will be, will be!" Personal prophecy always speaks to the potential, never to the inescapable. We must make a positive response.

Take responsibility for your blessing. Use the prophetic word to enter a dialogue with the Holy Spirit regarding your own preparation. Write a crafted prayer around the prophecy so that it is always in your heart expression to the Lord. Ask the two best questions that you can ever ask the Lord. They are found on the day of Pentecost (Acts 2:12, 37)what does this mean? What must we do?

What does this prophecy mean for me and my life? What must I do to cooperate with the Lord and partner with Him for its fulfillment? All personal prophecy is conditional on our response.

Prophecy Will Cause a Shaking

It's a hilarious fact that most prophecy is unpredictable! No one knows when a prophetic word is going to arrive in their life. When it does arrive, change will become a fact of life.

Prophecy is God's intention made clear. His avowed intent in Scripture is to make us in His own image. Prophecy works directly in alignment with that focus. It provides us with a specific opportunity for an upgrade. I have never known a personal prophecy that does not involve change. When prophecy comes into our lives and we remain unchanged, then that word has no possibility of fulfillment.

Prophecy is designed to shake our world. It disturbs our status quo; it is unsettling in the best possible way. Who really wants to stay the same? No true lover of God wants business as usual. We all want to become more! Prophecy moves us out of our safety and comfort zone. It provokes people. It gets us out of any spiritual rut that is holding us back. The very nature, especially of directional prophecy, is to get something moving that was motionless.

> *Order your life according to God's vision of you*

Change is necessary. Transformation is vital. Prophecy is essential to that end. Even prophecy that edifies, exhorts and comforts (1 Corinthians 14:3) will challenge us in our relationship with God. Inspirational prophecy enhances our understanding of who God is for us. It elevates His intentionality so that we are in no doubt about what His purpose is for us at this time.

Everything that is negative or contrary to our development will begin to be agitated by the prophetic word. All prophets hate complacency — whether it is the smug, self-satisfied attitude of the pharisee (Luke 18:10-12), or the foolishness of people who are unconcerned about their spiritual state and are therefore unprepared when something momentous occurs (Matthew 25:1-11).

One of my nicknames among my friends is "spin cycle," because I agitate the status quo. I like contentment with Godliness because it is relational. It demonstrates that we are upgrading and improving our rapport with the Father. It means that we are happy where we are with Him at the present but still want more of who He is in Himself. We are exploring our future relationship while we are enjoying our current fellowship.

Contentment outside of that context may lead us into complacency. My role is to stir people up into a new place of desire, to agitate for an upgrade. Prophecy shakes us up into something better.

Prophecy increases vision. Initially the entrance of vision sparks liberation. It breaks us out of the safe, narrow confines in which we see ourselves. It gives us a new horizon, lifts our viewpoint, and brings us into a much broader place in the Lord. We are free and our newfound liberty vastly improves our sense of wellbeing.

After that first euphoric flush of freedom, we begin to count the cost. In order for us to accomplish what liberation is offering, certain choices have to be made. An athlete called up to the Olympic team must now make decisions about lifestyle, health and fitness that are in agreement with a vision to win the gold.

Vision releases freedom but also brings restraint. Indeed there is no liberty without restraint. If I want to stay out of prison, my liberty depends upon restraining any criminal tendency to do something illegal. We have to order our lives in a different way.

We all must choose to live in a way that is aligned with God's purpose and permission. In order to generate accomplishments in some areas, I will have to curtail my involvement in areas that are dubious or unhelpful.

When I was first called to the prophetic ministry, I was elated. After the calling comes the training. Thankfully I had mentors who counseled me to count the cost. I gradually began to realize the scale of the calling God had given me. With that understanding came the comprehension that my life, as I had known it, was over.

At the time I was appalled. It seemed that everything I was doing was inappropriate to the vision I had received. I was in a daze for what seemed like months. My whole world was shaken. I wanted so badly to compromise a little here and there. Not much; just enough to have a life of my own.

Change had come into my life, and with it a period of unsettling and shaking. After a number of false starts, which I would have loved to blame on the enemy, I knew I had to get real with God. Frankly, I was not good enough to be attacked by the devil. My own flesh was doing his job well enough.

When I examined my heart, God's high calling was not matched by my low commitment. I evaluated everything and began the process of change. We only have one life, and this is not a dress rehearsal. We are on stage now and the curtain is up. Practice is not separate from life in spiritual terms.

I began to flow with different people, so my relationships changed. I had to finance my own development, so how I used my income changed. I wanted to learn the ways of faith, so being around people more familiar with doubt than trust was no longer an option. My study habits and subjects changed. So did my conversations and whom I conversed with at that time.

We count the cost initially, but we seldom get an accurate figure in the beginning. We pay the price in installments, which makes it bearable. We receive grace upon grace. Measure poured out into fullness. Every time we pay the next portion, we receive the next measure of God's allowance. It is more than enough. We are growing up into all things Christ.

When directional prophecy comes, change will not be far behind. That change will be both liberating and restrictive, hence the shaking and unsettling we will experience. Ironically, it is when we are shaken to our very core that we first discover the hunger to overturn everything contrary to the life God has ordained for us.

Shaking provokes a response toward God. It promotes a determination to lay aside every weight and pursue the life that God has promised. When we reach out for the prize of the high calling of God in Christ Jesus, we do so knowing what we have left behind, and counting it not at all.

Prophecy Will Cause a Shaking

If our eye is focused our whole body is full of light. Being single-minded is our only option because being double-minded is the height of instability (James 1:8).

God is Present–Future

Why does God give us prophetic words that can be so far into the future, we often feel that we cannot connect with them now? He loves us to have a horizon in our life; something to aim for and head toward in our relationship with Him.

"For I know the plans I have for you, plans for your welfare and not your calamity, to give you a future and a hope" (Jeremiah 29:11). These plans will connect us with our destiny, identity, and calling.

The principle of a future directive word is: The Father puts words into our long-term future because He wants to explore them in the Spirit and bring them into our present relationship with Him.

There are two ways that we walk in the natural. Firstly, we look at the ground around our feet so that we do not stumble or step into something nasty. Secondly, we look ahead at where we are going. Our horizon may be limited, but we look for landmarks of note to guide us.

What is true in the natural is also true in the Spirit. We look at where we are now in our fellowship with the Father, and we look ahead to where He is taking us in relationship. It is normal for us to have two perceptions on life; we live today and plan for the future. People who pay conscious attention to the interplay between present and future usually lead successful, productive lives. Those who only live for the moment seldom fulfill their potential and usually live with regret that they had not done enough with their life.

Present–future is also a way of thinking. It is a mentality that all fruitful people develop. We always make decisions now with the future in mind. We do not want to just move from crisis to crisis. We do not want our future to be a hostage of decisions we make in the present.

This is why meditation and reflection are so vital for us in life. The capacity to pause and calmly think about things (Selah) is an important part of our fellowship with the Holy Spirit, who is a genius at doing life!

If we really want to be transformed across the whole of our life in fellowship with the Lord, then we must be renewed in how we think (Romans 12:2). *"As a man thinks in his heart so is he"* (Proverbs 23:7).

What we think about God is the most important thing in life. Too many Christians are trying to have faith without being settled in their hearts about who God is for them and what He is really, really like in Himself. They have little chance of becoming men or women after God's heart because their own hearts are not fixed. When our hearts are unsure, our heads are double-minded.

Our testimony is always concerned not just with what Jesus has done (that's our history), but primarily with Who He is for us now. What are we discovering presently about God's nature? What are we exploring about the future in Him? Our present fellowship provides future assurances about our walk with Him. He who began a good work in us will perfect it in Christ Jesus (Philippians 1:6). Paul drew lots of confidence from his present–future way of relating to the Lord.

If what we think about God is most vital, then surely what He thinks about us is just as important. The Father's loving disposition toward us is absolutely essential to our wellbeing, both in the natural and in the Spirit. This revelatory knowledge when combined with actual physical, emotional, mental and spiritual encounters and experiences of God's nature becomes to us the very evidence of the incarnate Gospel. We are living proof of Good News!

> God is always present–future

Our thinking needs adjusting on two levels. Firstly, regarding our ongoing thoughts, ideas and reasoning about ourselves. Our innermost, heartfelt, emotional perceptions of ourselves must fit the way that God knows us and sees us in Christ.

Secondly, it is absolutely essential that we come to the place of understanding, agreeing with and consciously aligning ourselves with God's view of us both in the present and with the future. It is much more than an agreed perception; it's the basis of an upgraded relationship!

We see this, most particularly in God's fellowship and relationship with Abraham. In Genesis 18:17-19, we see the Lord visiting Abraham and Sarah. He tells them they will have a son by the next year and Sarah has a fit of the giggles inside the tent. As the Lord is leaving after lunch, He makes this statement about Abraham to the two angels who are traveling with Him: *"Shall I hide from Abraham what I am about to do, since Abraham will surely become a great and mighty nation, and in him shall all the nations of the earth will be blessed?"*

Firstly, *"Shall I hide"* really means: I choose to include Abraham. I will open something up to Abraham. I will hear his thoughts. God is taking Abraham into His confidence. This represents an upgrade in their relationship.

Secondly, the most powerful word in this statement is the word *"since."* God begins a dialogue, which obviously originated in Heaven concerning Abraham and his destiny. *"I will include Abraham in what I am doing next… since… (i.e. for the reason that) Abraham will become a great and mighty nation."*

It was a done deal in the heart of the Lord. He wanted to connect Abraham's present with his future. The Lord is going to include Abraham in what He is doing now because of what He sees Abraham will become in the future. He lives in the gap between our present and our future, relating to us easily in both contexts. Jesus, who ever lives to make intercession for us (Hebrews 7:25), stands in the gap between our present identity and our future destiny.

God speaks to us prophetically about our future and then relates to us in the present through our destiny. God begins to develop us **from** the place of our future toward where we are in the present. We partner with the Holy Spirit by cooperating **in** the present with our future in mind. In this way between our fellowship/relationship we always connect with our present–future.

All success is backwards. When developing a business, we start with a launch date in mind and then work backwards to the present to determine a pathway of development. It is called a critical path analysis that allows us to work out everything that must be accomplished and the order of sequence to ensure a timely launch of our product and resources.

> *All success is backwards*

When the Lord speaks prophetically, He has a date of fulfillment in mind. After the release of the word, He begins to work in our hearts and lives to ensure that the prophetic word comes to pass. When we fail to respond to that process of change and development, then the timing of fulfillment is delayed. Continuous not responding may postpone fulfillment indefinitely and could lead to cancellation.

He works from the future He has declared toward the present that we occupy. What attributes and character traits must I develop in line with the person that He perceives me to become? All discipleship is undertaken with the future in mind, not just the present. God begins with fullness in mind and takes us back to our present lack of resources in order to teach us about faith and provision.

If God has spoken prophetically about us, then we are not living in the present with no concept of our future. We have a God who knows our future and tells us how to align ourselves with Him to create a pathway from now to then and there.

Jesus loved to say, *"An hour is coming (future) and even now is (present)"* (John 4:23; 5:25; 16:32). The seeds of that hour to come are in the present with us now! The fruit of that future time will be realized if we nurture the seed that is currently present. God sees the end from the beginning and is always in both places at once. Which is precisely the reason why we can always know rest and peace.

He plans our journey by His own desire to be present with us! He is so trustworthy in this regard.

> *"The LORD your God who goes before you will Himself fight on your behalf, just as He did for you in Egypt before your eyes, and in the wilderness where you saw how the LORD your God carried you, just as a man carries his son, in all the way which you have walked until you came to this place. But for all this, you did not trust the LORD your God, who goes before you on your way, to seek out a place for you to encamp, in fire by night and cloud by day, to show you the way in which you should go."* (Deuteronomy 1:30-33)

He goes before us. He carries us through the difficult times. He seeks out a place for us to inhabit and He shows us the way. He is fully present–future with His people. Prophecy connects our present with His future. He speaks

The Promises of God and Our Development

to us from our future and works to develop us today so that we can become aligned with our truest identity as He perceives it. We then have the pleasure of cooperating and moving toward the future with the Holy Spirit.

Prophecy begins a process – a series of steps that will take us to our destiny. It is vital that we align ourselves with the process, rather than just the destiny. Many people want the outcome but not the journey of transformation. The process is concerned with establishing our identity. The outcome is focused on achieving destiny. No identity, no destiny. There is no future without process. It is the process that makes us rich.

Because He sees our potential for destiny and then speaks it to us, God begins to deal with us from the viewpoint of destiny perceived rather than destiny pronounced. Personal prophecy relates more to the possibility rather than the inevitability of fulfillment. All personal prophecy is conditional upon response and obedience.

The purpose of development time is to enable us to work with the Holy Spirit so that our prophetic future can become a present reality. Our prophetic word describes our next piece of territory, whether it is relational, personal, or ministerial. We have to go there, explore it, and bring into the present the attitude and persona required to respond, take ground and inherit the promise.

Israel had received prophetic promises regarding Canaan. They sent out a group of men (the best warrior in each tribe) to explore the territory and bring back a report (Numbers chapters 13-14). Only Joshua and Caleb had a right attitude toward what God had promised. They looked at Canaan in the light of God's nature and His prophetic promise. They saw nothing in the land that would prevent them from inheriting it. They realized all along that the fulfillment of prophecy depends upon alignment with God, not our own capacity to perform. Read their report:

> "Then Moses and Aaron fell on their faces in the presence of all the assembly of the congregation of the sons of Israel. Joshua the son of Nun and Caleb the son of Jephunneh, of those who had spied out the land, tore their clothes; and they spoke to all the congregation of the sons of Israel, saying, "The land which we passed through to spy out is an exceedingly good land. If the LORD is pleased with us, then He will bring us into this land and give it to us — a land which flows with milk and honey. Only do not rebel against the LORD; and do not fear the people of the land, for they will be our prey. Their protection has been removed from them, and the LORD is with us; do not fear them." (Numbers 14:5-9)

Alignment is only about pleasing the Lord. Development is about becoming the people that God perceives; turning potential into something actual. At the very least, do not rebel against God, and do not fear the opposition. Process is about experiencing the effect of God's favor. They shall be our prey. Their protection is removed. God is with us! Process is about developing confidence in God's name, nature and intentionality.

Joshua and Caleb explored the territory that God promised. They brought back courage, confidence, and faith. They
became stakeholders in their own future. All success is backwards. We must be in agreement with the end result before

> Alignment is only about pleasing the Lord

we start. When God shows us the finished article that He sees when He looks at us, we must take hold of that in our heart. Create a link between the person we are now and the one described in the prophecy.

When Moses was sent to Egypt to speak to Pharaoh and demand the release of Israel, understandably he had some misgivings about himself (Exodus chapters 4-6). He had many excuses and fears that caused his sense of inadequacy to be almost tangible. The only antidote to our lack of vision is the one that God is seeing when He looks at us!

"See, I have made you as God to Pharaoh, and your brother, Aaron, shall be your prophet" (Exodus 7:1). God sets markers down on our horizon. To fulfill that word we must develop a greater spiritual dimension in and around our-selves, particularly so that we can encounter and experience faith, favor, intimacy, and authority. If Moses does not see himself the way that God does, there is no possibility of him travelling to Egypt. If he does not agree and align himself with God's view of him, then he cannot generate enough faith to overcome his own fear. If he does not take on the characteristics of faith, power and authority, he cannot stand before Pharaoh. He must become the Deliverer in his heart before he steps into Egypt.

This is a Scriptural principle, not just a prophetic precept. Paul expounded it in Philippians 3:12-17:

> *"Not that I have already obtained it or have already become perfect, but I press on so that I may lay hold of that for which also I was laid hold of by Christ Jesus. Brethren, I do not regard myself as having laid hold of it yet; but one thing I do: forgetting what lies behind and reaching forward to what lies ahead, I press on toward the goal for the prize of the upward call of God in Christ Jesus. Let us therefore, as many as are perfect, have this attitude; and if in anything you have a different attitude, God will reveal that also to you; however, let us keep living by that same standard to which we have attained. Brethren, join in following my example, and observe those who walk according to the pattern you have in us."*

We are either enjoying our possession or actively pressing in to take it. The language here makes a powerful statement of intent. *"I press on, in order to take hold."* Real believers will always believe! They are honest, and they have a plan. "I am not there yet, but my strategy is to forget the past and reach out for my future." There is a pattern of behavior in faith that enables us to reach our destiny more quickly. It involves being present–future and not present–past in our outlook on life.

God speaks from the place of your future completion into the place of your present fullness. Take it on board. We can live from the past into our present and be undone by prior circumstances, or we can live from the future into our present and be edified by God's view of our real identity. But we cannot do both without destroying our momentum.

Our destiny does not come to meet us; we reach out for it and press toward it. We attract it to us by how we live our faith. We are learning to be as intentional about our future as the Lord is about our life in Christ in the present.

Prophecy promotes who we are in the Spirit. We learn confidence in that identity and God's intent. We develop the mindset, character and attributes that are in line with God's frame of reference. That mindset includes all the possibilities of ongoing victory. Whatever is going to oppose us on this level is smaller than God's perception of us.

"We can do all things through Christ who strengthens us" (Philippians 4:13). This is a mindset! A mindset dominates our personality so that we become that mentally, emotionally, and physically. The viewpoint of God toward us will release favor as we partner with Him, Rise up, take possession of identity and destiny. Own it. Wear it. Become involved with it!

Our favor attracts faith. We will need an upgraded provision of this new level of identity. This will be contested by the enemy who must surely be worried about a present–future disposition. He controls us when we live present–past, but has no authority when we press into the prophetic. We need a mindset that can receive under pressure. Crucially, our future self has never known defeat. Prophecy is history spoken and written in advance. In our mindset we must develop our identity from the place of advancement (future) and bring it into the present.

The crucial questions are:

1. What is the difference between where we are now and where we need to go?

2. What must change in our relationship with God and how we connect with Him in this new season of His will for us?

3. What must change in our personality as we pursue this mindset?

We have been present–past in our life for far too long. It is time to forget what lies behind and reach out to what is before us. If we are to really become significant people, we must live a prophetic lifestyle. We are present–future in Christ.

Christ is a Guaranteed Life

We are not given favor because of who we are but because of who Jesus is in the eyes of the Father. His favor is now ours because we have been placed in Him. We are not given favor because of our performance as Christians, but because of our placement in Christ.

We are given favor because of the Father's relationship with us in Christ and because of the Father's relationship with Christ in us. In Christ, we are a new creation, one that has never existed before in the earth. The first Adam was a living soul whom the Holy Spirit came upon so that he could fulfill God's purpose. The second Adam (Jesus) was a life-giving Spirit. When we were placed in Him on Calvary, the old nature passed away and all things became new. The old race of men passed away and anyone born again becomes part of an entirely new race of people that had never existed prior to Calvary.

> *Real believers always believe!*

The second Adam is from Heaven so that we now bear the image of the Heavenly (1 Corinthians 15:45-49). God has not restored us to the Garden of Eden. He has gone much further than that! He has placed us into the very heart of the Godhead where we are no longer looking at the earthly image but the Heavenly (2 Corinthians 5:16).

The first purpose of God was to make man in His own image (Genesis 1:26). That likeness is fully restored through death and resurrection (Romans 6:5). We are united with the likeness of Christ and given all the benefits of relationship with Him through the Father. Favor is attached to the image of Jesus, not our behavior. We are learning to grow in grace and favor. Grace is God's empowering presence to us in Christ. Favor is the right and privilege of sonship.

In Christ, the empowering Presence of God guarantees us all the rights and privileges of Jesus. The Father loves us as He loves Jesus. He has a relationship with Jesus, who is in us, as we are in Him. Therefore, I am a joint-heir with Christ.

We belonged to the Father who gave us to Jesus. Everything given to Jesus is from God, including us! All those who were given to Jesus by the Father also still belong to the Father. All things that belong to the Father also belong to Jesus and vice versa. John 17:6-10 is a fascinating study of joint ownership.

Everything that the Father has given to Jesus now automatically becomes part of our relationship with Him too. We are joint-heirs with Christ. Therefore, the origin of all our favor is in Christ's relationship with the Father and our inclusion into Christ. *"I am in the Father, and you in Me, and I in you"* (John 14:20).

"Just as the Father has loved me, I have also loved you, abide in My love" (John 15:9). Whatever the Father is to Jesus, He is to us. He has put us into Christ, so that He can enjoy the same relationship with us as He does with Jesus!!

This is not just the very heart of favor; it is the essential nature of the Gospel. *"You are dead and your life is hidden with Christ in God"* (Colossians 3:3). *"Even so (in the same way) consider yourselves dead to sin but alive to God in*

Christ Jesus" (Romans 6:11). *"We are a new creation, all the old things have passed away, behold, everything has become new, and all these things are of God"* (2 Corinthians 5:17-18).

All our favor is tied into the new creation, not the old. Because our old nature is dead, Father only relates to our new nature in Christ. When the Father looks at us, He does not see what is wrong with us. He sees what is missing in our relationship with Christ, and He is committed to developing that in us by the Holy Spirit. Our ongoing favor is a part of that development.

The Father honors the sacrifice of Jesus and He includes us, not only in His death, but also in His life. This means that when the Holy Spirit puts His finger on a part of our life that is not working, He is pointing to the site of our next transformation. We are looking at our next upgrade in the image of Jesus.

"But by His doing you are in Christ Jesus, who became to us wisdom from God, righteousness, sanctification and redemption." (1 Corinthians 1:30)

"Grace and peace be multiplied to you in the knowledge of God and of Jesus our Lord; seeing that His divine power has granted to us everything pertaining to life and godliness, through the true knowledge of Him who called us by His own glory and excellence." (2 Peter 1:2-3)

The true knowledge of Jesus involves an encounter and ongoing experiences of Christ that makes us in God's image as a transformational fact, not just as a mental assent.

Prophecy is a viable part of that transformational process. While we rely on Scripture for the whole and the particular truth of our progression into becoming like God, prophecy backs up a particular aspect of that work.

God always works from the whole to the particular. He sees the complete finished work of Christ but points us to the specific element that He intends to change now. Any personal prophecy will focus on the next stage of our transformation. We change by degrees. Upgrades take us to the next level of our conversion. The Gospel is always such fascinatingly GOOD NEWS in this regard. Who does not love changing for the better? The Holy Spirit does not touch our lives to make us miserable. He touches us to make us rejoice that change is possible.

The Good News is that Jesus has already claimed that part of our life that is not working properly. We have been granted everything pertaining to life and godliness. Prophecy makes that grant come alive in the present. It gives us a context and a fabulous opportunity to cooperate now and enjoy the process of change that is an offer.

Time Out!

What part of your life is under conviction from the Holy Spirit at this time? What Scriptures is He using to support the change He wishes to introduce? These will be blessings and promises that He will release to us as we respond joyfully to change. In addition to those, we may also have prophecy in our life that we may use in conjunction with Scripture. As we examine them, it may provide a significant catalyst for change.

We bear the image of the Heavenly and so we are blessed with every spiritual blessing in Heavenly places in Christ (Ephesians 1:3). We act in line with Colossians 3:1-3 and the Father locks us into the truth of who we are in the Spirit (Romans 8:16-17).

> *"Therefore, if you have been raised up with Christ, keep seeking the things above, where Christ is, seated at the right hand of God. Set your mind on the things above, not on the things that are on earth. For you have died and your life is hidden with Christ in God." (Colossians 3:1-3)*

> *"The Spirit Himself testifies with our spirit that we are children of God, and if children, heirs also, heirs of God and fellow heirs with Christ, if indeed we suffer with Him so that we may also be glorified with Him." (Romans 8:16-17).*

The Bible is a book of encounters that leads us into ongoing experiences of God's nature so that we become like Him. An encounter is a confrontation with God so powerful that we are propelled into another way of life. This opens up a whole new world of possibilities that will take us years of experiences to fully realize.

Favor is attracted to destiny

Jacob is a prime example — a cheat and a deceiver who robs his brother of his birthright and his inheritance. He has an encounter with God where he receives five specific prophetic blessings (Genesis 28). He later goes on to become Israel.

Saul is another example. Murderously engaged on destroying the early Church, he has an encounter with God on the Damascus Road. Humbled and blinded by the encounter, he has to wait in the dark before an experience of a miracle restores his sight and prophetically commissioned him for his work in the Kingdom (Acts 9). Later, he becomes Paul, a preeminent apostle.

There is also Mary — a humble maidservant who has an encounter with the Angel, Gabriel, who prophesies over her all the purposes of God for her life at that time. Later the Holy Spirit causes her to conceive and so begins her journey of experiences with God.

Encounters are the suddenlies of God that mostly come when you least expect them, though there are some that we can prepare for in earnest (Acts 1:1-15).

The Promises of God and Our Development

Prophecy and promises lift us up so that we become aware of God's heart toward us. We can do nothing to enter into encounters and experiences because God loves to initiate them. However, we must do everything to stay there. The chief spiritual discipline that establishes truth as a lifestyle is abiding (John 15:1-11). How we learn to stay, dwell and remain is most vital. Many people allow themselves to be taken out of blessings and promises that God has granted.

Often we treat words of God circumstantially. We allow circumstances to challenge our prophetic words or Scriptural promises often with the result that we abandon God's Word because the situation has overwhelmed our faith. Alternatively, we call our words down into our circumstances; which is okay, but we will only receive a measure of their true value. The words of God are designed to lift us up out of our circumstances into an experience of Heaven.

We are learning to live from Heaven to earth in our walk in the Spirit: to know what it is like to be seated with Christ in Heavenly places (Ephesians 2:6). That is, we have an attitude of rest about who we are and where we are in Christ. God's word (Scripture/prophecy) always calls us up to a higher place.

We practice our relationship with God based on the words that He speaks to us. As Christ is formed in us, our favor increases because of who He is for us. We do not earn favor; it is developed by Christ growing in us. Being conscious of our favor arises out of our true experience of the Presence of Jesus. Favor is the by-product of His life growing in our heart.

We position ourselves for fulfillment when we allow our lives to be defined only by what God says about us. The renewing of our mind empowers our thoughts to be in alignment and agreement with God's words over us. This creates transformation through our experience of God in the situations we face. We remind ourselves of God's promises and our inheritance in Christ. Meditation helps us to renew our minds and reframe our thinking (Luke 2:19). It produces a focused mind that is set on the Spirit. We can only change a mindset by replacing it with another. In Hebrew, the word "meditate" means to murmur or mutter aloud; in other words, to repeat what God has said. Repetition is a key to doing the word, not just hearing it. We declare the word back to God in praise, thanksgiving and rejoicing. We muse over it in His company. In so doing, we open up ourselves to further insight and input. When we declare God's word in this way, we make ourselves vulnerable to increase the anointing as a result.

Prophecy empowers our response to the Christ life that is developing within. It provides a now experience in the context of our overall journey. Jesus is the guarantor of our covenant (Hebrews 8:6), which is now (in Christ) based on better promises.

Time Out!

The Spirit of Disclosure

The Holy Spirit is the most enthusiastic, encouraging person that I have ever encountered. He loves the role that He has in our lives. He loves prophetically to disclose to us what is to come (John 16:13-15), and then to empower us in the process of becoming that in word and deed.

He is the Spirit of truth who loves to form Christ in the people of God. He adores Jesus and is determined that He would receive the full weight of glory that He deserves. He speaks to us prophetically to declare the intentions of the Godhead. He provokes us lovingly to partner with Him in establishing truth as a lifestyle.

There are many, many things that we must know, understand and experience about this life that we have received in Christ. It is the role of the Spirit to fully expose the Majesty of Jesus and to impart to us a sense of sovereignty in our own lives. He is the Spirit of Wisdom and Revelation who empowers us into encounters and experiences in the knowledge of Jesus. He is indispensable to us.

Our relationship with the Lord Jesus is sealed in our fellowship with the Holy Spirit (Ephesians 1:13). He is our Spirit of promise. All promises of God are "yes and amen" in Christ (2 Corinthians 1:20). The Holy Spirit is given to turn the possibility into a reality. He makes real to us all that Heaven would release into our hearts.

In my relationship with Him, I have found Him to be unfailingly good-tempered and wonderfully joyful.

He is present so that we may learn Christ and know who He is in Himself. Know His incarnate Presence in our own lives. Know the role of Jesus in Heaven toward us (Hebrews 7:25). He teaches us how to stand in Christ. He shows us how to walk confidently in this world in our fellowship with God. He reveals the majesty and sovereignty of Jesus. He declares to us the full power of the Cross and how joyful it is for us to live on the right side of it.

The Holy Spirit is a joyful, enthusiastic teacher. He renews us in the spirit of our mind (Ephesians 4:20-32). He empowers us to put on the new self, which is the likeness of Christ. All our negatives are done away in Christ on the Cross. We are dead to them because we have a new nature in Jesus.

We are not battling with our old nature; it is dead. We are learning how to undermine a sin habit by developing our righteousness. A renewed mind is essential in this struggle. The Holy Spirit is quite brilliant in unveiling the truth of Jesus and the power of the Good News in our development. He does not work against a negative in us, since we are dead to it. He does not deal with sin; it has been dealt with in Christ (Romans 6:10). The Holy Spirit deals exclusively with our righteousness in Christ. He shows us how to lay aside the negatives and become as Jesus is in our life and walk. He is fully focused on who Jesus is for us. He loves disclosure. He is most passionate about establishing the image of Christ in our lives. The way he speaks to us is essential to our confidence.

The Promises of God and Our Development

He is gracious, kind, gentle, faithful, powerful and restful. He is an incredible representative of the Godhead in His daily routine with us.

He has too much joy to be oversensitive. It is possible to grieve Him, but very difficult. He has been painted as hypersensitive, touchy and easily offended because of Ephesians 4:30: *"Do not grieve the Holy Spirit of God, by whom you were sealed for the day of redemption."*

Father, Son, and Holy Spirit are one person, each with different functions and purpose. The very idea that He is touchy, oversensitive and easily offended could not be further from the truth, in my experience. The Holy Spirit has the same temperament as the entire Godhead. His disposition is wonderfully loving. If I had to describe it in one word, I would use "affection". He is deeply affectionate. Affection is the vehicle for the Agape love of God. Affection involves a true understanding of my own struggles to be transformed and my intense desire to become more. He understands the pain I have to go through as I face up to my inadequacy and insecurity. He is my partner in the daily routines: Teaching me Christ, helping me put off the old and put on the new. When I get tired and cranky, His deep affection for me envelops me on days. His exuberance for me pulls me through.

> *Love never fails!*

His nature is to be happy. He has a wonderful sense of humor. I furnish Him with lots of material. His humor is often wry, dry, and full of irony and then it is audacious, infectious and hilarious. I love His infectious joy, especially in times of warfare. He has a never-say-die attitude that laughs at the enemy and circumstances. He smiles at adversity. His eyes sparkle with happy intent. He is the best encourager because He brings Himself into our circumstances. In the darkest moment He can fill us with joy and peace in believing and bring us to a sense of wonder about how our situation will be resolved. I have felt His joy completely diffuse my doubt. He is the bright ray of sunshine that breaks through on a cloudy day. He is full of joy and laughter.

He has this brilliant predisposition toward peace. In a changing, uncertain world, He has taught me to rest. He loves to establish Christ as my Prince of Peace. He is not situational in His outcomes with us. His intention is to establish us in relationship with the Lord. That means He is more concerned with our lifestyle spiritually than with how we simply respond to circumstances.

I love the fact that peace is always one of the main ingredients of our relationship with God. Peace eliminates any anxiety about negative issues and creates space for us to think properly. The Holy Spirit has taught me continuous peace, which is rest personified.

The way He speaks is restful, peaceful, and encouraging. He brings comfort without commiseration, which produces strength.

His character is to be loyally patient. He really deeply understands process as a way of life. He sees our life as a journey. His calmness always amazes me.

He is never under threat. Patience is the capacity to tolerate delay, trouble or suffering without becoming angry or upset. He models patience beautifully, that is why it is difficult to grieve Him. He has a capacity for forbearance and fortitude that makes me trust Him deeply with my own shortcomings.

Conviction does not mean that He is angry at something in our life that needs changing. It's His invitation for us to partner with the next level of our transformation. It signals His intent to be active in a specific area of our lives. Patience backs up His desire for us to adjust. It can take time for us to see all that He sees in our situation. Response can never be just a knee-jerk emotional reaction to conviction. Response is an affair of the heart supported by a change of mindset.

When our thinking is renewed, our heart response can really take us to the place of transformation. It can take a process of time before we make that adjustment. Impatience is demanding, hot tempered, intolerant and irritable. It is hasty, snappy, impetuous and rash. It can be abrupt, curt and indignant. It leads to anxiety and agitation, fretfulness and uneasiness. God is none of those things.

Surely it is important to know what the Holy Spirit is not. In His patience he displays a calm serenity. He is composed, enduring in His fellowship with us. He is forgiving, understanding and untiring in His application of truth. Rebellion may eventually grieve Him, but our stumbling toward freedom is always a delight.

As parents we need the same level of patience and kindness with a baby, preschooler, teenager, and young adult. Only the issues change. Life requires adaptation. Patience is critical to development.

The inclination of the Holy Spirit is always toward kindness. Love is patient and kind (1 Corinthians 13:4). I have found the Holy Spirit to be courteous and gentle, considerate and generous. He has been very compassionate toward me. Even His rebukes have been beneficial and always with favor attached. He does not withhold love or grace and mercy. He is our Helper and our Comforter. I can come to Him with all my issues and be received graciously. I love His clemency and His willingness to partner in my circumstances. He has demonstrated the kindness of the Godhead on hundreds of occasions in my life. Because of His disposition toward kindness, I have learned kindness myself as a way of life. I still have some way to go regarding consistency, but I have a wonderful role model. I value His goodwill and I prize His affection toward me. I want to be like Him, like all of them! The role of the Spirit is to make us Christ-like. Demonstrating kindness undergirds all His dealings with us. Ours is a partnership based on generosity and favor. When I have been struggling with my spirituality, kindness has often been the vehicle for me to receive the love, blessing and favor of God.

The Promises of God and Our Development

Goodness is God. He adores goodness and kindness. The Holy Spirit has a beautiful tendency to overwhelm us with good. Every thought, word and deed emanates from goodness. Even when He has to discipline us, it is for our own good (Hebrews 12:10). His discipline is in the context of proving and establishing us in Sonship. Goodness is the fertile ground in which our prayers bear fruit. Goodness is the seedbed for miracles to grow our trust and faith. He overcomes evil with good (Romans 12:21).

> *Goodness is God*

If His goodness can overcome evil, then surely it can overcome the flesh. People who judge others have not been captivated by goodness. They demonstrate their lack of Presence in their negativity toward others. Goodness is gracious goodwill; kindhearted mercy and benevolence to the undeserving especially.

When we realize the absolute significance of the goodness of God as a prerequisite for our ongoing encounter and experience of Him, then we will celebrate this wonderful virtue and revel in its place in our lives.

The Holy Spirit is incredibly faithful to us, our development, our growth as believers, and to the journey that we are on into the Lord Jesus. He is loyal and steadfast in His relationship with us. His disposition toward us is so healthy and wholesome it inspires trust and confidence.

He is constant. He is unchanging. He is unwavering. He is devoted, dependable, unswerving, staunch, immovable, truthful, true and trustworthy. He will never leave us nor forsake us. He is our Rock. We build our very lives on His faithful, dependent nature. He is the same yesterday, today and forever. We are learning to rely on and develop confidence in what God is really like in Himself and who He really is toward us.

His faithfulness has astonished me. The more I develop as a Christian, the more connected I become to His faithfulness. The more I become aware of His capacity to love me in all circumstances, the more I want to change. Love never fails.

When I am wrong about something, it is His patient, kind, loving faithfulness that walks with me and works with me until I get it. Those same attributes continue with me until I become it.

His gentleness has been gracing my life for a number of years. Mercy comes to us through gentleness. His nature is gentle, tranquil, serene, untroubled. He is a cool breeze on a hot day. He is thoughtful. His attention to detail is awesome. His interactions with us leave us joyful, humble and worshipful.

There are days when I tremble at His gentleness because of the power that it releases into my life. Jesus described Himself as meek and lowly of heart (other versions have gentle and humble). Meekness/gentleness is not weakness. It is strength under control.

It has often been the gentleness of the Holy Spirit toward me in a situation that has given me strength to resist and overcome what has been contending against me. His gentleness has mostly prevented me from reacting angrily or rashly toward people. I endure much criticism from people who are dispensationalists in their Biblical viewpoint — in other words, they do not believe in the person and work of the Holy Spirit today.

I am often savaged by people because I move in the prophetic gift. I live my life under restrictions that most people would find intolerable; purely because I want to speak a message of non-judgmental spirituality that I sincerely believe is the essence of the Gospel of Jesus Christ.

I am consistently ripped off financially by Christians, churches and organizations that illegally copyright material from my ministry but that have no passion for the missions I support from the distribution of our resources. The opportunities to be annoyed, exasperated and vexed are many.

Gentleness puts a stop to irritability. It prevents justifiable anger. I can be angry but not sin. Gentleness prevents my heart from becoming a vindictive wasteland. Gentleness is the only answer to super spiritual pharisaical people who are overly religious and love to demonize people. It's fascinating to study how Jesus conducted Himself with these people. He was forthright without being dictatorial, truthful without withholding grace, occasionally humorous at their expense, and honest in His appraisal of their spirituality. I am sure He was very conscious of the spirit that was operating behind their words and actions.

At best, that spirit is unloving, ungracious and unkind. At worst, it is hateful, deceiving, and manipulative. Gentleness keeps our hearts open to God under extreme provocation. It preserves our spirituality, ensuring that we do not have to repent or apologize later for our own words and actions.

Gentleness means we do not have to let our insides become an angry knot of anxiety, apprehension and wrathful thoughts. It allows me to bless, not curse. It gives me the power to count it as joy and to move in the opposite spirit. Gentleness has saved my sanity on more than one occasion. Crucially, it empowers me to become better rather than bitter.

The fruit of love, joy, peace, patience, kindness, goodness, faithfulness and gentleness acting together in our lives produces self-control. The Holy Spirit in all His mentoring of us seeks to establish us in the image of Jesus. When the Christ lifestyle is established, the self-life is destroyed. We do not crucify the flesh in order to become like Christ. The sin nature is dead already in Christ. When we abide in Christ, the flesh habit has no possibility of returning. The nature of the Christ life and the fruit of the Spirit produce an overall self-control that reduces the sin habit to nothing. The Holy Spirit works with us to establish righteousness into holiness.

His objective is that we thoroughly enjoy Christ and learn how to live in Him. He establishes our walk and our relationship into a powerful, peaceful reality. So the very idea that He is easily offended is preposterous!

It must be remembered that He bears the brunt of man's intransigence. He is the One with whom we are most engaged in the process of transformation. We can use the journey of Israel to Canaan as a metaphor for everyone's spiritual journey. It is symbolic of our journey out of darkness into the promise of relationship and interaction with Heaven. It depicts the journey out of bondage, personal oppression and enslavement into freedom, health and wholeness.

It shows the process required to shake off a slave mentality, overcome a victim mindset, and remove shame and blame as a way of life. It is the formation of a renewed mind; a willingness to trust and the capacity to walk by faith, not by logic or reason. They are learning God's nature as they are rebuilding their own. They are learning how to talk a new language, walk in a different way and practice new disciplines.

The journey of our transformation can be rough. We are challenged, lovingly confronted, tested, exhorted, encouraged, edified and comforted. Everything is about movement and momentum. Before we can become constantly victorious, we have to become the biggest loser. We have to learn to lay aside weight and encumbrance. We must say "no" to what would entangle us and learn to run with endurance the race that has been chosen for us (Hebrews 12:1).

In all of His dealings with us, the Holy Spirit has to overcome the flesh and establish Christ. We are babies, children, and rebellious teenagers before we become fully mature in Christ. There are many memories, hurts, wounds and betrayals that require new health and wholeness. There are sin habits, personality problems, fears, doubts and unbelief to overcome. A spiritual mindset that is not rooted in logic, rationale or reason must be established. The supernatural over the natural lifestyle must be developed or high levels of trust, faith and power are simply not possible.

He sees the worst of us and must establish the best in us. Rebellion can be simply opposition to His purpose. It is found in non-cooperation with our own development — crying out for rescue rather than being changed in a situation. It can be in our resistance to change and growth. We do not learn our current lessons and so we are destined to repeat them later. We have a defiance of authority, not just in our relationship with God, but also within the Church. Sometimes it is something simple like not seeking out a mentor locally. Some people circumvent that by asking travelling ministries to disciple them. I have been asked hundreds of times to mentor people. Discipling is relational first, functional second. The argument is that local people do not understand my calling or they are not spiritual enough to mentor me.

Faithfulness is astonishing

The Spirit of Disclosure

I have never found a perfect mentor yet, and I have worked with some amazing people — all of whom would acknowledge their own flaws as I do my own. There is no single mentor that can disciple us thoroughly. The best mentors teach us to think and to act from within our spirit.

When we enter a relationship with a mentor, we must define what we want from them. Be specific about what you want to learn from them. Then do not work with them to the exclusion of the Holy Spirit. A good mentor partners with the Holy Spirit and helps you to build a stronger relationship with Him.

Intransigence is about being unwilling to change. Most Christians want to change but do not put any real effort into the process. *That* is the nature of intransigence. People resist changing their mindset completely. They can be persuaded that something is true but not pursue it to the point where their behavior is altered.

We can be in agreement about the need for something but not develop our words into actions. Faith without works is a dead thing. The role of the Holy Spirit is to disclose firstly what is to come. He points out to us where we are going and how we must get there. Secondly, He discloses the process to us in which we need to partner with Him. Thirdly, He discloses the obedience required to attain the outcome. Finally, He establishes that outcome by testing our internal change and our external obedience.

He is the Spirit of Disclosure. He loves His role in our lives. Though He has ample opportunity, He is not easily grieved. He takes the likeness of Christ and makes Him real in our lives. We should honor His role and His commitment to us. He makes us complete, lacking in nothing.

When we speak to people prophetically, we must allow our own hearts to be filled by that same Spirit of Disclosure. We must love His Presence in our hearts. We need to enjoy the word that we are giving. It is important that we are fully aligned so that the heart that is speaking the Word is the same as the one that is behind it.

The Value of Faithfulness

Everything that we have is given to us by God first.

> "John answered and said, 'A man can receive nothing unless it has been given him from Heaven.'" (John 3:27)

> "OR WHO HAS FIRST GIVEN TO HIM THAT IT MIGHT BE PAID BACK TO HIM AGAIN? For from Him and through Him and to Him are all things. To Him be the glory forever. Amen." (Romans 11:35-36)

> "Every good thing bestowed and every perfect gift is from above, coming down from the Father of lights, with whom there is no variation, or shifting shadow." (James 1:17)

The Promises of God and Our Development

"We love because He first loved us." (1 John 4:19)

We are not given anything because of who we are or because of the quality of our performance. We receive from God because of who Jesus is and because of His relationship with the Father. We are not given anything because of our performance but because of our placement in Christ.

Whatever the Father is to Jesus, He is to us. The Father has put us into Christ so that He can enjoy the same relationship with us as he does with Jesus!

We bear the image of the Heavenly and so we are blessed with every spiritual blessing in the Heavenly places in Christ (Ephesians 1:3). This favor in Christ is not an event or merely an outcome of making a request. It is primarily a relationship that we have with the Godhead in Christ.

> *"Yet for us there is one God the Father **from whom** are all things and we exist **for** Him and for us there is one Lord, Jesus Christ, by whom are all things, and we exist **through** Him" (1 Corinthians 8:6).*

Everything comes from the Father and our very existence is for His pleasure and glory. He lives and loves to pour out on us all that we need to love, worship, know by experience, and serve His Presence.

Everything that comes to us from the Father comes because of Jesus. By His death and resurrection, we are a purchased possession. Life in Christ is surely about upgrading our capacity to live as He lives. We have a life that is solely and completely lived through His indwelling life and nature.

Everything comes from God

The faithfulness of God is established in and through the person of Christ. Heaven is open to us. Performance is dead. Placement is everything. As we live up to our position in Christ we will receive every blessing available in Him.

Too much emphasis on a negative prevents us from receiving all the promises and benefits of being in Christ. A life primarily focused on the avoidance of sin cannot receive fullness of blessing. A life focused on enjoying righteousness will inherit everything.

We do not give to God anything that originates in us. Everything comes from the Father, through the Son into our lives and then returns to the Father in praise, worship, adoration and glory by the indwelling power of the Holy Spirit.

Only God can love God. We love Him only because He first loved us. He fulfills the first commandment Himself in us. Because He loves us with all His heart, soul, mind and strength, we are fully empowered to return what we have received. The two biggest disciplines that we have to learn are *a)* to receive love from God daily, and *b)* how to abide, stay, dwell, and remain where He has placed us in Christ.

It takes God to love God. His love in us will free us up to adore Him, serve Him, live for Him. Faithfulness works in the same way. He is faithful to us and we return that devotion. Because of the quality of His dependability we can learn to be constant. Because of His unswerving reliability we can become steadfast. His unchanging Presence empowers us to become consistent in how we show up in Jesus. Faithful is He; faithful are we.

We must prize His faithfulness and develop a significant trust in this most beautiful attribute of the Father. We must rest in His faithfulness and never question it. Doubt provokes indecision. It causes us to be hesitant when we need to be confident. Doubt is the crack in the door that eventually leads us into misgiving, mistrust, apprehension, skepticism, and fear.

When we relax into His faithfulness, His nature promotes assurance. We know that we know. Our hearts lift in humble gratitude. Thankfulness produces appreciation. Confidence is the language of prayer. It leads to conviction of heart and a perspective rooted in certainty.

When we speak prophetically, we do so from a place of assurance, deep in God's heart. His faithfulness is tangible. Faithful is He who calls you, and He also will bring it to pass (1 Thessalonians 5:24). We are called into fellowship with Jesus through the faithfulness of the Father (1 Corinthians 1:9). Prophetic people must operate out of a place of faithfulness received rather than just faithfulness perceived. We need an encounter and experience of faithfulness rather than just a concept.

Faithfulness changes our heart. It guarantees both our humility and our confidence. Our prophesying is more heartfelt; we can impart Presence rather than just a form of words, however significant. I have lost count of the times I have heard powerful prophetic words delivered without heart. The initial impact of a prophecy is vital. The words that reach the head get put into a drawer. Those that impact our spirit, we carry everywhere like a letter from a loved one.

When we bask in the faithfulness of God, we can impart assurance, a confidence that God is with us. People relax around us. They discover God in the ordinary. The atmosphere we create is saturated with God's goodness, kindness and favor. When the faithfulness of God is present everyone can receive.

Faithfulness opens us up to the process that comes next. It provides us with an assurance of God's intent regarding the outcome. He will do it. As we partner with Him the outcome is guaranteed. The declaration of the Spirit places the promise in our account. Faithfulness will bring it about. His faithfulness empowers us to stand and cooperate with the process. Process is the work of the Holy Spirit in making the prophecy become a reality.

Faithfulness guarantees the outcome in God's heart. Faithfulness guarantees the process in ours. He gives us His faithfulness so that we can develop what needs to be cultivated in our hearts. The word is a seed that grows within. The faithfulness of God waters and nurtures that seed. When our devotion to personal change matches the faithfulness of God there is only one outcome. The Holy Spirit works toward that end.

The Promises of God and Our Development

All Prophecy Contains a Moral Imperative

All personal prophecy is conditional. It requires a faith and a character response. Prophecy does not have to express those ideals in the content. They are explicit enough already in our approach to Scripture. We base the pattern of our lives on the revealed Word of God in Scripture. We base the direction of our lives on the proceeding word of the Lord as the Holy Spirit proclaims it.

Keeping the revealed Word of Scripture is a major element of all prophetic teaching. If we cannot obey Scripture, it will be even harder to see prophecy fulfilled in our lives. We must remain diligent in our partnership with the Lord. All prophecy has a moral imperative. Obedience to righteousness is implicit in all that God speaks and commands in our lives.

When prophecy is spoken over us, we must take the opportunity to examine ourselves. Is there anything in our life that would prevent this word coming to pass? What needs to change in us as we pursue our response to the now word of God? We cannot just sit around waiting for the prophecy to fulfill itself. Prophecy comes to completion through partnership. God has invaded our time-space world with an invitation to move further into our future destiny.

What skills, attributes and giftings must be acquired in us in order that we may see that particular destiny unfold? What character defects must come under renewed grace so that obedience may achieve its just reward?

Personal prophecy declares the possibility, not the inevitability of fulfillment. We will probably need to make some new adjustments in our lifestyle and approach to God as a result of the prophetic word spoken over us.

I absolutely love the excitement that is created by the prophetic gift. I love the entrance of a personal word from God into someone's life and the internal rise of faith and enthusiasm. However, after the high point of the revelation, God often plunges us into a place of confrontation. We are faced with our deficiency. These are the irregularities in our life currently that will, if they are not dealt with, become the biggest opposition to our forward momentum.

On the journey from revelation to manifestation, i.e. prophecy spoke to prophecy fulfilled; the Lord confronts us with the things in our lives that presently just do not work. He points out the area of change that He will require. This confrontation is designed to produce a transformation as we respond.

The Holy Spirit does not torment us with things; however, He does convict us for our good. When He highlights a deficiency, He also points to Christ's sufficiency. Whatever He spotlights, He has a plan for its change. Firstly, God wants to confront us with Who He is for us in regard to this situation. Secondly, His grace, His empowering Presence begins to work on us to enable our faith to move in the right direction. Thirdly, He invites us into partnership with Him so that we can experience fresh momentum in our relationship. Finally, it

> *It takes God to love God*

is important to understand and experience that confrontation is intended to bring us into a place of renewal and refreshing.

It is immature and foolish to become despondent when the Lord is dealing with us. He is good and His goodness has extended to cover a part of our life that we probably do not like or want anyway! We get through this sequence of events by focusing on what He is giving to us, not what we are giving up.

Love the learning. As we go after renewal in our thinking, so we upgrade our thanksgiving. Be refreshed. The plans He has for us are for our welfare, not for our calamity, to give us a future and a hope (Jeremiah 29:11).

God's grace is amazing and abundant. When He points out a deficiency, He is pointing out His sufficiency by declaring to us the diametrical opposite. He always moves in the opposite spirit to our flesh. If we are not being generous, He shows us His generosity. If we lack compassion, He shows us His compassionate nature.

When He shows us something we hate about ourselves, He also shows us something wonderful about Himself, that we can love and desire. When we see that incredible part of God's nature, it provokes us to give up the thing we hate. The Holy Spirit, in effect, displaces the bad with the good.

In God's economy a moral imperative means that when He confronts us with our weakness, He is wonderfully obligated in His righteousness to show us His strength that is made available to us in Christ. He is righteous because He can only do what is right.

When we understand what the Father is really like, it seriously affects our capacity to prophesy into people's lives. Our experience of the nature of God is what we impart into the lives of another through the prophetic word.

People who have no current experience of grace, mercy, kindness or the love of God will not be able to convey the heart of the Father when it matters most. They should keep silent for a season and explore their personal relationship with God in order to take it into a new place of compassion and mercy.

All prophetic people have a moral imperative to speak out of the fullness of God's heart. A prophet must be GOOD NEWS, even if that news is REPENT! A call to repentance is to invite people into a deeper experience of the Gospel. It cannot just be a command to stop doing something negative or hurtful. It is a call to return to first love. It is an announcement of glad tidings of great joy. It is designed to arouse people to receive a fresh encounter and experience of the Living God.

How we speak to people prophetically must line their hearts up with the Gospel of the Lord Jesus Christ. The Good News is that transformation is available, accessible and attainable.

The Promises of God and Our Development

Prophecy and Mentoring

Prophecy always precedes change. Its very entrance signifies that an adjustment must follow. All prophecy leads to process, and the identifying of new development in the lives of both individuals and people groups. At some point, in the reception of prophecy, we must consider the state of our lives.

Prophecy can give us a different horizon. We may see something that we have never previously visualized. A variety of questions will spring to mind as we seek to understand and respond to the prophetic word. We can only experience God in the present. We must therefore use prophecy as a compass heading to check our progress in our walk with the Lord.

Are we going in the right direction? Are we moving fast enough? What obstacles are ahead of us? What needs to change in us so that we can conform to what God is saying? Do we have the required faith and anointing to fulfill this calling? What upgrade is required in order for us to be repositioned in the ministry?

Questions need to be asked if we are to refocus. The Father always has an agenda and prophecy will bring it to the forefront. Prophecies and promises are often interchangeable dynamics of God's intentionality. He is intensely practical and always wants to get on with our development. Once He has shown us the horizon He will want to fix our attention on the next series of steps immediately in front of us.

We must consider the obstacles we will face both internally and externally. Having shown us the future, He will want to work with us in the present to ensure the correct response, lifestyle, and preparation. We walk with God by seeing what He is seeing, hearing what He is speaking, and doing what He is doing. A prophecy can put our head in the clouds initially. It is important that we get our feet on the ground as soon as possible.

When directional prophecy occurs, it provides us with opportunities to get a handle on the lives of people around us. All prophecy must have follow-up! Prophecy can be a significant discipling tool. It provides us with opportunities for questions, dialogue, and prayer input.

Directional prophecy involves an examination of the present with regard to the future. It creates a window of opportunity that enables us to honestly assess the discrepancy between where we are now and where want to go in the future. It is one thing to aspire to that prophetic future and quite another to achieve that outcome. The gap between aspiration and achievement is always filled with development. Sometimes mentoring people in this process is a pleasure from first to last. At other times it is difficult because the response from the one being discipled needs a two-stage process. Firstly, to reframe their thinking and perception, often from a place of unreality to a place of reality and faith and secondly, for them to see that active participation is mandatory, not optional. We have to work out our salvation in fear and trembling (Philippians 2:12).

Fear and trembling (*phobos* and *tromos* in the Greek) is a paradox of raw emotion. *Tromos* is used to describe the anxiety of one who distrusts completely in his own ability to meet all the requirements of God. *Phobos* is the reverential fear of God that will inspire a constant carefulness in our dealings with Him. Combined, they put us squarely in the place of dependence and grace as a foundation for our fellowship with God. It is important that we know what we can be like without Jesus and also what we are like when we abide in Him.

It is so wonderful to have a constant and conscious appreciation of grace; to revel in God's kindness and put the whole of life, past, present and future under the enormity of His grace. Love covers a multitude of sins. Grace is both the protection and the patronage of God that covers our life as we work through the issues of righteousness and Christ-likeness. Our stumbling, faltering lifestyle is not only forgiven, but grace empowers us in our weakness to see and know the Lord Jesus (1 Corinthians 15:9-10; Ephesians 3:8; 1 Timothy 1:15-16).

Grace allows us to have a good opinion of ourselves in Christ (Romans 12:3). We know that it is God who makes us fit for His task (2 Corinthians 3:5), because He works in us to will and to work for His good pleasure (2 Philippians 2:13).

This is our lifestyle of grace. These are also the tools of grace that every leader and mentor requires in order to disciple another human being. Grace is a process of life. We embrace it and we must grow in it.

We mentor people in grace. That is, we use grace in our conversations with them and we also teach them how to live in grace for themselves. However, they must see grace in action in us. Grace is demonstrated in our heart toward them.

We are all learning to become whole in every part of our lives. Sin has damaged us all. It has decimated our character, impaired our perceptions, ruined relationships and injured our self-esteem. We have been hurt, wounded, betrayed and suffered loss in many areas.

We are in recovery. We are being lovingly restored, renewed, and refreshed. We are learning to put off the old and put on the new. The enemy is still making mischief, still seeking that opportunity to steal, kill and destroy. He flies around our lives looking for a landing strip. We are all pharisees being healed. By that I mean we are quick to judge, lay blame and believe the worst of people. We see people as they are and not through the lens of the Father. He sees people's potential in Jesus because He looks at them through the person of His Beloved Son.

People may give us a hard time as we mentor them. It is a process of teaching, speaking and demonstrating grace that will be most beneficial in their development.

I have worked through this process several times. I knew a particular individual (who we will call Luke) who was resisting all attempts at character development, personal accountability and lifestyle change. For several weeks I had chosen not to see him, preferring to pray and ask God to break his resistance.

Sometimes we can pursue things with people almost to the point of personal vendetta, losing kindness and grace in the process. I recognized that I was in danger of taking his refusal as a personal insult to my leadership and ministry. In prayer, I asked that the Lord would bless Luke. In my experience I have learned that blessing opens people up to God just as much as affliction. As a father in the church, I would rather have people in favor with God than disfavor. Giving people over to affliction through prayer has to be a last resort. It occurs only when all else has failed and we are genuinely fearful of losing them to acute godlessness.

I enjoy praying blessing over people. Everyone has a vulnerability to goodness which needs to be increased. When people see genuine goodness, they are touched in the deepest places where they hide their true self. The real skill of mentoring is getting beyond the mask to discover the essential person behind it.

In Luke's case, I prayed for the Lord to bless him. After all, a gift makes way for the giver. Several weeks later, he received a major prophetic word that I immediately witnessed to, as did others. Luke was ecstatic; this word spoke to all of his dreams and aspirations. For days afterward, he was on cloud nine. I recognized that the Lord had given me an opportunity with this man, and I arranged a time to speak with him.

The humble approach is always best. It is non-threatening and completely disarming. People cannot maintain a defense against humility without coming across as arrogant and ungodly. Luke was wary, thinking I was going to deny him my approval of his prophecy. He was taken aback when I did the very opposite. I was delighted for him and wanted him to know that. I congratulated him and declared my approval. I told him I believed in him and wanted to serve him in the development of his gift and ministry. We talked about training and opportunity to grow in his calling. We looked at a potential action plan for his progress. He thawed noticeably as we eagerly discussed his future.

At some point in the conversation, I casually asked him what percentage of the prophecy he wanted to be fulfilled. When he looked blank, I mentioned Jesus' parable of the sower and how thirty percent, sixty percent, or one hundred percent could be harvested from a seed. As kindly as I could, I told him that I felt there was only a realistic possibility of forty percent fulfillment of his particular prophetic word. I asked him what kind of character he would need to demonstrate in order to fulfill God's heart in this new calling.

We talked about that for a few minutes. I told him that God obviously believed in him, and I reiterated my own faith in him, and my desire to serve him. In this spirit, I asked him to think about our previous, unfruitful conversations. I pointed out gently that these were the very areas of character that would prevent his word from being fulfilled. These things, not me, were the obstacles. I asked him if I could have the privilege of helping him work these things through. He sat there in silence.

I further stunned him by saying, "Luke, I believe you want to be a man of honesty and integrity. I believe the Lord has His hand on you right now. After the calling comes the training. This is now a time to sit down and work out the cost. I don't want to put you through an emotional wringer to elicit some response. I want you to think hard over the next few days. The decision you make now should be based on your desire for obedience, not emotionalism. Let me know how you feel."

> Judgment
> helps no one

Within two weeks we had real movement in those areas. Luke has gone on to real maturity in both his character and his gift.

Mentoring Through Paradox

In mentoring, we must deal with people in a paradox rather than a paradigm. A paradox is two apparently conflicting ideas contained in the same truth. We must die in order to live. We must give in order to receive. We must be last to be first. Paradox is both/and, not either/or. A paradigm is a one-dimensional way of perception and action that makes it easy for us to become annoyed or vexed in our dealings with people.

For example, a mentor needs to have no compromise with regard to righteousness. By itself, "no compromise" will back people into a corner, become angry at their non-response, and may treat them harshly. Judgment helps no one. It is the end result of an incontrovertible breakdown. However, love never ceases and goodness overcomes. As long as there is breath there is hope of change.

The concept and practice of "no compromise" must be rooted in love. That is an excellent paradox. All spirituality is paradoxical. Therefore, both the mentor and the disciple need to be moving in paradox. A loving attitude plus no compromise allows people to face their issues in the right environment. Love is atmospheric. God surrounds us with it, involves us in it, and influences us by it.

We need holiness with humility so that our gentleness supports people to come to a right conclusion and take the appropriate action. We need strength with patience. It can take time to change. It can take time to adjust. We force people to change when only strength is present. If change is to be permanent, it must be internal; otherwise they will return to their weakness later. Many times I have sensed resistance and I have pushed as far as God gives permission and then I have stepped back. Sometimes people need to go around the wilderness one more time. Patience is not giving up. It is saying that "time is on my side." It creates the promise of a revisit at some point in the near/distant future.

Leadership with partnership is a powerful paradox. Without creating a sense of togetherness, our leadership can sometimes be overly authoritative to the point of bullying. I have had the misfortune to see some leadership bullying. It never works. It can produce acquiescence, but never wholeness. A partnership is a joint approach, an undertaking for a specific purpose. Good leadership supports the partnership that creates internal change.

We need to influence with joy. It is hard to spend time with mentors who do not help us to enjoy the process of changing and becoming more. Change can be exciting, stimulating and inspiring. People need to love the learning.

| Influence with joy |

We need to establish a present–future element in the conversation. Where are we now, where do we want to go in the future? Who are we in the present, who do we want to become? We are moving people out of their past–present lifestyle where they are governed currently by issues and prior circumstances. The antidote to someone's past is not the present, it is the future. That is why prophecy is essential to counseling. God gives us *"a future and a hope"* (Jeremiah 29:11). Pastoring people is easier when we are working from freedom rather than toward it. We work from the future back into the present.

Finally, we need a dialogue with questions. Mentoring only becomes a discussion when the disciple is ready to make a decision. Until that time we must keep the dialogue moving forward. A dialogue is an opportunity to explore, discover and enquire of the Lord. It asks the right questions that empower people to examine who and where they are effectively. So often we have discussions simply because we are trying to get people to a certain point. It is contrived, too planned and artificial.

People change best when they arrive at an internal place of desire and willingness to be transformed. It is a metamorphosis, not a behavior modification.

Prophecy enables us to experience God's heart in a now sense. The knowledge of God's love and care will cause us to become more deeply attached to His person. To become like Jesus is the goal of the Holy Spirit's work in our lives. The aim of the prophet is always to release people to know, love, and yield to the person of Jesus.

God speaks prophetically to enable us to enter into His divine nature. Careful attention to our character response will ensure that we are cooperating with the Holy Spirit to achieve this aim.

Maintaining Our Distinctives

We are learning to grow up into all things in Christ. Our avowed intent is an alignment with the purpose of God to make us in His image. All our words and actions must be evaluated through that outcome. Do our words reveal Jesus? Do our actions demonstrate His Presence?

The mentoring of believers falls into two main categories. Firstly, the character recognition that determines if a person is wholly following after God's name and nature, and secondly, the ministry designation which determines their capacity to move in a high level of spiritual authority and power. The following are the distinctives that we must protect and propagate if we are to walk in His footsteps.

Character recognition involves **Compassion**. If we are intent upon demonstrating the true personality of God, we must deal with other people the way we want the Lord to deal with us. Real believers work hard at grace. We examine it, meditate on it, and embrace the beauty of it in our own relationship with the Father. What we enjoy from the Father we must celebrate everywhere we go. Grace is about empowerment. Enabling people to see themselves as God sees them is an essential requirement for anyone who loves the Lord Jesus.

Grace extends both mercy and forgiveness. What would it look like for us to be known for the quality of mercy that truly represents the Lord Jesus? Compassion is the companion of clemency. Fruit is always in the cluster, like grapes. The fruits of the Spirit hang together. They overlap easily. That is their strength. They can never be isolated.

Truthfully, we never now where one ends and another begins. When one is practiced strongly it will reveal another in the action. Grace reveals mercy which in turn promotes clemency; a readiness to forgive. Compassion without remission of sins is defunct.

Unforgiveness hardens the heart, which makes people vulnerable to bitterness, resentment, and cynicism. The Father is making our hearts soft so that the fruit of the Spirit can grow easily. The fruit of the Spirit is a more powerful weapon against the enemy than the gifts of the Spirit. Internal fruit creates an environment within that overcomes anything external.

When the environment within is established thoroughly in Christ, then the external atmosphere it creates will overcome anything against it. One person walking with God is always in the majority, because Presence is majestic and sovereign. Every knee must bow to Presence.

Grace, mercy and forgiveness travel together in compassion. It is a major distinctive that we need to pursue, develop and make our own. Without compassion our character will destroy what our gift has built.

Another distinctive cluster is **Humility**, which is accompanied by gentleness, kindness and goodness. Without a softness of heart, the people around us are not safe. The majesty of God is always attached to His goodness. God is good! He is supreme above all lords and kings and He is good. He is sovereign, far above all, and He is *good*.

He is benevolent and beneficial. Everyone He touches in grace is strengthened immeasurably. His love is beneficial to every area of life. His goodness nourishes our soul. His kind, gracious, unselfish disposition empowers us to trust His nature. His righteousness means that He is only able to do what is right.

We must receive goodness in order to demonstrate it. People who love truth more than goodness just don't get it! Real truth is focused on God's nature. What God says comes out of who He is in Himself. Words reveal nature. Pharisees are incapable of becoming like God. Nicodemus had to sneak out at night just to have a conversation (John 3). Pharisaical relationships are toxic. People who love truth but have no grace are devoutly to be avoided. They are harsh, dictatorial, and unwholesome. They seek the detriment of others, not their redemption. A Pharisee is mostly self-righteous and superior. They lack humility and that is their undoing.

Without humility, our attempts at spirituality aid the enemy at the expense of the people of God. Humility is rooted in goodness, kindness and gentleness. That is a powerful combination which is full of empowerment, release and freedom. We cannot speak change without loving people into freedom. Even the way that we speak truth must represent God's heart.

Speaking the truth in love is a sign of growth in the nature of God (Ephesians 4:15). Anyone can speak truth, even the enemy (2 Corinthians 11:14-15). Speaking truth in love is a credential of true spirituality. It informs people that we have not just met Christ, but that we have given ourselves gladly to the process of being made in His image. Loving-kindness is a wonderful attribute of God. We are protected as we grow in Him. His kindness is considerate (He remembers that we are dust and knows our weaknesses), generous, thoughtful and affectionate. When He disciplines us, it is for the sake of love. Discipline without love is punishment. Christ has been punished on our behalf. We are free to make mistakes and learn of Him.

> *Christ centered people love grace*

If we are not free to make mistakes then we are captive. Children growing up are encouraged to try, to learn and to become confident. Such children will make well balanced, thoughtful, decent adults. The joyful part of learning would never make shame or blame a tactic in development. Kindness loves growth and freedom. It is for freedom that Christ has set us free. When we are mentoring distinctives in people, we are cultivating growth in the very nature of God. Gentleness is a huge part of vocal ministry. Paul often used the language of entreaty. The word beseech is seen constantly in his writings and his approach to people.

Scripture is clear — Ephesians 4:29-5:2, Colossians 3:12-17, 1 Peter 4:8-9 and of course the classic 1 Corinthians 13 — all entreat us to live in compassion and its associate affections. We are to clothe ourselves in humility toward one another (1 Peter 5:5). Humility and its characteristics are a distinctive that requires careful fellowship with the Holy Spirit.

A third distinctive is **Intimacy**. We can tell a lot about a church just by sitting in the worship service for a few weeks. Does the worship team have to work hard to encourage people to praise and rejoice? Are the songs up to date with what the Holy Spirit is doing? How many people are engaged in thanksgiving? What is the atmosphere that the congregation has developed in praise? Is it inspiring and influential? Or is it flat and slightly depressing?

Maintaining Our Distinctives

When mentoring people, we should give careful consideration to the quality of their thanks, praise and rejoicing. Joy is who God is; rejoicing is our response to who God is. What are they thankful for at this time? What aspect of the nature of God would bring them easily and powerfully to praise? Spend some time rejoicing with them and listen to their heart. Go in cold (no warning) and ask for a time of personal praise. People can get themselves ready for praise if they are forewarned. That's good. We should be able to call up our distinctives when required. However, a true character distinctive is always a lifestyle choice, not merely a life support option.

Rejoicing is ongoing and contagious. Rejoice always. In everything, give thanks. Praise the Lord at all times. God is looking for worshippers. Intimacy is the lifeblood of faith. If we practice intimacy, trust is ever-present and faith always accessible. We all need to be gently challenged about our practice of intimacy and our intention to upgrade our practice into a custom.

Ideally, every disciple should be able to give a short talk on the importance and power in rejoicing as a lifestyle. If they are not confident at speaking, they should be able to write an inspiring and influential piece. It must come from the heart, not the head, that's the point. What are we doing this year in intimacy that is new? What difference has our latest upgrade meant in our relationship with the Lord?

Another distinctive is obviously **Righteousness**, particularly in connection with integrity and honor. Doing the right thing is important training and development for all of us. The world will always weasel its way out of commitment. It will choose expediency rather than integrity. We live in a blame and shame culture where someone is always at fault and everyone looks for a scapegoat.

Honor is vital in the Kingdom. A culture of honor that seeks to uplift, encourage, speak well of and esteem others, produces superb growth conditions. Being principled and fair is important. Creating an environment of mutual respect and dignity where we can guard one another's reputations and provide favor to those in need is the essence of a good church community.

Guard against insincerity, meanness, and disrespect. Do not allow shame, condemnation, scorn, or any other behavior that is offensive to the Lord Jesus Christ. Can a fountain bring forth sweet water and bitter (James 3:12)? Can a fig tree produce olives or a vine produce figs? We are known by our fruits. What fruit of the Spirit is operating in a person's life? That signifies currently who they are in Jesus and where they are in relation to the Holy Spirit.

Lack of honor makes us potentially dangerous. Honor is a clear sense of what is morally right and it is acting toward others from a place of moral obligation. Honor is not situational. It is about who we are within our own hearts. It is concerned with how we personally show up. It is doing the right thing, even to our own disadvantage.

Integrity is concerned with internal consistency. It is the state of being whole in terms of Christ's righteousness and operating from that place instinctively. If we have to weigh up the options before choosing to be full of integrity, then we have further development to make.

Integrity and honor do not require praise or any form of acclaim. To do right is the least we can do, not the best. Integrity is the minimum requirement to be an Ambassador of Christ. It's nice to have something profound to look up to, aim for, and measure oneself against. Our intention in the progression and improvement of honor is to make it an intuitive, instinctive response of the heart. I admire anyone who is learning to be mastered by honor. In today's climate of mendacity, it is a hard road.

We all need mentors who model honor and integrity and who will lovingly challenge us to become instinctive in our righteousness.

Another powerful distinctive is **Persistence**. This is the ability to continue firmly in a course of action no matter what is standing against us. Endurance is a time-honored sign of maturity and consistent behavior.

Words reveal our nature

The attributes of persistence are patience, faithfulness, and self-control. Patience is the capacity to remain even-tempered in the face of extreme provocation and injustice. Those who will live Godly lives in Christ Jesus will suffer persecution. As well as the normal problems of delays, strife, tribulation, warfare and life in an increasingly troubled world, there is the constant sniping around the ministry from a variety of people. Patience is essential. It must be wholeheartedly embraced. It needs to be thought through from every angle. Patience creates the internal space to buy us time to make sure we can respond cheerfully.

Self-control is the key to negativity. Anyone can become angry, negative, reactionary, and harsh. Restraint is the prime part of patience. It allows us to compose ourselves internally. Self-control and joy make good partners. When we count it all joy and shout for joy at persecution, we are routinely protecting our hearts. Consider this passage:

> "Beloved, do not be surprised at the fiery ordeal among you, which comes upon you for your testing, as though some strange thing were happening to you; but to the degree that you share the sufferings of Christ, keep on rejoicing; so that also at the revelation of His glory, you may rejoice with exultation. If you are reviled for the name of Christ, you are blessed, because the Spirit of glory and of God rests upon you." (1 Peter 4:12-14)

Fellowship affects character. When our fellowship is in a low place we tend to look at difficult circumstances as negatives to avoid. When our relationship is good, we see them rightly as shortcuts to be taken into a higher realm of fellowship. They create momentum by accelerating our growth by the Spirit.

The difficult aspects here are: fiery ordeal, testing, strange things, sufferings of Christ and reviled for the name of Jesus. The positives are: revelation of His glory, rejoice with exultation, you are blessed. The Spirit of glory and of God rests upon you.

In the place where the enemy is doing his best to bring us low, the Father commits His best to bring us to a higher place of encounter and experience. I am persecuted relentlessly by well-meaning Christians who firmly believe that I am apostate and leading people astray. My life is constantly harassed by unkind, ungracious, unloving judgmental comment. I am so happy.

Many years ago, the Father showed me how to respond to Him when these things occurred. He taught me to dance. He taught me to celebrate in Him. He taught me to ask for my next upgrade in revelation, glory and exultation. Patience is easier when we are celebrants. He taught me how to use opposition to receive blessing.

My life is undeniably more blessed, not because of my detractors, but because of how the Holy Spirit uses them to my advantage.

Detractors never realize that when they are pointing out someone's shortcomings they are also revealing their own, only much more emphatically. It is possible to read what they write and feel sorry for them. It is possible to hear how they speak and realize that often their heart is in a worse place than the person they are opposing.

It is ironic that the critic may be in for a tougher time than the one they are criticizing (Matthew 7:1-5). One who is criticized will receive the grace to be transformed by it. The critic may not perceive the grace available to repent and be changed themselves. When we justify unloving behavior because of the truth, we make our hearts more accessible to the enemy than we do to God. This is the beginning of pharisaism.

Patience harasses the enemy. Rejoicing makes him weaker. Peace affects his focus. The enemy feeds off our reaction. It stimulates and energizes him. He loves hate, abuse, anger, bitterness, rejection, and rage. He loves Christians to be enraged, especially at other believers. It makes his day. He loves accusation, strife, backbiting, jealousy and envy. He feeds off every negative that we manifest. It fuels our carnality and strips us of grace and anointing.

On the back covers of *The Way of the Warrior* series I wrote these words:

"There is a place in the Spirit set aside for us where we make the enemy confused. We weary him by our rest. We discourage him by our faith. We demoralize him with our joy. We depress him by our endurance. He is dispirited by our favor; defeated by our grace. Warriors win by staying fresher, longer."

–Qualities of a Spiritual Warrior

"In the heat of battle, when faced with difficult circumstances, contending against impossible odds, warriors call up the majesty and supremacy of God that is already present in the secret place of their Spirit. They have a warrior's perception of the reality of God in the midst of provocation, attack and opposition."

–Manifesting Your Spirit

"We are learning to work with God who schedules our conflicts so that we can practice the art of overcoming. It is vital that we do not blur our focus. Warriors have clear perceptions, great insight and a heightened level of intuition because they follow the path of continual Presence."

–Coming Into Alignment

The issues of strife, trouble, slander, persecution and opposition will always be with us. Use them well. Treat yourself to some self-control and patience. Be faithful to people who are hostile to our identity and message. God is kind, let us be the same. Persistence in these things can only accelerate our journey. Imagine using all that the enemy is doing, even through "friendly fire" to make us in God's image. It is extremely satisfying.

> *Patience harasses the enemy*

One of our prime areas of distinctiveness is in our **Personal Disposition** in Christ. If we have to set a guard on certain areas of our life that would indicate that we still have serious ground to take regarding our spiritual lifestyle.

Setting a guard is responsible behavior as we are growing and developing. However it is part of the process and not the outcome of it. Many people imagine that they are properly covered if they have safeguards in place. The only effective deterrent to the flesh is death. The way we crucify the flesh is to only live in our new nature. Holiness is the only forceful deterrent to carnality. Sanctification is not just about making sure we are not vulnerable to the flesh. It is the process whereby the flesh is removed forever as a tangible hold on the base line of our character.

When our personal disposition is to love God with all our heart, soul, mind and strength, then we develop a mindset that loves Him above all else. Otherwise we have a duality about us where we withhold a part of ourselves. It is a back door into our fortress that makes us susceptible to the sin habit. Our old nature is dead. The flesh is our sin habit. It too must be crucified from our mind and heart.

Love God outrageously and we will discover what it means to be the Beloved. Love, joy and peace are the biggest signs of a personal disposition that is fully Christ centered. Our rejoicing in the Lord in any situation witnesses to people concerning the state of our heart. Our peace reduces negative personality to nothing as we lose the ability to be worried, anxious, or fearful.

Our mind is refreshed out of our personal disposition. We are renewed by our internal predisposition toward the nature of God. Every decision is made long before the circumstances arise that force us to choose. Do not wait for sin to appear before a decision is made about how to respond to its overture. Settle it in the heart now. Pray over it and align yourself with the Holy Spirit. Then simply learn the pleasure in abiding. Dwelling and remaining in love, joy and peace is a simple, childlike discipline. Stay in the place of being the Beloved. Do not allow the new man to move away from being Presence-oriented. We crucify the flesh, the sin habit, when we not only declare it dead with our sin nature on the Cross, but we also live as one fully alive to God. *"We have died and our life is hidden with Christ in God"* (Colossians 3:3).

Our personal disposition of love, joy and peace carries us through each day and every circumstance. We abide in His nature and our own changes into His image. We greet the world with a broad grin, happy heart and good thoughts. It is our pleasure to learn the joy of abiding.

The final distinctive is concerned with **Power**; not anointing or authority (they belong to our ministry designation), but the way we use our personal strengths in our interactions with people. Obviously, there are positive and negative strengths that play a huge part in our decision-making and relationships with people around us.

Our positive strengths of courage, fortitude, focus, stamina, energy, wellness and boldness are all a powerful help and support to the people we travel with in the course of life. It is important to face everything with courage; otherwise circumstances will intimidate us into giving up and not pressing through. Positive strengths ensure that we do not become victim minded and weak. Focus empowers our concentration, improves our personal vision, and creates the necessary energy to realize fulfillment. Positive strength enables us to become confident, assertive and bold in our approach to possibilities.

Confident people go out to meet life rather than waiting for it to come to them.

Positive strength has submitted to the Holy Spirit and therefore aligns itself to the encouragement and edification of others. We love people to do well. We do not merely consider our own lives but think positively about how we may upgrade, increase, and advantage other people. We love how the Lord works with us and we are willing partners in the development of people around us.

As each strength is proven, we must use it to mentor and disciple others. A mentor is more of a fully orbed teacher, adviser, coach and friend to people, across a wide range of issues and circumstances. Generally, they have an experience of life that is broad and deep. A discipler of others may have a few areas of skill, instruction and expertise to pass on, but willingly give what they have.

The Promises of God and Our Development

Negative strength occurs because we have not fully embraced the power of the Cross in our personal lives. There has been no point of real brokenness that has taken place in our relationship with the Lord. Brokenness comes to us all. It is absolutely vital. Without it, we cannot enter the high places of God's trust and Presence.

There are two things that He is doing with us in regard to trust. Firstly, we are learning to trust God in all things. We are learning dependency on His faithfulness. We are learning not to panic, be anxious or fretful. Secondly, He is bringing us to a place where He can trust us. The Father trusts what is manifested of the Son in our lives. He does not trust our flesh or our carnal behavior.

When our natural powers are not broken into the way of the Spirit, then we are a liability in the work of the Kingdom. We will use our natural strength, our learned behavior, and the ways of "successful" people, particularly in the world, to get what we want and to have our way.

We strong-arm people. We push them into a corner. We intimidate and brow-beat. We project our own image and presence. We criticize, use sarcasm, and negative humor to humiliate and bully people into submission. We ridicule people with our intelligence, erudition and education. We belittle people, make them feel inferior. We make them over-awed by who we are instead of upgrading how they can perceive themselves in the Spirit.

We do not have to be forceful to be strong. We can just withdraw our affection and approval. Withdrawing love and support is often what a strong person does when things are not going their way. We become a strong person masquerading as a weak one. We sulk, whine and play the victim. We can use exasperation and frustration to point out problems but we take no responsibility in the issue. Our line is: "It wasn't my fault that this happened." Negative strength is the bane of the church and ministries in general. These are the character flaws that need to be broken. When our natural powers are not yoked with the Holy Spirit's character, we are a handicap to the work of God we represent.

Meekness is strength under control

The antidote to negative strength is meekness. We need to be firm and decisive but with peaceful, patient intent. Meekness is not weakness; it is strength under control. Meekness encapsulates all of our strengths and puts our shortcomings firmly under the rule of the Holy Spirit. Meekness is the consciousness of God's true nature uppermost in our heart and mind. It does not see people as obstacles, or objects to move around at our own whim. It views people as partners who can be inspired and influenced by the Holy Spirit. A mindset rooted in meekness looks for opportunities not obstructions. It listens, learns and empowers people to refocus.

Meekness allows other people to find a place of rest and peace as they are developed. Meekness can provide a joy, an energy and a desire to be cultivated in the hearts of people.

The meekness (gentleness and humility) of Jesus takes away our weariness and false burden bearing (Matthew 11:28-30).

Our life in Christ is essentially an exploration and discovery of delight. We rest in His acceptance of us in Christ (Ephesians 1:3-8). When people are living from God instead of toward Him, the meekness of Christ will powerfully confirm and establish our identity in Jesus.

Meekness is the ability to create alignments by investing the atmosphere with an attitude of togetherness. It is a paradox of being firm and decisive with humility and fairness. It does not take control, but has the capacity to create movement and momentum. It seeks agreement without coercion and cooperation without being domineering. Meekness has no ego.

Negative strength is often full of self-interest and self-awareness. We view ourselves as more important than others and believe that our voice must be heard. Meekness believes that we are part of the dialogue but not the only contributor.

When we examine ourselves, we must take an honest look at the positives and negatives regarding the strengths in our personality. What needs to be broken in us so that we can lead without power? If we do not value influence and inspiration, we may not be as powerful in our organizations as we think.

Every situation and circumstance is about power, love, relationship, integrity and the nature of God. Negative strength defines our limitations and reveals our weaknesses, often in a glaring manner. Strength plus meekness is a creative power that overcomes through loving relationships, inspirational dialogue, and partnerships of mutual love and support.

When we examine our personal distinctives, there is seldom a decent hiding place! The best way to determine how we are doing in character terms is to go through these distinctives with friends, leaders, and mentors. We need objective honesty. Often our own assessment is too subjective. What is our normal pattern of behavior? We can all be amazing in short bursts. However, life is a marathon, not a sprint.

The personal distinctives are:

- Compassion — involving grace, mercy and forgiveness

- Humility — including kindness, goodness and gentleness

- Intimacy — embracing rejoicing, thanksgiving, praise and worship

- Righteousness — comprising honor and integrity

- Persistence — incorporating patience, faithfulness and self-control

- Personal Disposition — comprising love, joy and peace

- Power — encompassing strength with meekness

As a mentor, that is my own personal checklist regarding the development of character. There is another checklist regarding our ministry designation which we will examine next.

Maintaining our distinctives makes us hard to beat and much more likely to become overcomers in our battle against the world, the flesh and the devil.

Designations of Ministry

All true mentors would never place the emphasis on character before gift, simply because God is not inclined that way. He works life and gifting together. He produces character out of our anointing as He works character into our gifting. Ministry supplies us with lots of opportunity to develop our personal disposition and cultivate honor, integrity, and holiness. God does not develop character in a vacuum. He does not take us out of His plan and purpose so that He can deal with us unless it is an absolute last resort with no other possibility of redemption.

He kept faith with Abraham even when he lied about Sarah being his sister because he was afraid for his own life (Genesis 12). He appeared to lying, cheating, swindling Jacob who later became Israel (Genesis 27:36). When Samson was blind, humiliated, and beaten in the camp of the enemy because of his own sinfulness, God answered his final prayer and fulfilled his calling (Judges 16:28-30). When David committed adultery and murdered the woman's husband, God did not take him out of being king for a season (2 Samuel 11). He dealt with him in the continuance of his role and calling. Similarly, with the Apostle Peter, who was guilty of racism and hypocrisy against the Greek believers (Galatians 2:11-14). Judas remained as a team member and a friend even when looking for opportunity to betray Jesus (Matthew 2:14-16, 48-50). In their arrogance, immaturity and abuse of authority James and John wanted judgment and to call down fire from Heaven. Jesus rebuked them by saying, *"You do not know what kind of spirit you are of"* (Luke 9:51-55). He did not dismiss them from the apostolic team.

For the most part, the Father seems content to handle our growth issues in the course of life in all its fullness. All of life is spiritual. We do not have a ministry separate from life, but one that is wholly integrated with how God sees us and who we are becoming. Eli the priest remained in his place despite the facts that his sons were a disgrace (1 Samuel 2:12), that he himself could not discern the word of the Lord (1 Samuel 3:1) and that he misunderstood the purposes of God (1 Samuel 1:12-16). Yet God remained faithful to him and would not cut him off from the altar (1 Samuel 2:33).

All of life is spiritual

What makes Christianity so compelling in the earth is the fact that it is the story of God's journey with people in the course of life with all its ups and downs, majesty and stupidity, mercy and truth, grace and sin, greed and glory. Through it all, God stands supreme in His loving-kindness, compassion and goodness. Slow to anger, full of patience and wonderfully faithful. Yes, eventually people would either reap what they sow and become transformed, or harvest their own bad fruit and fall away. Yet, the Father is always leaning toward repentance, redemption, restoration, renewal, sanctification, reconciliation, atonement, rehabilitation, absolution, freedom and favor. He does not compartmentalize our lives.

Many times I have received input into a pressing need in my own life while on a platform teaching or prophesying or praying with people. Out of my own mouth has come the answer that I needed or I have received an impartation myself while laying hands on someone else. We are in Christ all the time, even when we are being stupid. The Father will not take us out of our position in Christ because He is our freedom!

I have lost count of the times that God had spoken to me as I have been speaking to others about Him. I am profoundly grateful that God is not like the Church, and so the Holy Spirit has the final say in all matters of development.

There is no finer place to be than in a church that really understands the nature of God and is committed to cultivating a spiritual environment that is like Heaven on Earth. I am blessed and fortunate to be part of such a community at The Mission, Vacaville, California. People are developed across the whole of life, not just a part of it.

I enjoy mentoring people. I love talking about life and personal distinctives and also practicing designations of ministry. Both together make up our truest identity. I have several areas that I like to talk about regarding ministry designation.

The first is **Devotion**. Our first ministry is always to the Lord. One of my earliest mentors taught me to spend eighty percent of my anointing on adoration of Jesus. I typically spend four months of the year in meditation. Sitting quietly in His Presence, attending, listening and exploring in dialogue form the things that are on the heart of the Father. That is in addition to my normal routines of prayer and praise, which is in addition to my lifestyle of lifting my heart to God at every opportunity.

Many years ago when I was a business development manager for a very exciting, thriving company, I had a different routine. Usually the base line for me is ten percent of my day, 154 minutes as a guaranteed minimum for prayer and praise. Reading Scripture and study were extra. I love reading Scripture aloud to the Father. When necessary, I would ask the Father to bless me with one hour less sleep so I could be with Him. Never underestimate the desire for relationship in the heart of the Lord. Do not miscalculate the genius of the Holy Spirit in making those relational times both interesting and rewarding.

Always approach a devotional time from the heart of God. Many people make the mistake of trying to get somewhere with God. You are already there! *"But of Him, you are in Christ Jesus"* (1 Corinthians 1:30). We do not, by our own strength, move toward God devotionally. We are already in Christ so we relax at the point of acceptance. We are the Beloved (Ephesians 1:3-8). We are blessed, chosen, and are made full sons by God's kind intention. In Him we are forgiven, redeemed, and seen as holy and blameless because of the astonishing riches of His grace.

Without grace we are always looking at the downside, preoccupied by a negative. In grace, we are lavished with wisdom and insight regarding our true place of identity in Christ. Our chief role in devotion is to allow ourselves to be loved. We must receive from God so that we can give to Him. Thanksgiving is brilliant here because we can thank God in anticipation of His grace being poured out on us today.

Everything originates in God, and comes to us from God. We can only return to God what He gives us in the first place. Read and devotionally study these Scriptures and ask the Holy Spirit to give you insight so that you can revel in the truth: John 3:27; Romans 11:35-36; James 1:17; 1 John 4:19.

We are in Christ in God. It is an authentic, cast iron, bottom-line fact which must be established in us by experience. We are starting from a place of truth and working back to a point of need. We are not starting from a point of need attempting to establish a point of truth. *"But by His doing you are in Christ Jesus who became to us wisdom from God, and righteousness and sanctification, and redemption, so that just as it is written: LET HIM WHO BOASTS, BOAST IN THE LORD"* (1 Corinthians 1:30-31).

Passionate devotional experiences arise simply out of a heartfelt encounter from within our position in Christ. A mentor loves to explore and upgrade the devotional relationship of a disciple to his/her Maker.

Another of our ministry designations is **Inspiration**. We inspire people both consciously and unconsciously. It is true that many people do not read their Bibles, but they do read their Christians. We are being watched. Years ago, in an airport on the East Coast, we were faced with storm delays. Everyone was encouraged to go to the desk at their respective gate. I had a ticket for the next flight out only to discover my seat had been allocated to another and I could not even get on stand-by.

The agent was harassed, stressed to the max and obdurate. I had a legitimate ticket — too bad. I talked, she argued. I am a firm believer that if anger rises up big time then it was already there anyway and this person is only bringing to the surface what was already present. No one makes us angry. They either expose our disposition, or we choose to call it up. Positive anger is righteous indignation usually on behalf of another. It is useful only at certain times and must not lead us to sin.

Negative anger emanates from our own internal disposition and often makes its presence felt when we are under threat or thwarted in some way.

I knew she was having an awful day and had probably drawn a mental, emotional line in the sand. I quietly thanked her and spoke some appreciation into her life. Possibly throughout that day people had been taking value out of her life. Esteem is vital to all of us. I wanted my interaction with her to be memorable for the right reason. I did not fly out that day; there was no a room to be had within forty miles. I spent a horrible night at the airport.

There was a person behind me that day who was a disillusioned believer. We never spoke. I have no personal recollection of him. Months later, someone handed him one of my journals, *The Nature of God*. He enjoyed it, got on my website, saw my photograph, and remembered me at the gate. Apparently, I impressed him that day as the only non-stressed, non-angry person at the gate. In his language, what he saw made him think of Jesus.

A lifestyle approach to spirituality is more powerful than a situational attitude. When we are focused on being rather than doing, then our life is being established rather than our posture. The front that we erect can be undermined in less controlled situations. When the fruits of the Spirit become established, they form the basis of our ingrained behavior.

Imagine if I had been in the flesh that day and he had read my books months later. Further disillusionment may have resulted. I am not a super saint. I am sure that I have disillusioned people and may do so again in the future. This story, and others like it, arrest my perspective and create a stronger desire to unconsciously manifest the Lord Jesus Christ.

From the authentic basis we can move into the arena of consciously and deliberately wanting to inspire other people. If what we think about God is the single most important thing in the world, then how we think of others is also of huge significance. How we actually express that in word and deed is the very essence of the Good News! A good mindset must be continually practiced and expressed. A mind set on the Spirit brings life and peace (Romans 8:6). When we allow ourselves to be renewed in the spirit of our mind (Ephesians 4:23), then it is other people who catch the benefit of what has wonderfully changed in us.

To deliberately inspire other people is a joy that makes Christ more real to us in the interaction. The art of ministry is encouragement. The purpose is edification. The process is elevation in their relationship with the Lord. When we inspire, we provide another human being with the urge or the ability to feel or do something that they would perhaps not undertake without our encouragement.

Inspiration is the breath of life

We literally breathe life into them. There is a principle of respiration involved. We provide an atmosphere for people to reconnect with God and their true self. A person of deliberate inspiration sets the pervading tone for an upgrade in persona and personality. We make life more pleasurable, interesting and exciting. When I speak at an event I want to encourage and stimulate people to fall in love with Jesus at a deeper level.

We carry an anointing to quicken, arouse and awaken people to the Lord Jesus Christ. Everything we say and do should reveal God's true nature and inspire people to believe. We carry an anointing to reassure people of the love of God. We inspire faith in God's grace, mercy, and forgiveness. We do not hang people with a negative. We cut them free from it.

When we elevate a negative above a positive, we discourage and demoralize. We beat down people's self perception and dampen faith. People focus on sin rather than righteousness. What we focus on, we become. Inspiration never inhibits; it sets people free to discover the radiant nature of God and be transformed.

It is important that we check ourselves out in terms of the quality of our inspirational output. A good mentor provides great lessons in the art of upgrading. It is time for us to think clearly about the people around us, both those we like and those who represent a struggle to our heart.

Ask the Father to show His perception of them. Fine tune your appreciation and add value to someone's life. Create a good habit of communicating what you see, either by speaking or writing. The lies of the enemy and the disparaging comments of others will stick less and less to us as we practice being an inspiration. *"Give and it will be given to you"* (Luke 6:38). That works both ways, positively and negatively.

Our third ministry designation is **Influence**. Who are we influencing? What does our influence look like? How is it affecting the individual and corporate life of people around us?

Influence is the capacity to have an effect upon the character or behavior of someone or something. In the world it is power arising out of status. In the Kingdom it is power emanating from Presence. Influence in spiritual terms is connected to the flow of the Holy Spirit.

If we think of a brick wall and focus on one brick in particular, we note that it has a particular relationship with each brick in its vicinity. Firstly, it is resting on two bricks, which denotes a mentoring relationship with people who undergird and support. We all need people to depend upon for advice, input and accountability. Such people empower us to connect our future with our present.

They are concerned with destiny; where we are now and where we are going. They ensure that we are built up in regard to life itself in Jesus, in the body, in the world, and in the Kingdom. They provide a valuable imprint on our identity and calling. They are significant in our development. I am privileged to have a number of people, both recent additions and people of long standing (over twenty years), who heavily influence my life.

Secondly, that particular brick is in line with other bricks on the same level. This speaks of working relationships and peer level friendships that operate around our lives.

There are a large number of speakers that I work with on varying events around the world. It's good to catch up on news, ask advice, receive prayer, and talk about good practice. I love the leadership and itinerant teams at The Mission in Vacaville where I can share life, receive input, and be a part of a learning circle that has real significance. I am part of a friendship group called The Tribe, where we practice community and life in the Spirit. I am also part of a teachers/free thinking forum called The Room, where we dialogue only about the Nature of God. We explore the Agapé love of God across all areas of life.

We should all make efforts to know, relate, and commune with fellow travelers. I am very intentional about supporting, edifying and encouraging people who are on a similar journey and have the same type of warfare and pressure that I am learning to joyfully endure. It is important that we stand with people irrespective of how well or badly they are doing. If we only give support when people are doing well, then we are not much of a friend. Jesus is not ashamed to call us brethren (Hebrews 2:11).

It is a privilege to be attacked in defense of a friend or fellow minister who is failing, struggling and making poor decisions. We must not shoot our wounded. Everyone has the right of restoration and redemption. It is a joy to watch the Holy Spirit turn someone's mess into a message that defines their life and glorifies Jesus.

I am very happy with the hits I have taken from well-meaning Christians because I chose to stand with someone who was making big mistakes. I have felt the kiss of God, who understands commitment and faithfulness. It is possible to separate the man from the message on those occasions so that we uphold the person while not condoning the message. Doctors say that a broken bone, when healed, can become much stronger. When people are restored and have changed in the process, they often carry a greater threat to the enemy.

The final brick supports two others, which are indicative of our need to be discipling someone else. It is right for us to take responsibility to pass on what we have received in Christ. Iron sharpens iron. Often those I have been discipling have been the people that have pushed me further into the realm of the Spirit. I have discipled some people in the prophetic for around twenty years. Some are in full-time ministry, traveling and speaking. All have become part of my development process.

Apart from the regular people that I am routinely discipling at home, there are others that I connect with on my travels. I usually have times set aside for certain people at events so we can dialogue about the process that they are experiencing. I have people traveling in to see me when I am in Vacaville. I do conference calls with groups of people around specific issues.

The Promises of God and Our Development

I love having coffee with people in the late afternoon sun, or a glass of red wine (à la Jesus) in the late evening, talking about the Lord and what comes next. Influence: we all have it and we all need it.

A fourth ministry designation is **Identity**. We have a space to occupy in the battle; a given role in the Kingdom, a relationship in the church family, a particular part of the Body of Christ to become. Identities are attached to everything we are and all that we do.

In the natural world we have multiple identities but only one personality. A man can be a son, brother, cousin, nephew, uncle, husband, father, grandfather, friend, colleague, and employer – all of which are relational. A woman has the female equivalent. When we get together at family events we naturally fall into expressing many of these identities intuitively. We would not speak to our grandfather as we would our nephew, or our brother as if he were our uncle.

> *Identity is the fact of being who we are*

Add to these identities our functional relationships of apostle, prophet, pastor, teacher, evangelist, elder, counselor, mentor, *et al*. We have multiple identities in Christ that enable us to relate to people within the context of both friendship and function.

We have two distinctive relationships with God. Mary represents our personal intimacy, devotional relationships, and is primarily concerned with learning to be with God. Martha represents our ministry designation and the role of giftings He has provided as we learn to work with God. True identity is the blend between both of these distinctives.

Jesus constantly proclaimed His identity in His "I AM" statements. I AM, Bread of Life, Light of the World, Door, Good Shepherd, Son of God, Lord and Teacher, Resurrection and the Life, Way, Truth and Life, The True Vine.

Paul spoke of his identity as a bond-slave, apostle, wise master builder, father, farmer, leader. He was a teacher, evangelist, ground-breaker, and ambassador of reconciliation.

God gives us identities so that we can discover what He wants to be for us in those specific areas. Each identity has its own distinctive anointing, favor, and relationship with God attached to it. When the Father speaks to us from Scripture, He begins to declare to us how He sees us in Christ. Out of that declaration He begins to shape a life that is congruent with His image.

It is part of the Law of Life in Christ Jesus that favor is attached to identity and that alone can mark us out as different. Favor is God's intentional bias toward us. It is important to know the intentionality of God within the specific identities that He is cultivating within us. The Law of the Spirit of Life in Christ Jesus relates to fullness and abundance. Multiple identities in Jesus enable us to experience fullness on a much broader front. *"Of His fullness have we all received"* (John 1:6).

In ministry, when we call up our identity in a particular situation, we also call up the favor that is attached. That specific favor has resources attached. It will provoke an experience of God. Favor is about embracing the power of God's goodness and provides permission and authority in ministry.

Identity is the fact of being who we are. It is the practice of that which brings us into harmony with the life that the Father has chosen for us. It is the development of these characteristics which determine our contribution in the Kingdom. We bear a close similarity to the person of Jesus and we have an affinity with His ministry.

Practicing our identity is what makes us consistent in life. Conformity to Jesus means that we live, move, and have our being according to His personal disposition (Acts 17:28). A good mentor will ask a disciple questions about their identity, both in character and function.

The natural progression to dialogue about identity would be the establishing of a **Calling**. This is a strong sense of being chosen for a specific purpose or set of purposes. It is an assignment that carries with it a sense of particular mission and a specific role and ministry. I do not take speaking engagements. I only take assignments. Churches and conference hosts have to complete a specific questionnaire on my website. Our prayer partners pray over them. I only accept invitations to places where I believe the Lord has given me a specific assignment. Otherwise I would rather stay in Vacaville and hang out with the Lord. He does not pay me to do ministry. He pays me to be His friend. Mostly that is private, often it can be public.

When I go to a place, it is usually to establish or release something. Occasionally it can be to overthrow something perpetrated by the enemy. The assignment can be to equip, arouse or awaken. It can be to open up the next level of the Spirit or to strengthen a work that is under attack. I love assignments and the fight that goes with them. I have hundreds of prayer warriors wonderfully commanded by Alison Bown, who is my International Prayer Director. She has regional commanders and captains who are discipling and empowering a whole bunch of people to make sure that I cause enough trouble for the kingdom of darkness.

We need our eyes opened. An illumination within that sheds purposeful light on who we are, and what we are called to do (Ephesians 1:18). We must cultivate a favorable and confident expectation of breakthrough wherever our assignment takes us. It is important to have a significant expectation of good around the ministry. We are at our sharpest and best when we live in anticipation with pleasure regarding what God is going to do.

> Favor is attached to identity

There is no pressure in ministry. There is a distinct pleasure in being in Christ and partnering with the genius who is the Holy Spirit. Ministry is our reward. It is a prize that we constantly move toward as we continually define our upward call in Christ (Philippians 3:14). Receiving the next upgrade of our calling at the time of its release is vital. I know many ministries with unclaimed upgrades that have become weary and disillusioned. Life in Christ is forever upwardly mobile. Most of our upgrades become available to us in times of adversity since the Father loves to crown difficulty with blessing. Only unchanging, ineffable Goodness would think and act in such a wonderful way. Whatever God is, He is relentlessly. His actions when we are under pressure are the source of legends. He works everything out for our good. Our part is to abide in the beauty and power of His love and remain firmly on purpose. Everything comes to the one who is wonderfully loved and who loves in return.

Part of our partnership with the Holy Spirit is to learn faithfulness and commitment to God's nature. In this way we can walk worthy of our calling which is always to represent His heart to others. His goodness needs to be uppermost in our hearts and minds. Our ministry is surely to fulfill every desire for goodness to triumph and overcome (2 Thessalonians 1:11).

The need to treat our calling as holy and to establish a public life in grace is absolutely crucial. We are in ministry to serve His purpose with outstanding grace (2 Timothy 1:9). We represent Heaven, not the church (Hebrews 3:1), therefore our encounters and testimony is more profound and glorious. All ministry must have a radiant testimony of God or it cannot rise to the height of God's fullness and intention. It is the always astonishing Holy Spirit who encourages us to become diligent with regard to our calling. His enthusiasm for us and our calling is our main source of motivation. His intentionality empowers our diligence (2 Peter 1:10).

Mentors impart the sense of privilege that all disciples should feel at being invited to serve the Lord. Within the realm of that invitation we must discover the **power source** that is readily available to each of us. We should never separate power from Presence. We are not merely prophesying as much as releasing the life of the Prophet within. We can all prophesy simply because Jesus within us is our Prophet, Priest and King. We release Christ the Healer, Christ the Deliverer, Christ the Redeemer, because we do everything in His Name and Nature. Our source for power is our own intimacy with Him supported by the person of the Holy Spirit. Our foremost passion is to receive Jesus in His fullness and release that to everyone, everywhere we go.

When we are filled with the Spirit, we live in His passion to reveal Jesus. We embrace that same Spirit of disclosure. All ministers live in the glory of covenant with the Father. That covenant is revealed and released to us joyfully in Christ and wonderfully supported and empowered through the indwelling Holy Spirit. To be filled with the Spirit is to be overflowing with covenant.

Obedience to the Spirit of covenant releases Presence. Rather, it pours out of us. Obedience makes the Christ life uncontained, free flowing. Abiding is the key New Testament practice. More than a discipline, it is a passion that calls us to joyfully remain in the center of God's affection. We obey covenant by living up to God's nature in all circumstances. The New Testament teaches relentlessly about relationships and the nature of God.

His promise is incredibly trusting and full of permission: *"If you abide in Me, and My words abide in you, ask whatever you wish, and it shall be done for you"* (John 15:7). Abiding releases exponential life while keeping us grounded in God's nature. Our goal in abiding is to come to the place where we are so one with His heart that there is little difference between our desire and His; freedom in and through relationship; power revealed in and through the passion of intimacy.

The Father cannot be properly represented aside from goodness. God is Good. It is the goodness and kindness of God that leads us to repentance. We overcome evil with good. God's glory is that He is amazingly and most wonderfully full of goodness. He causes His goodness to pass before us and it makes our face shine. His goodness is our radiance. Jesus went about doing good and healing all who were oppressed by the devil.

In Christ, we are learning to *"fulfill every desire for goodness"* (2 Thessalonians 1:11) and the work of faith with power. The work of faith is love (Galatians 5:6). Love and goodness are two of the most powerful representatives of Kingdom life. God is slow to anger and so cannot be represented by it. If we have not fully embraced love as the passion of our hearts, then we will most assuredly sin when we become angry (Ephesians 4:20-27). People who have not been taught to live in Christ are vulnerable to their own sin habit. We must lay aside everything that does not represent life, love, and godliness. Our thinking must be renewed so that the way we live our life is transformed. The likeness of God is everything! Only in the context of His true nature can we afford to speak the truth. Speaking the truth without love empowers the enemy. It provides him with an entrance and an opportunity.

A religious spirit can never represent God, only its own denominations or network. Whenever we see or hear a ministry moving in anger, judgment, or negativity we are observing a person whose own life has not been upgraded by love. Something is missing.

Anointing and revelation must emanate from an encounter with Presence, or we simply are watching a person moving in God rather than enjoying God moving in that individual.

Power is God confirming what we speak about Him. He exhibits what we expound. Our declarations put His beauty on display. He follows through on our faith in Him. Nothing happens without proclamation, which is why our testimony is so vital. Our testimony of Jesus is the very essence of prophecy (Revelation 19:10). Testimony releases people to see God differently.

A testimony is a revelation of God's nature and passion for us combined with the anointing to pass on that intentionality. This is what God did for me and now He will do the same for you!

The Promises of God and Our Development

Jesus partnered with the Father. He said what the Father was saying and Heaven demonstrated that truth. Faith comes by hearing the very words of God. We have a responsibility to live out our relationship in public, with or without a microphone!

Presence and Kingdom are intertwined. The affection of God is the beginning of maturity. Growing in love and grace is the maintenance of maturity. Expressing the heart of the Father is the evidence of a mature personal covenant. As He is, so are we in this world.

Good mentors help disciples to desire and seek after Presence as a way of life and the only POWER source for ministry.

Our final ministry designation is **Authority**. In apostolic language there are two types of authority. *"For even if I boast somewhat further about our authority, which the Lord gave for building you up and not for destroying you, I will not be put to shame"* (2 Corinthians 10:8).

The authority that edifies does so by seeking the highest good of another. It builds up, releases and empowers by providing permission and approval. Let all things be done for the purpose of edifying (1 Corinthians 14:26). We want to lead people as God leads us. All shepherds (with the notable exception of Jesus) are sheep also.

> *Authority is connected to example*

To be sure, in our authority it is necessary to bring a measure of correction specific to the problem we encounter in people. We do so with great patience and instruction (2 Timothy 4:2). The best authority is used in the context of coaching, training and discipling. Effective discipling requires a learning environment. Without it, we may be administering punishment rather than development.

In the world, authority chiefly stands for the power or right to give orders and enforce obedience. It is concerned with exerting control in a particular sphere. Jesus declared that human authority without Godly influence would cause leaders to lord it over people in their exercise of authority. When people feel a right or privilege over another, then an abuse of authority is about to take place.

Jesus presented an alternative to worldly authority when he placed authority squarely in the place of authentic servanthood (Matthew 20:25-28). Real leaders serve others; they do not exercise mastery and control over them.

When we use worldly habits of authority, then we can become spiritually authoritarian. We enforce strict obedience to our authority at the expense of personal freedom. We use censure, judgment, and fault-finding over people, to exert pressure on their lifestyle. Instead of provoking people to love and good works, we put a heavy tax on their behavior that provides the enemy with an opportunity to increase disobedience. When we are heavy handed, we create a hard heart. There is a place for rebuke with strength, but it is only when all other avenues have been carefully explored.

In the Corinthian church, the gross immorality of one individual necessitated direct action. In this case, although authority is used strongly, it still does not include punishment; but that the flesh (sin habit) is destroyed so that the spirit may be saved (1 Corinthians 5). Paul wrote it in tears and with great sorrow, which is revealed in his second message on the matter (2 Corinthians 2:1-8) where he urges the church to reaffirm their love for the individual and restore fellowship. The language that Paul uses in this incident is hugely indicative of the heart relationship that He has both with the Lord and with God's people.

Authority with people lies in the power to influence others through our own exemplary behavior. When the issue of personal greatness caused a dispute amongst the disciples, Jesus asked a couple of questions.

"For who is greater, the one who reclines at table, or the one who serves? Is it not the one who reclines at table? But I am among you as the one who serves." (Luke 22:27)

The attitude and approach of Jesus regarding personal position and authority provides us with the clearest example concerning our personal approach. Great people have certain expectations, yet He was among us as one who serves.

Authority is not connected to age, but example. The way in which we speak to people is of equal importance to how we conduct ourselves before them. Our pattern of behavior includes an object lesson in loving people, demonstrating faith and exhibiting purity in all things (1 Timothy 4:12). If we have to rebuke, the objective is to create a greater respect and reverence for God in the hearts of all who witness that incident (1 Timothy 5:20).

Authority is connected to destruction, but only in the context of the enemy, not people. We do not fight against flesh and blood but against rulers, powers, world forces of darkness and spiritual forces of wickedness in the Heavenly places (Ephesians 6:12). Jesus came to destroy the works of the devil (1 John 3:8) while not judging the world (John 12:4), but acting as Savior (John 3:16-17).

When we judge people it can often be according to our own flesh (sin habit), which is a carnal standard of behavior. Jesus is not judging anyone in that context (John 8:15-16). Judgment in the flesh involves condemnation, but by the Spirit becomes an assessment of where people are and how they may upgrade their lifestyle.

This is of critical importance to the work of the ministry. If we include people in our judgments then our authority over the devil is weakened. If our authority with people does not involve their freedom, then we are less likely to release captives and open prison doors. No ministry involving people can act as advocate and jailer. That is double-minded and will only produce instability in those we minister among.

The Promises of God and Our Development

Destructive authority is reserved for our battle with the enemy (Luke 9:1). The true expression of the Kingdom is found in Matthew 10:7-8 and Mark 16:16-18:

"And as you go, preach, saying, 'The Kingdom of heaven is at hand.' "Heal the sick, raise the dead, cleanse the lepers, cast out demons; freely you received, freely give." (Matthew 10:7-8)

"He who has believed and has been baptized shall be saved; but he who has disbelieved shall be condemned. And these signs will accompany those who have believed: in My name they will cast out demons, they will speak with new tongues; they will pick up serpents, and if they drink any deadly poison, it will not hurt them, they will lay hands on the sick, and they will recover." (Mark 16:16-18)

Peter's original testimony to the Gentiles was that Jesus was anointed with the Holy Spirit and with power and went about doing good and healing all those who were oppressed by the devil, for God was with Him (Acts 10:38).

Authority that involves destruction is concerned with two things in regard to the enemy. These are ascendency and jurisdiction. Ascendency is connected to the resurrection and the surpassing greatness of God's power to those in Christ. All key ministries have a revelation of Ephesians 1:18-23 in regard to their own anointing.

Good mentors check out people's credentials in the Spirit regarding authority over the enemy. Is there enlightenment within, concerning the substructure of our whole approach to ministry, and the clash between two kingdoms? Everything that we do for God, we automatically do against the enemy. Our rejoicing blesses the Lord while grieving the enemy. Our goodness glorifies the Lord and weakens the devil. Any time we move in the opposite spirit, we depress the devil.

To work with the Lord and know the conscious damage to the kingdom of darkness that our service creates, that is a powerful weapon, and most enjoyable.

Does this disciple have a reasonable, rational approach to spirituality or have the eyes of their inner man of the spirit become truly acquainted with the demands and modus operandi of Heaven on earth? Does this individual really comprehend, by experience, the full anticipation and expectation that they can have permission for in Christ? If the glory of God is that He is good (Exodus 33:18-19), then what has this person encountered of the riches of God's glory?

Are we familiar with our own inheritance as a joint-heir with Christ? Do we have any revelation regarding God's inheritance in us, and what that may mean in connection with the capability of Heaven on earth? Do our experiences include becoming overwhelmed by majesty? Do we have any inkling about the surpassing greatness of His power and what it might look like in a modern world?

Are we encountering Heaven in any usual way? From our seat with Christ in Heavenly places, what is our viewpoint on the warfare that is being waged from our side? In our engagement with the enemy, what is changing regarding his subjection to Christ in the earth?

Good mentors do not disciple people in the sub-routines of life in the Spirit. If we expect to fulfill Isaiah 61:4 in reality, then we need to ascend to the right place in the Spirit. From that vantage point, when we spy out the land that God is giving to us, we must recognize that it now belongs to Christ and we have jurisdiction. We have imputed power and authority over that territory. We say what happens in a city or region, state or province, nation and continent. The power of the one with the One is all embracing. God is the One, True, Great Territorial Spirit who marked out Israel's territory as part of their inheritance in Him (Joshua chapters 13-21).

Every believer has territory assigned to them. It may be our street or place of work. It may be a people group or an institution of society. It could be an event or a gathering. My friends at New Earth Tribe in Australia have claimed all the new age festivals in that nation as belonging to them. The favor they have with God is phenomenal in that territory.

When I speak at an event or church, my prayer warriors and I claim that place and people for the purpose of breakthrough. I want jurisdiction. I want official power to make legal decisions and judgments over the enemy. The ruler of this world has been judged (John 16:11), we are enforcing that conviction and passing out sentence. We have authority to cast him out.

Authority gives us territorial jurisdiction

Part of our inheritance is land. Jurisdiction is having and exercising authority over assigned territory and empowering believers to rise up and occupy the space around them. That territory may be a neighborhood, a business, local government, a culture, or society.

We have a favorable and confident expectation of something good. We anticipate with pleasure the majesty of God to overcome the enemy. God's Word comes fully equipped. We shut off access to that power by defining our lives outside of what God is saying and doing. A powerless Gospel is of considerable benefit to the enemy. A non-relationship with the Holy Spirit seriously empowers the darkness around us. The natural mind with its predisposition to logic, reason and rationale is a formidable impediment to faith and a supernatural lifestyle. I am not against logic, reason or rationale. I love them. I use them daily. In my experience, being renewed in the Spirit of the mind is of paramount importance in developing the mind of Christ.

I have chosen a mindset on the Spirit to determine my way into revelatory truth and experience. Wisdom is the key to life in the Spirit.

Logic and reason often talk us out of supernatural encounter. Wisdom enables us to behold and become what the Father sees in Heaven.

Authority over the devil is concerned with ascendency and jurisdiction. We are made alive in Christ and raised up with Him and seated with Him in Heavenly places (Ephesians 2:5-6). Being in Christ in actuality is everything. It is a specific encounter and an ongoing series of experiences to enable us to grow up in all things in Christ.

We must examine our ministry designations as an important part of our growth in the function of anointing and ministry. Visit them with friends and colleagues in the Kingdom who understand and practice such attributes. Our ministry designations are:

- Devotion involving prayer, meditation and praise.

- Inspiration whether conscious or unconsciously applied.

- Influence throughout all of our relationships.

- Identity compatible with God's perception of us.

- Calling that has a specific rather than general burden.

- A power source that fulfills every desire for goodness.

- Authority that has ascendency and jurisdiction.

There are many questions that we may ask in the context of defining ministry and calling. There are other designations also. These are the ones that I have found most useful in my development of people. There is a huge area of overlap within the dialogue that they generate. These are but the headlines.

Joyful Accountability

There are many perceptions of accountability in the wider Body of Christ. Most of these seem to encompass the notion that people need to be governed in the process of developing righteousness. This idea that we need to be in a partnership where one individual (or a group) have the power to call the shots over another does not originate in Heaven. It is largely a worldly construct with some Bible verses tacked on.

The idea of "covering" comes from the Old Testament where the sons of Noah covered the nakedness of their father without looking at him (Genesis 9:23). Nothing to do with authority or accountability, and everything to do with the preservation of modesty and respect.

The notion that we all need authority to tell us what to do and how to live is not really conducive to personal responsibility. The popular idea that people need someone else to hold their feet to the fire would seem to guarantee immaturity and a certain non-development of our new nature.

People do not require oversight to teach them not to sin; that can only arise out of their love and passion for the Lord Jesus Christ. It's a wonderful by-product of a devoted, loving relationship with the Father. People need over-sight to empower them to love righteousness and adore freedom. It is for freedom that Christ has set us free (Galatians 5:1).

The old nature is dead. We are co-crucified with Christ, every bit as much as the two thieves on either side of Him at Calvary. The wonderful difference is that the Father put us into Christ on the Cross (Romans 6:3-11). All true discipling must involve a passion to empower people to walk in newness of life. We are seeking to establish people in the likeness of Christ. We teach and example the privilege of being alive to God. Galatians 2:19-20 captures the stun-ning boldness of our inclusion in Christ. It is an astonishing partnership that we are thrust into in Christ by the Father. It is audacious, daring, adventurous, definite, eye catching, enterprising and awesome. The whole concept, prac-tice, and lifestyle of being in Christ is breathtaking in its liberty. The freedom is bright, shiny and powerful.

"It is no longer I that live but Christ that lives in me." This is the essence of accountability. The bottom line regarding accountability is concerned with what we are doing with our freedom. *"For you were called to freedom, brethren; only do not turn your freedom into an opportunity for the flesh but through love serve one another."* (Galatians 5:13)

There are no excuses. There is no one else to blame. We are responsible to live in Christ. All the times when I have been stupid and sinful are because I chose something else above my freedom. I may have been tempted or beguiled by someone or something. I may have been pressured by the enemy. That is irrelevant. I chose to act outside of Christ. I must take responsibility for not abiding in my freedom.

> *Accountability imposes God's freedom*

I chose my sin habit above my new nature in Jesus. If it happens again, it is because I made the same stupid, selfish mistake.

We are partakers of Christ. We are joyfully obligated to live as free people (1 Peter 1:16). Abiding in Christ is the key passion of all New Covenant peo-ple. In all our interaction with the Holy Spirit, we are learning how to live in Christ, and He lives in us (Ephesians 3:17; 4:20). The goal of the Spirit is to present everyone as mature in Christ (Colossians 1:28). To do that effectively, He seeks to empower us in our desires through His own passionate persua-sion. The enemy seeks to make sin attractive so that resistance becomes more difficult. It is called the process of temptation. This involved planting a key thought in the mind that worms its way into the heart over time. It creates a longing and a justification. The longing turns to looking and the justifica-tion to excuse. The freedom is reduced every time we entertain a thought or take an opportunity to look. We are being enticed. Job put it this way: *"My heart has walked after my eyes"* and *"My heart has been secretly enticed"* (Job 31:7, 27). This finds an echo in James' apostolic heart when he writes, *"But each one is tempted when he is drawn away by his own desires and enticed."* (James 1:13-16)

James does not mention Satan's role in temptation. The enemy may be an external agitator, yet we are free within to follow Christ. Our nature in Christ is no longer drawn to sin. We are learning to crucify the sin habit by remaining in our new nature of Christ in us, the expectation of glory. The enemy seeks to take advantage of weakness unrefined.

The Holy Spirit loves to promote the beauty of the Christ life (John 16:14). For us to live is Christ, and to die is gain (Philippians 1:21). This truth works well on all levels. Accountability loves freedom and revels in the truth that death to self is to be highly prized as part of our freedom in Christ.

Our goal is to discover the length, breadth, height and depth of God's love for us, so that we are rooted and grounded in love by His indwelling Christ. To encounter and fully experience the love of Jesus that miraculously passes knowledge.

A true encounter with overwhelming love will make mystics of all of us to a greater or lesser degree. I am often amused by the accusation that I am a mystic. It makes me grin from ear to ear, mostly because the accusation is so silly. It is people betraying their own lack of encounter and ongoing experience. We are not created anew in Christ to remain earthbound in our natural, logical perceptions (1 Corinthians 2:6-10).

The Spirit searches the depths of God and seeks to empower us so that we develop a new way of thinking and perception in alignment with Christ Himself. It is the thinking that comes by way of relationship with Jesus and not academic study. The theologians of the day marveled at Peter and John being uneducated and untrained, yet had obviously prospered in Christ (Acts 4:13).

I love the study of Scripture (2 Timothy 2:15), but to know the truth and not be set free by it is surely grossly immature. Knowledge not combined with experience is not knowledge in spiritual terms.

A mystic is someone who, by meditation and self-surrender, seeks a union with God that is out of the ordinary. They seek to reach truths beyond mere rational, intellectual understanding. The life they choose will inspire a sense of spiritual mystery, awe, and fascination about God. If we are truly living from Heaven to earth rather than the reverse, then we are going to perceive and receive truth in a profoundly different manner. People who are earthly minded are no Heavenly good in spiritual terms.

I know many intellectual Christians who have never moved in supernatural gifts or power. Their intellect does not allow it. They will seldom, if ever, move into any great level of faith — their brain will talk them out of it. When we are accountable, we become responsible for our freedom, not our spiritual poverty. We must give an answer regarding why we live in measure and not fullness.

Accountability is concerned with our whole person and the whole person of Christ glorified. We are obligated to explain our lack of majesty and our non-enjoyment of God's sovereignty. Through the ongoing experience of the abundance of grace and the gift of righteousness, we are empowered to reign in life by Christ Jesus (Romans 5:17).

Our biggest problem is that our belief system is not challenged by the quality of our life in Christ. We make allowances for mediocrity and powerlessness. When we turn away from simple trust, we make doubt an intellectual art form.

Our spiritual reality is that we boast in our confident expectation of the glory of God. Eternal life has begun. It is here and we are in it. As He is (in Heaven), so are we in this world (1 John 4:17). On earth as it is in Heaven, Jesus prayed. We reign in life by the One.

Exuberance, not careful argument, is required. When we are justified by faith, we live out of abundance in grace and not the mediocrity of our own resources. Boast is a noisy word. We boast in God through our Lord Jesus Christ (Romans 5:11). Everything about God is extravagant; therefore exuberance can be our only real response. We should be accountable for the level of our excitement, cheerfulness and exhilaration.

Accountability could never be about something so mundane as a code of conduct. If righteousness can only come by rules and performance, then we can never become the Beloved. Unless our righteousness exceeds the righteousness of our denomination, network or church group, then we cannot enter the Kingdom (Matthew 5:20). We cannot be judged by the good efforts of man, the double standards of the hypocritical, or the external legalism of the religious minded. We are worth so much more than that in the heart of God.

The key to oversight is to find a way to lead people without ruling their lives or dreams. We cannot impose accountability on people. Accountability is best provoked from below. The role of a leader revolves around inspiration and influence. There are leaders out there who are decisive, commanding, and effective, but I would not trust them with my life. There are some who are friendly but not relational, so it is hard to confide in them. We want leaders who see something in us of real value and who can inspire us into becoming that person. Everyone wants to be great; no one wants to be controlled. That, perhaps, is one of the core issues of leadership and true accountability. Freedom is a key; permission is another.

Accountability is about release, not restraint. When we set people free, the liberty and support we provide should cause self-discipline. Self-control is the only acceptable form of control in the church. When it is visible, we can openly trust people. When it is absent, we must be cautious in our dealings with those individuals. Imposed control can never cultivate the values we love. It can only curtail improper behavior, but the individual cannot grow beyond a certain point.

The Promises of God and Our Development

Abiding in Christ means taking responsibility for how we show up in life: taking responsibility for our own blessings, promises, behavior and lifestyle. There is no liberty without self-control. If people are going to love accountability, then they must trust that their freedom will always be in their own hands. It is fairly impossible to impose control on others without developing controlling behavior in ourselves. Controlling people are often out of control in their own behavior. We become what we impose on others.

It is interesting that when Jesus first spoke about proclaiming liberty to captives and release to the prisoners, the setting for this message was His hometown church. Religious oppression is extremely harsh and controlling. These kinds of leaders use shame, blame, condemnation, contempt, guilt and humiliation to embarrass and manipulate people into following the party line. I have witnessed enough church politics to know a penal establishment when I see one. A church prison is one where the congregations are the inmates, the leadership team the jailers and the pastor is the warden, and the Bible is the stick they use to beat people.

The philosophies of control and freedom cannot coexist. The more we try to control people, the less accountable and responsible they become. However, the real problem is much worse. When our only role models are control freaks, then all we can learn is how to become a control freak! When people are victimized by their leaders and organizations, the level of resentment and rebellion actually increases. The flesh cannot be dealt with in these circumstances, it is merely driven underground. People will fight back, mostly in ways that we cannot see. Lack of commitment is usually a sign. Withholding finance, support, and love is a personal demonstration of non-engagement.

Accountability is about release, not restraint

To create real personal accountability at every level of church, we must establish freedom at every level of human behavior. Freedom-based leadership creates free people who are responsible, committed, and engaged. Leading without using personal power and authority eliminates hierarchy as a form of oversight. Individual freedom is the epitome of the Good News. People are free to make choices in line with their love for God and His people.

Discipling involves empowering people to become personally responsible. Good mentoring necessitates having faith in people. Leaders control what they do not trust. People cannot grow without faith. Whatever is not born of faith cannot please God. Control guarantees displeasure to all concerned. Control freaks are never happy. The controlled are always oppressed. God is not glorified. People are not leaving the church because they have lost faith in God. They are leaving so that they can upgrade their relationship with Him.

Great leaders believe that everyone wants to be great. Poor churches have developed a system of oversight that controls how the organization grows. Often, these are a mild to mean version of enforced relationship that is more functional than relational. It is meant well, but imposed authority will not produce the people that God wants to see.

Good leadership creates the environment for people to discover God and become responsible to fulfill His vision of them, trust people to do the right thing, and encourage them at every opportunity to act within the love of God. Every chance we get we should advocate the bottom line of personal responsibility. That is to do to others what we would most value for ourselves. We reap what we sow. Do not ask people to do things right. Ask them to do the right thing.

Everyone has the ability to be great in the Lord Jesus. Really good leaders help people to lay aside every weight and hindrance. They remove the things that prevent people from becoming great. Poor leaders heap rules, systems, and expectations on people.

Accountability is about intentionality. God is the most consistently intentional person I know. The bottom line of His intention is found in Jeremiah 29:11:

> *"'For I know the plans I have for you, declares the* LORD, *'plans for welfare and not for calamity, to give you a future and a hope.'"*

Empowerment creates good habits that determine our future. Empowerment is a choice. What are the beliefs that we have about ourselves that actually assist in cultivating a relationship with the Lord? In discipleship we encourage people constantly to look at the nature of God and to study what it means to be in Christ.

Disempowerment is also a choice. What are the beliefs that we have about ourselves that prevent us from having a good relationship with the Lord? I am not good at prayer. God will not meet me. He is displeased. I am not good at being a Christian. I do not feel His Presence. I am not worthy of being loved.

Disempowerment begins with our performance. Empowerment is rooted in God's essential nature. Mentoring involves discovering what God wants to be for me. It involves a true understanding of how He really sees me. It includes His strengths and not my weaknesses. He enables me to *"do all things in Christ."* As I behold Him, I can become like Him.

Accountability is the joyful development of good habits. Successful people have good habits; unsuccessful people do not. A habit is something that we do so often it becomes easy. It becomes a behavior that we keep repeating. The Holy Spirit is in the business of reprogramming us to be like Jesus. We are moving from being self-conscious to becoming God-conscious. We are leaving the flesh lifestyle behind as we develop our spirituality. We are cultivating our new nature as we abandon our sin habits. We are being renewed in the spirit of our mind.

In real, accountable relationships, we learn not to dabble at change. People do not drift to the top of a mountain, they climb. Accountability is taking the time to nourish our own spirit. It is concerned with exploring and expanding who we are in Christ. It involves knowing our true purpose and having the highest level of awareness regarding the Lord, ourselves and our calling.

Accountable relationships shape us in the present while preparing us for the future. We learn that all of life has consequences, so we work together with the Holy Spirit for good. Being led by the Spirit involves planning to be anointed, powerful, and formidable. The Holy Spirit is planning our significance now! Consistency requires a checklist, just like a pilot or astronaut. What habits need changing? What part of our lifestyle requires an upgrade? Write a list and assign priorities. At least we will know the areas that are under construction.

Quality is not an act. It is a habit. Approximately ninety percent of our normal behavior is based on habits, good or bad. An often-used question in accountability is: "Who do you want to be regardless of circumstances?" How do we want to show up on a good or bad day? Inconsistency is a habit too. Good routines are vital. Enjoying the journey is therefore a vital part of an accountable lifestyle. Everyone will always do exactly what they want. Passion is fueled by delight. When we delight ourselves in the Lord, the upgrade we receive includes the fulfillment of our own internal desire (Psalm 37:4).

Be delighted with the Father. Rejoice in the Lord always. Be filled with the Spirit. Let this mind be in you, enjoy thinking like Jesus. Be open and honest about current situations. Being economical with the truth is the best way to protect the enemy against the Holy Spirit. We provide shelter so he can harass us unopposed!

What makes us unproductive? Be honest! Bad habits are our obstacles, and therefore our own personal oppression where we stress ourselves and other people. They can become our trapdoor or our springboard. In accountability, the Holy Spirit empowers us to turn bad habits into successful strategies.

We can identify habits by asking for feedback. Invite comment and observation by people who know us well. Look for consistency in the feedback. Do not get mad if some of the feedback is difficult. Outward behavior is the truth. Our inner perception of our behavior can often be an illusion.

The environment we create is the one that influences us the greatest. The environment we allow affects us the most. Accountability is living from the Author and toward the Finisher (Hebrews 12:2). Enjoy the journey. Celebrate the process that allows growth and development. Love the learning that is involved in each situation. The process of how we become like Jesus needs to be joyful. It is a happy partnership that we have with the Holy Spirit. We are learning to cultivate the right mindsets that elevate our conscious spirituality. All things are for our sakes (2 Corinthians 4:15-18). Process is about seeing God's love for us at a higher, deeper level consistently. It is concerned with cooperating with what God is doing in our present circumstances.

> *Disempowerment is a choice*

Taking ownership of the revelation of what the Father is doing in and through us. Allowing ourselves to be exposed to the love of God. We must declare and reveal His love for us and accept the upgrade that enables us to return that love to Him. Accountability becomes our confession to people around us who love us! "This is my current situation. This is what I am learning. This is what the Lord is doing in me. I give you permission to help me in this process."

Accountability means giving people permission to be a part of our learning. We want them to help us enjoy the journey and achieve all the outcomes that God has planned. Accountability is not a battle of wills. It is not about one person being under the control of another. It is not a contest, and therefore does not require a confrontation. It is cooperation; a partnership between friends who seek one another's highest good.

Our process always has witnesses! It can be easy or light (Matthew 11:29-30). If we take on the character of gentleness and humility, we are blessed in both directions.

Firstly, as a mentor, our gentleness and humility will provide confidence and trust in the heart of the disciple. Firmness can still be present, but it has been rightly captured by inspiration and influence. It's a paradox that means we do not have to pull our punches, but we have no intention of putting anyone down or knocking them out!

Secondly, as a disciple, our heart becomes open as we engage in gentle humility. We are not resistant or closed in our demeanor, and are much more willing to engage in a dialogue that explores all possibilities.

All process is designed to touch what can never live in the Presence of God. Process touches habits and thought patterns that are ingrained in us, but wrong. Process will afflict us unless we have a positive approach based on joy and loving the learning. Process will harass the part that we need to give up next. The flesh is enmity against the Spirit and the Spirit will always go after the flesh. Process is part of that encounter, and our ability to choose properly is vital.

In partnership with the Holy Spirit we must lose track of time. We cannot be obsessed with when! When will it be over? When will God break through? When can I move on from this? At times the *when* question will mean that we are not really enjoying the process, but are more set on the outcome. We must allow our hearts to be drawn back into partnership, both with the Holy Spirit and chosen mentors. If we are outcome-focused, rather than process-centered, then our focus can cause us to become weary and ineffective in our relationship.

When we lose sight of the objective, we become more vulnerable to the enemy. Our flesh does not want to be changed. It schemes to be able to remain untouched. It whines, throws a pity party and seeks undue sympathy. It draws attention to its suffering. It wants mercy (really to be left alone). Such an attitude prevents accountable behavior.

The inner man of the Spirit does not whine when the flesh is put under pressure; he rejoices. He is energized, happy, diligent and ruthless toward the enemy. The inner man of the Spirit loves the nature of God and is excited and blessed with every opportunity to become like Him.

> "For all things are for your sakes, that the grace which is spreading to more and more people may cause the giving of thanks to abound to the glory of God. Therefore we do not lose heart, but though our outer man is decaying, yet our inner man is being renewed day by day. For our momentary, light affliction is producing for us an eternal weight of glory for beyond all comparison." (2 Corinthians 4:15-17)

Process can be difficult. Big transitions are not easy. However, with a poor attitude they are almost impossible. Never take the pressure off the flesh. The process will stop if we ignore our part in it. However, by doing so, we guarantee that it will come around again, and next time it will be more expensive for us. There is always inflation with the truth.

If people have the wrong mindset about the process, they will resist it because it is too hard. People turn away from the outcome when they do not understand the development required to attain it. Paul describes process as a light and momentary affliction. The word "momentary" (Greek: *parrar-hueo*) means to get through this faster than we think. It is a unique and wonderful paradox that patience will speed up the process, while impatience will slow it down. If we are overly concerned about time, we are generally displaying our impatience and possibly not putting enough energy and focus into the partnership. It is important always to compare process to outcome and to be accountable to someone for both.

Most of our process is delightful. Process makes me happy. I discover the goodness of God in His essential nature. Process is where we explore the territory that is God's heart for us. We get to know how He thinks about us. He shows us how He sees us in Jesus. We learn His ways. We find ourselves changing and adapting, conforming to His pattern of thought and behavior.

> *Never take the pressure off the flesh*

He delights in us. He takes pleasure in us. He loves us. Process is the manner in which He chooses for us to know Him. Accountability ensures the learning and empowers the upgrade in relationship. A lot of process is repetition and reinforcement. The same lessons over and over until we are transformed and His nature is embedded. God never tires of it. He loves it so much.

Accountability is about loving the process as much as God loves us. When we love the learning, we consistently put ourselves into the place where we have the potential to grow quickly.

Prophecy Empowers Our Testing

The life that we are chosen for must, by definition of that calling, provide us with tests to enable us to fulfill that vocation. We begin every endeavor with a discovery of what we lack in ourselves and our resources. We have a shortfall within ourselves that can only be filled by God Himself. Prophecy tells us that we will survive the process. It gives us an outcome beyond the testing.

Prophecy does not come to test us in the process. It comes to test our faith in the outcome! Prophecy is given to enable us to focus when our lifestyle and calling are tested to the full. Prophecy provides us with an outcome that is fixed when the circumstances of our life resemble a roller coaster ride.

All times of testing are beneficial to us and therefore need to be met with joy. Testing is designed to prove who God is for us and who we are becoming in Him. Testing is the Father's designated method for producing all the qualities that truly represent His Name and Nature (James 1:2-4).

Testing is concerned with receiving, so that we lack nothing. The joy in testing is that if we remain true to God's nature it is impossible not to receive. Always focus on the outcome first, then seek to understand the process that will achieve that objective. The outcome provides necessary focus. The end result is guaranteed, provided I stay with the process. The series of steps that make up any particular process are always concerned with development. It is the process, therefore, that makes us rich in Christ, not the outcome. Focusing on outcome and not cooperating with process will register us for disappointment.

God cannot give us the outcome if we remain in the same state we were in when we first received the prophecy.

If our father bought us a new car and said, "You can have the keys when you pass your driving test," our process is clear. Process is a series of steps. Fill out the form, pay the fee, pass the written test, take driving lessons, pass your test!

Looking at the car (outcome), longing for the car, wishing for the car, are all useless activities without process.

After the prophecy comes the problem — a set of circumstances that are designed to enable us to hold onto the words we have received. The same prophecy may well see us through several tests. Prophecy does not bring us testing, it brings us necessary focus so that we can pass the tests of our character, lifestyle, and belief. Because prophecy and problems occur in the same context, it is easier to feel that the one produces the other. Prophecy is the North Star in a turbulent sky. It provides a fixed heading. The Father is always our true north.

Each phase of testing is devised to bring us into deeper levels of faith and encounter, trust and experience of God. Testing is the territory where we learn to put off the old and put on the new. Prophecy provides focus so that we can walk in the newness of life. Testing times can vary in length and power.

Joseph had a dream about his own future:

"Then Joseph had a dream, and when he told it to his brothers, they hated him even more. He said to them, 'Please listen to this dream which I have had; for behold, we were binding sheaves in the field, and lo, my sheaf rose up and also stood erect; and behold, your sheaves gathered around and bowed down to my sheaf.' Then his brothers said to him, 'Are you actually going to reign over us? Or are you really going to rule over us?' So they hated him even more for his dreams and for his words. Now he had still another dream, and related it to his brothers, and said, 'Lo, I have had still another dream; and behold, the sun and the moon and eleven stars were bowing down to me.' He related it to his father and to his brothers; and his father rebuked him and said to him, 'What is this dream that you have had? Shall I and your mother and your brothers actually come to bow ourselves down before you to the ground?' His brothers were jealous of him, but his father kept the saying in mind." (Genesis 37:5-11)

The dream was concerned with ruling, reigning, and being in a place of power and authority. In order for Joseph to be entrusted with high office he must learn some humility. It appears that he is his father's favorite, no doubt spoiled, and certainly a tattletale. He seemed to stay at home while his brothers were out working (Genesis 37:2-4, 12-17).

His first test concerned his own brothers and his **relationship** with those around him. Our own arrogance and poor behavior can dig a hole for us in some relationships. Also, it is true that one of the major tests that we all face is how we handle betrayal, rejection, and being misunderstood. The flesh is vindictive, judgmental, quick to anger, and proud. It is also a victim that whines, throws pity parties, wants its own way and sulks. We can take none of these traits with us on our journey into God's heart. Some of our tests are about unloading these characteristics so that our relationships can truly reflect the nature of God.

Joseph probably thought that his brothers were just going to frighten him. Picture him thinking about his next bad report to his father. He expected to be returned to the family and also get his brothers into trouble. No doubt this was in the mind of his brothers also. Joseph's betrayal at the hands of those he is supposedly in relationship with is hard for him to take. To be so thoroughly rejected and dismissed is harsh. It kills us. It is supposed to kill something in us.

Prophecy provides favor in the test

Sadly, in lots of cases, what dies in us is love, trust and values. Betrayal in truth is a short cut to the elimination of anger, bitterness, judgmentalism, self-pity, and a victim mindset, to name but a few. To go through betrayal and not kill the flesh in ourselves, but instead to allow a woundedness to flourish is a travesty in and of itself. We justify the continuation of our fleshly mindset and behavior through self-pity and anger. That is a deadly combination which keeps us locked into a present–past lifestyle and immobilizes our walk in the Spirit. Heads, the enemy wins; tails, we lose. We keep ourselves in prison by our own justification and desire for vindication.

Vindication can never set us free. God will simply not allow it. If vindication comes, it will only arrive when we do not want it or have ceased to think about it. Mostly, it never comes! Forgiveness sets us free. So does grace, mercy and humility. The fruit of the Spirit is often a more potent weapon against the enemy than any supernatural gifting.

An open sore has disease within. It is infected by poison and constantly inflamed by touching. We have all had to deal with that kind of bitterness in ourselves and other people.

The next test involves **Status**. A slave is the lowest form of human life. To be the property of another is to have no personal rights or freedom. The desire for status, position and renown will warp our spirituality if unchecked. All spirituality is earthed in a paradox, two apparently conflicting ideas contained in the same truth. One such paradox is sonship combined with servanthood. One is relational, the other functional. We are the beloved, Children of God, sons of the Father, and joint-heirs with Christ. We are also bond-slaves, servants and stewards of God.

I am beloved, but I take orders too. We are His friends (relational) if we do whatever He commands us (functional) (John 15:14). Joseph is fixed on the prophetic interpretation of his dream. The outcome is concerned with ruling and reigning. Prophecy is tested by our faith in the outcome. *"All things work together for good"* (Romans 8:28). This either takes us into freedom or fatalism. Freedom is only found by fulfilling the two conditions in that Scripture. Love God in the circumstances and stay within the purpose that He has designated. Otherwise, Romans 8:28 is merely a memory verse, a fatalistic quote that has no power.

When Joseph remained fixed on the outcome, it gave him power in the process. Ruling and reigning is the fixed purpose of God in his life. He begins to learn the language, customs, and the business of the house. He became increasingly significant in his servanthood. Our lives will always have value to someone if they have value to us. Joseph became excellent at everything he did regardless of his own personal circumstances. His prophecy was related to prominence. He rose to influence and importance through his attitude and behavior in trying circumstances. When we are fixed on the outcome, we gain favor in the process. Fulfillment is attracted to identity. We see how keen the favor is to accumulate to us. All prophecy has partial attainment before total completion because the Father loves to encourage and empower us.

Prophecy provides favor in the test. Joseph became prominent because the people around him could recognize that he had favor (Genesis 38:2-6). Prominence results in promotion. Self-pity destroys destiny. It robs us of our favor. Joseph stayed true to the Lord in his own heart. He stayed fixed on the outcome. He ruled in Potiphar's house and over all his businesses. Everything was left to him because his skills and aptitude were so excellent, favor walked with him as a result.

When we fix our eyes on the outcome, we do not make it a destination. It is not a fixed point on our horizon and we are not working to get there. We do not move toward a prophetic fulfillment. We live from it. Prophecy gives us a unique capacity to live in the truth of God's word while it is unfolding. It becomes true in our hearts first. Then it flows with us through the process with which God engages our life, faith and obedience. We know the truth by our life experience of it now, and it sets us free as we move from heart attachment to lifestyle implementation (John 8:32). We confirm the prophecy is true in our hearts, and then we live from that realization by our actions.

David became kingly long before he was crowned. He ran to meet Goliath because he knew that he could not die, because as yet, he was a king, but without a crown. His kingdom was as real to him as the promise was to God.

A prophecy is first consummated in our hearts and then it births the lifestyle that completes the cycle. A prophecy comes to us from God as an outcome that we embrace. See figure 1:

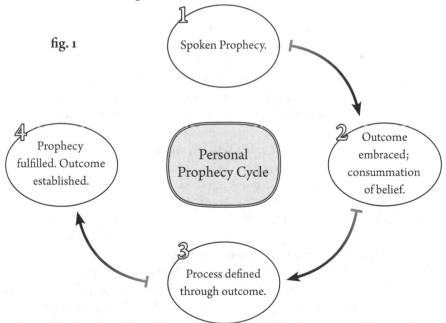

fig. 1

1. Spoken Prophecy.

Personal Prophecy Cycle

2. Outcome embraced; consummation of belief.

3. Process defined through outcome.

4. Prophecy fulfilled. Outcome established.

Before we engage with the process, we must consummate the word as true in our hearts. Our relationship with God is present–future. His relationship with us is future–present, which is part of the reason He is ever-present. Jesus put this prophetic lifestyle in this context.

"An hour is coming and now is" (John 4:23; 5:25). When God gives us prophecy, He speaks from the outcome to the outworking. Therefore, to be with His Word in the same way, we need to adopt the same strategy. The outcome is settled first in our hearts, and then it is outworked in our lives by the process of our obedience and partnership.

Prophecy requires a "this is true now" approach in our hearts. Then as we act from the embrace, it becomes established in our behavior. Joseph became a ruler in his own heart, so then his slavery actually became his opportunity. His obstacle became his advantage. When we embrace the prophetic word, we begin to stand up on the inside. Our attachment to the outcome now defines the way we navigate the process. Favor is the result of that belief system in action. Potiphar recognized the present–future dimension of Joseph's lifestyle. He saw evidence of God's hand on Joseph. God's hand becomes visible when we get it together with His word.

The third test is **Personal Purity**. Sanctification is vital if we are to go high and deep with the Lord. Holiness is not an option, but a necessity. When confronted by an amoral woman, Joseph has the right attitude and does the right thing. He could have said, "My brothers have betrayed me. My family thinks I am dead. I am far from home and may never return. All that I once knew and loved is no more. I have managed to rise up into a place of influence and promise. I am lonely with no comfort. A beautiful woman wants me. After all that I have been through, I deserve some comfort and release. Why shouldn't I lie with this woman? I deserve some excitement and pleasure."

However, he has embraced the prophetic word over his life. We cannot become an exception if we are making excuses. He realizes that she will be angry and spiteful. He knows the cost of rejecting her. It will mean the loss of all he has attained to this point. He takes fresh hold of the outcome; to rule and reign. It came once, it will come again. His relationship with God is the most important thing to him. *"How then could I do this great evil and sin against my God"* (Genesis 39:9). Day after day he was pursued. He always tried to have other people around him when she was present (Genesis 39:11), but one day they were absent and so he did the only thing possible, he ran. She lied to protect

> Do not call time
> on your dream

her own position, and because of a vindictive spirit, Joseph came into the lowest place of his journey.

He is sent to prison as a slave rapist. This is lower than the pit of his brothers. Lower still than his initial slavery. Innocent, but wronged. This final test is both subtle and elegant. It is the test of our **Enduring Mindset**; our true thinking. He could be forgiven for giving up at this point. He has lost everything. He has worked hard and is now in a worse place than ever. The temptation to give up is huge. After all that he has gone through, to have to start all over again. Every door is closed. He is on the bottom rung on the lowest ladder in the basement of humanity and civilized society.

What do you do? Your flesh wants to call time on the dream. The unfairness is huge. The stories about your circumstances run riot with rumor. Everyone talks about you, no one talks to you. Everyone discusses your guilt. Believers are quite brilliant at believing the worst. People whom you thought were friends do not speak up for you. Instead they do the expedient thing and wash their hands of you. You cannot defend your life without attacking someone else. It is death by a thousand cuts and it goes on for years.

When we have not checked out the facts from both sides, then we cannot represent Jesus by speaking into the issue. We can only represent our own carnality. Misinformation and misrepresentation do more to dishonor the Lord Jesus than the lies of the enemy. An innuendo is a subtle lie calculated to destroy. Only the devil steals, robs, kills and destroys. We are givers of life. Even if a person has sinned, they need grace, love and mercy to find forgiveness and healing. Judgment prevents redemption. Goodness and kindness empowers repentance.

It seems that the Church are the worst people in the world at forgiving and forgetting. Pharisees always turn a sin, a mistake or an error of judgment into a stigma. No one does shame like the Church. They put marks of shame on people that consign them to ongoing disgrace. It is as though, at our essential core, we do not believe in the power of the Gospel. We do not believe that the blood can cleanse people or that believers can be transformed. We remember sin when God does not.

Then we question everything that the individual says or does, both back into the past and forward into the future. There is no grace, no mercy and no kindness. Only the blunt force trauma of truth applied without a vestige of love. In these situations the Church pays lip service to the true nature of God. We are the only army on earth that shoots our own wounded.

Are all these comments true? Yes, but they are also misplaced. The last four paragraphs are also a victim mindset. They represent the mind and heart of a person who still does not get what it truly means to be in Christ. These comments come from a poverty mindset. Victim language can never glorify Jesus. We can never use the sins of others to draw attention to our own suffering.

All those comments have happened to me personally, but they do not define who I am in Jesus, nor how the Father perceives me in the Spirit. Every one of us will need forgiveness, healing and restoration many times before we face our Maker in Heaven. Not to extend love and grace to people is a crime against the Cross. We tread underfoot the sacrifice of Jesus.

There is only one way to deal with this level of Christian unkindness. We must ensure that we overcome it and not just survive the onslaught. The best way is to rejoice and give thanks (1 Thessalonians 5:16-18). Pray for people who despitefully use us (Matthew 5:44). The world is in the church and the only antidote is the Kingdom. Abusive treatment must itself be met with real forgiveness, grace and loving-kindness. If we meet an accusation with an accusation, then we do the work of the accuser. Only the enemy and carnal Christians are the accuser of the brethren. If we, in self-justification, take sides with the enemy against God's people, then we are no better than a Pharisee ourselves.

We need an **enduring mindset** that can put God's overall purpose into every circumstance. Everything is concerned with becoming Christ-like. A true lover of God will not waste any circumstance to grow. The purpose is of far more consequence than the circumstance. In our own immaturity we pay more attention to what people say and do than to the advantage behind it. Everything forms Christ in us. Little children don't get it. Mature people know that we are ultimately in Christ learning to be made in His image. Everything is useful. When we humbly rejoice at our treatment by others, we lose the ability to react in the flesh because we are choosing a response in the Spirit. Joseph's response is seen when he meets his brothers later in the story. *"It was not you, it was God."*

> *"Then Joseph said to his brothers, 'Please come closer to me.' And they came closer. And he said, 'I am your brother Joseph, whom you sold into Egypt. Now do not be grieved or angry with yourselves, because you sold me here, for God sent me before you to preserve life. For the famine has been in the land these two years and there are still five years in which there will be neither plowing nor harvesting. God sent me before you to preserve for you a remnant in the earth, and to keep you alive by a great deliverance. Now, therefore, it was not you who sent me here, but God; and He has made me a father to Pharaoh and lord of all his household and ruler over all the land of Egypt.'" (Genesis 45:4-8)*

Everything out of his mouth demonstrates his own enduring mindset. A mind set on the Spirit cannot be overcome by the flesh. It can however, receive an abundance of life and peace (Romans 8:5-8). Fleshly thinking is hostile and displeasing to God. Joseph is healed and whole in his own personality. He is focused on ultimate purpose. We can endure when we know our circumstances can form Christ in us, if we partner with the Holy Spirit. However, we must not endure by default but by design. There is a teaching CD on the Brilliant Book House website entitled *Why Wounded and Betrayed Believers are so Useful to God.* This is where I first really discovered the kindness of God.

We are being trained for a dynamic purpose

We can get through something and be a little changed or we can walk in it with the desire to be transformed. Choose a powerful response!

In the prison as a convicted slave rapist, Joseph does not let go of his prophetic destiny. He does not focus on the injustice done to him. He does not lose it, give up or walk away from his identity. This is what it really means to trust the Lord and to believe the Word. The prophecy is concerned with ruling and reigning. Joseph is still connected to favor and prominence if he chooses! Circumstances cannot rob us of our life decisions if we are focused on prophetic purpose. Joseph was diligent in the prison to conspire with his destiny and not against it. It is never too late to return to destiny. Identity grows when we are fixed on destiny because we make present decisions in the light of a fixed future outcome. He learned about government administrative systems. He increased his business skills, leadership and strategic planning capability. He partnered with God and overcame the circumstances of his personal tragedy. Joseph is the epitome of an enduring mindset.

He came to prominence three times on his journey. Two of those occasions were primarily about his development. We must complete the training! If we do not have the faith or passion to train well, we can never be trusted with a high office. If we allow the petty mindsets of others to rob us of rightful responses to God, then we have just proved that we have the same mental processes of our detractors. Rise up. Rise above the antipathy.

We are being schooled for a life of dynamic purpose. Joseph did not merely allow his development times to change him. His is no passive response. He seized the day. He apprehended his own response. He took responsibility for his choices. He conquered things within himself. He arrested any notion of decline. He embraced his prophetic destiny to rule and reign. He overwhelmed negativity. He refused to live in the past. He always looked ahead. Destiny forms identity. In this regard it is like the Apostle Paul:

> *"Not that I have already obtained it or have already become perfect, but I press on so that I may lay hold of that for which also I was laid hold of by Christ Jesus. Brethren, I do not regard myself as having laid hold of it yet; but one thing I do: forgetting what lies behind and reaching forward to what lies ahead, I press on toward the goal for the prize of the upward call of God in Christ Jesus. Let us therefore, as many as are perfect, have this attitude; and if in anything you have a different attitude, God will reveal that also to you; however, let us keep living by that same standard to which we have attained." (Philippians 3:12-16)*

Our ministry is our reward. If we do not fully prize our calling, we will fall away from destiny when hard times arrive on our doorstep. We will see situations as trouble, problems or difficulties rather than opportunities that propel us toward fulfillment of prophecy. Identity often unfolds in the mundane. Destiny gives everything purpose.

Joseph never lost sight of God's perception of him as one who rules and reigns. He became a forerunner, one who pays a price to bring other people into life, breakthrough and release. We can take the highest place when we have used the lowest place effectively. The humility we gain in the valley becomes our authority on the mountain.

Prominence arises out of internal significance. We seldom get to choose our circumstances, but we always get to choose our responses. Only immature people consistently fail to see the hand of God in their own situations. Men and women of God not only see behind the scenes, they understand that nothing is coincidental. Identity and destiny is all around us. The best people take advantage of everything in order to discover God and find themselves.

"Until the time that his word came to pass, the word of the Lord tested him" (Psalm 105:16-19). Prophecy does not come to test us in the process. It comes to test our faith in the outcome.

What has been spoken over you? That is your destiny. Now you must cooperate with the formation of your identity. Prophecy creates focus so that you can pass the tests of your character, lifestyle and belief. It empowers you to develop the enduring mindset that sees God in everything and rejoices at His Presence.

Focus On the Steps, Not Just the Goal

To fully respond to a prophetic word, our thinking and approach to believing must change. In our approach to the Word we must be responsible, clear, and strategic about what faith in this Word will mean for our very lifestyle. We treat prophecy the same way as we do Scripture. It is the proceeding word. Prophecy never contradicts, but compliments the written Word.

Many believers read Scripture but do not believe it. If they did, the Church would be in a more significant place in the Spirit. If we believed Scripture we would practice its truth and be radically changed. Sadly, most Scripture never gets to the place in us where it transforms our mind and heart enough to establish a likeness of the Lord Jesus Christ.

Prophecy works in conjunction with Scripture to empower us to move into a place of refreshing, anointing and renewal. Timing and preparation are key elements in the fulfilling of God's Word. When God speaks through Scripture and prophecy, a new place is opened up to us in the grace of Jesus. We are being introduced to the next version of ourselves in Christ. Growth in the Spirit is incremental and we must take the necessary steps.

Most prophecy on a personal level is not self-fulfilling. It needs our cooperation. All personal prophecy is conditional, whether any conditions are stated or implied. We have a responsibility to be involved in the working out of the word by our obedience. A prophecy tells us how God sees us now. He is in our future looking at us and relaying what He sees into our present. In our present, we move into the future when we adopt how He sees us in that dimension. We do not work toward fulfillment of prophecy — prophecy works from the outcome to the outworking.

Overwhelm negativity

We start with what God sees and we claim it as our own. It is truth or God would not have spoken it. We confess truth even if we do not thoroughly understand it. This, after all, is the process of the Gospel in our salvation. We are expected to believe that an event 2,000 years in our past can have a bearing upon our present–future life. We are encouraged to believe that blood shed 2,000 years ago can cleanse us of our sin in the modern world.

We are inspired to believe that when Jesus hung on a cross, we hung there with Him. When He died, we died. When He was buried and then raised to newness of life, so were we. The Father empowers us to confess and claim something for ourselves that is most illogical, irrational, and unreasonable. It is simply life in the Spirit that is utterly dependent on faith. Not remotely intellectual, but deeply spiritual. The same process which is true of the Gospel is also true regarding prophecy.

In the Gospel we accept the fact that we are in Christ, learning to be Christlike. We claim what He has done for us as our own. His finishing point is our starting place. We are in Christ, and we work from that truth into our experience. We are not trying to be different. We recognize that we are, and we prove it by abiding in the Truth that sets us free. There is a difference between what is true and Truth. It may be true that we are struggling with some habits. However, Truth is a person and He has included us in Himself. Therefore, as we confess Him, His Truth abides in us and we are empowered from within to overcome all external issues. Truth overcomes from the inside out. We are not trying to get anywhere with God, we are already there. We believe His perception of us. Abiding enables us to behave as though we actually are who and what God declares us to be in Christ.

Jesus is made unto us wisdom and righteousness, sanctification, and redemption (1 Corinthians 1:30). He is our righteousness. That means we rest in His righteousness. We behave righteously because we believe we are righteous in Christ. Our abiding empowers us to live from a place, not toward it. It takes all the stress and strain out of performance. We are not trying to do anything. We are simply learning to rest in who we already are in Christ. Abiding is the key part of process. We walk out our salvation because it is already established in us. We work out our salvation in rest, peace and confession. We do not become a new person by trying to change our behavior. We recognize who we are already in Christ and behave accordingly.

It is the same principle and process for the prophetic. The Cross connects our past with our present, bringing freedom, release, and power. The prophetic connects our future with our present, bringing destiny into our identity. The key element in the reception of Truth is agreement and confession. Confess means to say the same as another. We agree with God and we confess that we are who He says we are and that we have what He says we have.

When God speaks prophetically, our reception to the Word is earthed in our agreement. We evaluate the prophecy and we adopt the persona that God describes as belonging to our identity. As we abide in that by confession and growing experience, then our exposure to the Truth transforms us into its

Focus On the Steps, Not Just the Goal

likeness. We become what we behold. How we respond to prophecy dictates what will happen to the word. Will it be fulfilled or discarded?

Rejoicing and thanksgiving establish God's reality. Agreement with God must always be joyful if we are to fully endorse the process of transformation. If change is good, shouldn't it therefore also be joyful? If change is joyful, then obedience cannot be miserable. If we enjoy the journey with the Father, then possible joy will make things considerably less difficult. Change is only onerous because the enemy loves to make it appear that way. If change is wonderful, desirable, and joyful, then our experience of it can be the same. Do not let the enemy mess with the emotions. Rejoicing keeps our emotions in the safest place of God's heart. A heart not cultivated by praise, rejoicing and giving of thanks is vulnerable to weariness, boredom, stress and discontent. These are all characteristics of resistance that flow out of a resigned state of being.

Obedience opens up the way for God to bless us. Obedience is joyful compliance to the One who knows us best and who loves us the most. Obedience enables us to live in partnership with the Living Word that empowers us to grow, flourish, and be fulfilled. *"Let the word of Christ dwell in you richly."* (Colossians 3:16)

We must, out of necessity, form strategies for the fulfillment of words. If the prophecy is directional, giving vision for the future, it must be accompanied by a God-given plan to enable us to get from a receptive beginning to a successful completion. Vision can be frustrating unless we agree with it. If we allow our current self-perception to clash with God's vision of us, we will usually hold onto what is familiar. That is like driving around in a clunker for years that keeps breaking down and is hugely unreliable and often embarrassing. One day someone offers us a brand new vehicle for free as an exchange for the old. Tough decision!

Some people would believe God for money to restore the old. Others would believe it's more holy to struggle on with the old. Still more would not feel worthy enough to be in something new and wonderful. A religious mindset is a weird place from which to live. Obedience lies in receiving gladly all that God has done for us in Christ. It is a cool drink on a hot day. Obedience is desire. Obedience is hunger and thirst. Obedience is instinctive passion. When hungry and presented with food, we eat joyfully. Our eyes are bright, our mouth waters, our stomach growls in joyful anticipation of what is to come. Thirst is similar. We love the reviving presence of water. We sigh with pleasure in the refreshing. *"Blessed are those who hunger and thirst for righteousness, for they shall be satisfied"* (Matthew 5:6). When we put obedience into partnership with joy, a desire forms that will overcome every obstacle. We form strategies that enable us to become more of what we want to be.

Simple prophecy often comes to us at particular points of the journey. It is the joyful, general encouragement that pours out of Heaven like a river.

The Promises of God and Our Development

Everyone born-again has a well of encouragement within their own spirit. It edifies, encourages, exhorts and brings comfort. The more we use it to bless others, the more we are encouraged ourselves. Encouragement is a lifestyle. No one is safe from our refreshing optimism. We are our own stimulus package. We travel with inspiration, influence and invigoration. We are of good cheer because Christ has overcome. Eeyore will always have a burst balloon. Pooh will always find honey. Eeyore will complain about the snow. Pooh will make a song about it and sing it to his friends. Please, can we just get happy!

Simple prophecy affirms us in the heart of God. It is a dynamic release from stress, a joyful bridge to a fresh disposition. It affirms us in the present. Directional prophecy lifts our eyes to the future. It declares what will be in God's heart into the "what is not" of our current state. He replaces it with something new, different or better. We accept it, receive it with joy and have the pleasure of using our new identity on our current circumstances. Simple steps that have immediate impact, not just goals to look forward to achieving.

> *There is joy in change*

When the Lord speaks of the future He provides a goal, a horizon for our journey. He also provides all the initial steps to get moving. In finance, if we look after the cents, then the dollars take care of themselves. On the journey, if we pay attention to the steps, any goal can be achieved. Many Christians receiving prophecy think about goals, but never the steps. We are fixed on the outcome, but not partnering with the outworking.

The key steps in prophecy are firstly to accept that the word is from God to me, and that He has declared His intention for me in this next season. Secondly, receive it as an upgrade for the present. It starts immediately. Personal prophecy does not wait. It may take time to come into full fruition, but it takes hold of our life the moment it appears. We must take hold of it.

Thirdly, we keep the Word alive and real through praise, rejoicing and thanksgiving. We rejoice that this word is true and that we have an open invitation to become the embodiment of that word in the present. Fourthly, we examine the goal of the prophetic word. What is the outcome? The conclusion must become the payback now. The outcome is our destiny. Bring destiny into the light of today and examine it. What steps must we take to become that person? What attributes must be realized in order to act like that person? Those steps and attributes form our identity in the present. Our current state is renewed when we take hold of our future standing and bring it into the present.

State is how we see ourselves. Standing is how God perceives us in Christ. Our standing must always impact our state. Prophecy provides a standing that changes our behavior. Destiny impacts identity. We own the destiny now. If we accept that destiny, how do we change in the present because of it? David acted like a king long before he was crowned. Jesus, when a child, acted like the Savior long before He came to the cross (Luke 2:41-52).

Focus On the Steps, Not Just the Goal

If we are that destiny now in God's heart, then we must become it in ours also. How should we behave then in the present? We behave as though the future were already true. We always live from the truth, never toward it. We abide in God's perception of us. We become the truth by abiding in its reality. We are a new creation. As we abide in that truth, the reality is that all the old things pass away and everything does become new (2 Corinthians 5:17). If we do not abide in it, then we are still troubled by the old. We grow by becoming fixed on what God has said, done and provided.

When we live from our destiny, our identity unfolds. We develop a strategy that cooperates with the Holy Spirit. If we do not, we will experience frustration and eventually failure and defeat. We are not trying to develop anything in our own strength. We are growing into our next upgrade by joyful obedience. The Lord gives us the essential steps so that we can make progress in our believing and becoming.

If we are looking at prophecies and cannot possibly imagine them coming to pass, we are in the wrong mindset. A prophecy is a guaranteed outcome, the steps must follow. As we pursue destiny, identity is revealed. We take steps of obedience in line with that identity and behavior changes. God will do the things we cannot. It is a partnership that produces newness of life.

For prophecy to work fully, we must become entirely occupied with what God has spoken. This is His word and needs to be treated with every ounce of respect and honor possible. Whether it's already revealed truth or a prophetic word, the Holy Spirit takes us up on our response, transforming us into becoming one with God's word.

In order to enter that fullness, we must *open the prophecy for comment by mature people.* In 1 Timothy 4:14-15, Paul gave some good advice to his friend Timothy: *"Do not neglect the gift that is in you, which was given to you by prophecy with the laying on the hands of the eldership,"* he said. *"Meditate on these things; give yourself entirely to them, that your progress may be evident to all."*

Whenever we receive a prophecy, we should ask spiritually mature people to discuss the word and its implications. What advice do they have for us? What are the things we should be studying and watching for? This not only gleans wisdom from others, but commits us to the application of the prophetic word. The advice of significant people will be of great benefit; we need others to judge and weigh the prophecy and to correctly identify what the Lord is really saying. We should never keep prophecy to ourselves — doing so could lead us into deception.

Most prophecy is not self-fulfilling. A young man once received a prophetic word about evangelism and the Lord's blessing. His personal interpretation was that he had received a call to be an international evangelist with a massive ministry. He saw himself as the next Billy Graham. Suddenly, the very ordinary work of church-based

The future does not wait

evangelism was beneath his consideration because he felt the Lord had called him to greater things.

However, when those with a good deal more maturity and seasoning examined the prophetic word, they found that it related to a significant success in evangelism, not the calling to be an evangelist. After some counsel and prayer that diminished his delusions of grandeur and released him to pursue a more low-key style of ministry, he has become extremely successful in the area of personal evangelism. To date he has led scores of people to Christ, including his friends, colleagues, coworkers and neighbors.

Prophecy should not be worked out in isolation unless there is no other option (as with Joseph). It is best worked through in fellowship with people who have some understanding of prophecy and the ways of God. It requires fellowship, not association. If we are surrounded by people who have little or no concept of these things, our words may be received in just the same way as Joseph's. At best, people will not understand and may try to talk us into being sensible.

Prophecy is not attracted to common sense. It cannot be understood by the natural mind. It can only be spiritually discerned by those who are spiritually minded. That is why we use wisdom, not common sense. Our understanding of God makes us uncommon in the world. In Christ, He is made unto us wisdom (1 Corinthians 1:30) from God. Wisdom is the ability to see as God sees and to speak and act in faith, beyond the place of rationality and what is reasonable.

Jesus came walking on the water inviting people to join Him. Wisdom says it must be possible because God's nature would not take Jesus where we cannot go too. Logic would stay in the boat because surely it must be a ghost. We need fellowship in wisdom, not the association of natural mindsets.

Our identity and destiny are too important to be entrusted to people who lack spiritual perception. God will provide input as we pursue the next installment of our journey.

Faith and Patience

Once we are convinced that a prophecy is true, we must prepare ourselves for the outworking. Some words take a process of time to come to fulfillment because a number of things have to change. The process of time and change is where we find the Holy Spirit working for us. It is also the place where the enemy seeks to work against us. We must not allow ourselves to be robbed.

In this instant world people want everything on tap and in hand immediately. Our life is both a story and a journey. To inherit the promises of God, we will require faith and patience combining together (Hebrews 6:12). Faith requires the ability in the Holy Spirit to possess **now** in our faith. In some situations that is all we require for completion and reception of what was promised.

In other circumstances, we need faith allied to patience. Faith operates in the same way, confession and possession. Patience provides us with the strength to endure and remain fixed to the faith and the outworking. Sometimes our growth involves difficulty, adversity and warfare. Faith and patience allow us to receive under pressure and continue to abide in the promise when faced with intractable circumstances. If we do not gain the capacity to be patient, we cannot become fully developed in the Spirit. We damage our confidence when we refuse to learn patience.

"Therefore, do not throw away your confidence, which has a great reward. For you have need of endurance, so that when you have done the will of God, you may receive what was promised." (Hebrews 10:35-36)

In between the prophecy and the fulfillment usually lies a set of circumstances that demands an ongoing response. Faith keeps our confidence high while patience keeps the enemy at bay. It is wonderful to know that the fruit of the Spirit is so powerful against the enemy. He has no answer to the nature of God. He left all that behind when he fell from Heaven.

The Holy Spirit seeks to make us like God. The enemy wants to make us in his image. Heaven is a very particular environment; healthy, joyful, loving, restful, celebratory, wise, beautiful and good. Hell is diseased, bitter, malignant, fearful, and resentful. Spirituality is mostly concerned about creating the right atmosphere and environment so that people can grow and flourish. There is a negative spirituality that wants to establish a climate of discord, intolerance, and ungenerous behavior so that people are reduced, not increased.

The enemy moves in the opposite spirit to the nature of God. What are the opposites of love, joy, peace, patience, kindness, goodness, faithfulness, gentleness, self control, grace, mercy and forbearance? What atmosphere would they create?

These are the attributes of hell. These are the opposite to the nature of God. Hatred, malevolence, enmity, malignance, despair, distress, rage, bitterness, pessimism, depression, misery, grief, resentment, disharmony, frustration, disagreement, agitation, upset, anxiety, worry, fear, unrest, impatience, intolerance, turmoil, discontent, irritability, outrage, discouragement, harsh, cruel, mean, abusive, inconsiderate, ungenerous, unfriendly, acidic, sarcastic, contemptible, disagreeable, unpleasant, wicked, evil, rotten, unreliable, vicious, hateful, dishonest, disloyal, false, treacherous, betrayal, fickle, untrue, rude, unkind, crude, rough, harsh, sharp, rigid, severe, stern, sour, powerless, helpless, weak, giving up, letting go, victim, renounce, disabled, insensitive, hard-hearted, uncaring, unfeeling, disadvantaged, fake, ruthless, feeble, disenfranchised, incapable, brutal, comfortless, punitive, merciless, unforgiving, iron-fisted, forbidding, strict, authoritarian, oppressive, unsparing, callous, compassionless, without pity, ungodly.

The Promises of God and Our Development

That is a horrible, horrid list. It is a horrendous environment to live in, even if only a part of it is true. If only ten percent of that were true of us, what would we represent to others? Wherever a negative is allowed to rule, we become warped in our personality. Why rail against sin when we can promote righteousness? Why castigate uncleanness when we can dignify purity? Why rant against someone's deficiency when we can elevate the beauty of Jesus?

When we take a stand against something, we place ourselves closer to where the enemy can take us captive. The enemy is obsessed with sin, it is his business. God is consumed by love, grace, mercy, life, joy and holiness. We cannot fight a negative with another negative without becoming a negative ourselves. We move in the opposite spirit to the enemy.

When we take a stand against someone, we cannot demonstrate Jesus to them. We create a gap beloved by the enemy; a cruel divide that he can easily exploit.

All negativity slows down our development. If people are intolerant, they are more likely to be impatient also. If they are impatient, they can be frustrated, then angry and harsh. Fruit comes in clusters.

If we can add diligence, faith, moral excellence, knowledge, self-control, perseverance, godliness, brotherly kindness and love together (2 Peter 1:5-11), surely we can also do the opposite? Not paying attention to the nature of God in our own behavior makes us blind and vulnerable to the opposite spirit. Our lives are never neutral (Luke 11:23).

> *Our lives are never neutral*

It is imperative that we deal with the frustration and irritation that is in our lives because they are the seed bed of intolerance and impatience. In an instant society, we have no means of learning how to wait on the Lord. It simply does not occur to most believers. Faith and patience are an incredible paradox that allows us to inherit the promise.

We maintain faith in the promise while we patiently go through the process of change that brings it closer to fulfillment. Often, between the prophecy and its fulfillment, the Holy Spirit is dealing with our lifestyle and our character. Are we responding to that? Patience relates to our personal attitudes. It is a calm endurance; a standing still under the hand of God. Not resisting at all what the Lord wants to do. Not anxious, but unworried and trusting in the Lord's goodness and timing.

> *"Yet those who wait for the LORD will gain new strength; they will mount up with wings like eagles, they will run and not get tired, they will walk and not become weary." (Isaiah 40:31)*

Patience is most concerned about the attitude we have to endurance; literally, the spirit in which we wait. The Greek word *hupomone* speaks of a cheerful constancy, a calm endurance, a peaceful abiding, a self-restraint and a sense of being opposed to despondency.

Faith and Patience

Patience compels us not to lose heart but to become even-tempered. Not agitated, frustrated or irritated with people or circumstances. It is active, not passive. It means to be steadfast under trial, to have a willingness to overcome obstacles, and to continue moving forward in spite of events or discouragement from people.

Rejoicing and thanksgiving empower us to be still and to remain, dwelling in Christ. Without rejoicing, patience can wear thin. Rejoicing and giving thanks require focus. It keeps God's purpose in the forefront of our conscious response.

Prophecy gives us initiative. It serves us notice of God's intention. Patience allows us never to surrender that initiative. Faith and patience combine so many times in our experience. They help us to keep our eyes on God through what He has spoken.

I was first given prophetic words about being an author in the late 1970s. At the time it was so far off my grid I found it difficult to even think about it. Fortunately, a mentor at the time encouraged me to see it as a future word that I needed to start preparing for in the present. He encouraged me to start writing short articles and to take writing classes. I went to night school and wrote simple articles on faith, devotion and life in the Spirit for my friends for many years. I had been running Schools of Prophecy in England since 1986. Friends, family, and disciples began to encourage me to write a book on prophetic development. It was like pulling teeth. I was utterly convinced that I would never make it as a writer. It was here that I was introduced to patience as a cheerful pursuit of all that God is in Himself. I began to learn calm endurance and my particular favorite, peaceful abiding. At the time, I was learning how to rest in the Lord and be still. Patience fits well with rest.

My first attempt at the book was awful. I did learn how not to write! I realized that my lack of patience was contributing to the stress that I felt about writing. I began to rejoice in the outcome. God promised me that I would write lots of books. I declared that I was a writer now. I had nothing to prove and everything to enjoy. I focused on writing with God and not for Him. I worshipped. I meditated. I took notes. I waited on Him. I wanted it to be a relational experience with the Father. I wrote when He wanted to write. I came into a place of calm, tranquility, and joy in the process. I wrote with Him, for His enjoyment. Patience became a conscious part of the process.

Developing Your Prophetic Gifting was finished in 1991. I asked the Lord about a publisher. He just said, "Wait." It stayed in my desk drawer for two years. I never looked for a publisher. The Father brought one to me. It became a classic book on prophecy and has been reprinted many times since 1994. I still get letters from around the world. The process took sixteen years from prophecy spoken to first book published. Since then I have written sixteen books and numerous articles. Patience has become stronger in my heart. Faith has more substance. When we are conscious of moving in patience, we should rejoice. When we are not focused on endurance, we should rejoice.

Rejoice always, in everything give thanks. It's God's will for us. Make sure that your attitude does not neutralize the prophecy. Speak His promises back to Him. Quote them in praise and thanks. I love speaking my prophecies to Him. I love to read the Bible to the Father. Speaking His promises in an expressive way aligns my heart to His. Doubt is difficult. Faith is much easier when we live a celebratory life.

Faith and patience are perfect companions. More importantly, they annoy the enemy intensely. When combined in our heart, they upgrade our potential to something actual. Patience is not concerned with time because faith makes everything now. Faith brings the Word close. Patience provides the cheerful disposition that keeps it fresh.

Prophecy Empowers Abiding

Some prophetic words are so big it is hard to live with them. They overwhelm us. The implications for our life are massive. They open up such a huge space around us that we feel small and insignificant inside it. We realize that we have just discovered our growing room. God has spoken and we must grow to fit what He has seen in us. After prophecy comes the process of development.

David is just a shepherd; a son in a good family with older brothers who are taller and more handsome. He is behind his brothers in hierarchy, until the prophet comes to visit. The first that David knows about Samuel's visit is when he is summoned by his father. All his brothers are lined up looking glum. His dad makes a "don't embarrass me or I'll kill you" face at him. There stands Samuel with a flask of oil, pointing a finger at him, saying, "He is the one." "The one what?" thinks David. "Now what have I done?"

To his utter astonishment, he finds himself being anointed king "in time," and the world that he knew vanished in a split second, never to return. One moment his life was fairly mapped out and then it was blasted wide open. He was dumbfounded and overwhelmed.

Mary is busy putting things aside for her marriage to Joseph, planning the wedding, excited, happy, with so much to look forward to in her life. It all comes crashing down in a few moments of visitation with an angel — Gabriel, no less. What she hears next will shatter her world to pieces, bring her to the brink of defamation and thrust her into a prominence she could barely imagine. How does she explain that to people? She is pregnant and still a virgin. The Father is the Holy Spirit! The child is to be the Son of God! God has to save her marriage by talking to Joseph (Matthew 1:18-25). So many things happened around her; all she could do was ponder them in her heart (Luke 2:19).

Patience is mostly a cheerful disposition

Before prophecy can be fulfilled in its entirety, it must live in our hearts. We need to Abide in the Word, think deeply, meditate over it, and make it an occasion for praise and worship. The announced word of prophecy must be compatible in spirit and character with the revealed word of Scripture. We meditate on both together. They both concern identity and destiny which are found only in Christ. We need to interact with the promise in our inner man. Keep the word alive, fresh and dynamic. We need creative thinking to learn how to live with it. God gave us imagination so we would never be earthbound in our thinking. Part of being renewed in the spirit of our mind (Ephesians 4:23) is the restoration of creative thinking as an essential for spiritual journey. Jesus spoke in parables so that people could capture truth in picture form. We give testimony so that people can see what God did for others. We use anecdotes in teaching so that people can get a visual handle on the truth and see it for themselves. Prophecy is part of that cycle of hearing and seeing.

When Moses was anxious about returning to Egypt and standing before Pharaoh in a packed palace court, God spoke to his vision: *"See, I have made you as God to Pharaoh, and your brother Aaron shall be your prophet"* (Exodus 7:1-6). Unless Moses saw himself as God did, he would not have the courage to stand before Pharaoh, let alone perform signs and wonders in the presence of his anger and hard heart. Moses would face incredible opposition and needed to be living from a place far above anxiety and fear. "I have made you as God," means that the only way that Pharaoh could understand what just happened to him would be to conclude that Moses must be God in human form. In Egyptology that was the prevailing wisdom about the Pharaohs, that they were all descended from the Sun god, Ra. Pharaoh, therefore, could only be beaten by another, more powerful god.

Moses' ministry was to bring a nation out of bondage and oppression. The plan of God was to destroy an occult power behind a despotic regime. Each plague destroyed a household god and brought all occult religious practice to a complete halt. The spiritual power behind Pharaoh was defeated so thoroughly it has not risen to the same level again in that nation.

Imagine being in that place before God. Imagine preparing your own heart on your journey toward Egypt. What do you say to the leaders of Israel? How do you gather yourself to stand in a packed court before Pharaoh? You know that every word will be resisted and actively contested. You know that their sorcerers have real occult power. It will be a fight, a contest, a battle — the like of which you have never seen! Imagine.

Prophecy empowers creative thinking. It opens up our inner man to see. The eyes of our heart are enlightened (Ephesians 1:17-18) so that we may know (by beholding and becoming) all that the Father wishes us to understand. Prophecy is part of the Spirit of wisdom and revelation. It activates our creative thinking by unveiling our eyes. Revelation is the receiving of "insight" into the way that

God's word is intended to work in our lives. When the Holy Spirit opens the eyes of our inner man, we learn to see what He is seeing. It is the same perception that empowered Elisha to understand what was happening around him (2 Kings 6:15-17). His servant could only perceive through his natural mind and senses, which made him fearful.

Elisha could see that the enemy was seriously outnumbered. What he saw in the Spirit empowered him to walk out to the Syrians, engage in conversation, and then physically lead them on a 14 mile hike to where the King of Israel was waiting. At this point, the enemy was done, defeated, and they departed, never to return. Imagination, as well as natural thinking, outside of God, is surely not to be trusted. The Spirit of revelation enlightens us so that our normal thinking is renewed to a higher level and our creative thinking provides wisdom and insight that enables us to rise up and overcome every obstacle.

We can abide in what we see. Revelation is so powerful that the insight inspires us to a level of confidence that we had not previously employed. In the Far East, many years ago, I was speaking at a conference in a strong Islamic region. The daily intimidation was extremely rough. The spiritual assault was a blanket of oppression. I was sick, confidence low, and fighting to stay on my feet. If this had been a boxing match, the referee would have stopped the fight. I don't think I had laid a glove on the enemy in two days of spiritual warfare. Back home in the UK, my personal assistant Carol had gone into battle joined by our intercessory team. They broke through where I could not. She sent me a fax simply saying, "God is sending lots of angels to your location" (not the actual words but the very sentiment!). She faxed the message. The fax came through on a broken machine, in the middle of a power cut to our venue.

As I read, something seized me on the inside. Revelation got hold of me. We do not receive revelation in our mind. We receive it in our spirit and faith explodes into our conscious thinking. What we see elevates our thinking and believing. We do not need to understand something fully in order to believe. We all got saved on a fragment of the truth. The biggest decision of our life came because we saw and heard something and believed it with confidence.

I was gripped in my spirit. It was lunch time on the third day. Normally, we did not leave the venue during the day because the crowd waiting outside was too intimidating. A brooding malignancy surrounded the building. We only subjected ourselves to it twice per day, on the way in and out. Holding the fax in my hand, I pushed open the door to the street. It was empty. Light shone where before had only been brooding menace. Looking up, I saw angels standing on every building, swords sheathed, watching. A battle had already been fought. We picked up the spoils in the remaining two days. I learned a valuable lesson about air cover. The devil is the prince of the power of the air (Ephesians 2:2); he lives in the atmosphere. People moving in their unregenerate nature, or Christians moving in the flesh, support the environment that the accuser wishes to present.

The intimidation and menace of unregenerate man outside the conference had joined the fear of man (fear is one of the signs of the flesh) inside the event. When the Spirit rose within me, my own flesh disappeared and I became super confident, bold, and full of authority. Over the years since that time, that same revelation is present because I have practiced abiding in that truth. Abiding enables us to call up the truth and the power that goes with it.

Previous to that Far East event, I had received prophetic words about being a warrior, standing alone and overcoming against significant odds. I had not been living in the outcome, but had allowed the circumstances to dim my vision of how God saw me. Prophecy gives us a vision of how God sees us. The declared word of prophecy must be combined with the disclosed word of Scripture. Prophecy consolidates with the revealed Word of God and provides a more intimate and personal vision of how the Lord sees us as an individual. Our next set of circumstances are designed to establish that vision into an internal reality. Had I followed through on those prophecies, I would not have needed the fax message. That was God's gracious wake-up call to the next part of my identity. Things of value are always formed under pressure. Gold, diamonds and coal are fashioned in extremes of heat and cold. So it is with character and gifting.

Abiding is the key discipline of revelation. What we see, we must take care to become. Abiding is the practice of beholding and becoming. Abiding creates the platform to move from being a doer of the word and not just one who hears. To see something in Christ and not become it is very immature. When we think that knowledge without experience is still relevant spiritually, then we have taken leave of our senses. Knowledge must result in one action. It must change behavior or we cannot embrace our identity in the Spirit.

Knowledge without experience produces deception (James 1:22). The Holy Spirit shows us our next level of identity and we must partner with Him to establish it or lose sight of how God sees us. The law of life in Christ Jesus is incremental; we must grow in grace and favor. We are putting on Christ in ever-increasing stages, literally growing up in Christ in all things. Being active in our ongoing experience is vital. As we put on the next phase of our spiritual identity, we are adding new dimensions of spiritual character, perception, and power (2 Peter 2:2-11).

Abiding is the key to becoming

Abiding is the key to successful becoming. As we engage with "doing the word," our experience becomes the ground of our being. We abide in what we become and we learn to stay and operate from that place. There is no breakthrough without follow-through. What is established by the Holy Spirit must become our place of abiding. Lessons learned, upgrade established and now maintained by abiding. We get to call up what has been received and established.

Abiding adds an ever-growing substance and weight to our faith, our praying, and our position in the earth.

Faith and trust are established in what we abide in before the Lord. When God puts a prophetic promise into our lives, He puts a weapon into our hands. By *"these prophecies previously made concerning you, that by them you wage a good warfare"* (1 Timothy 1:18). This injunction is given in the form of a charge, a command from Paul to Timothy. He will no doubt have to give account to Paul regarding how he is using his prophetic promises. Fight a good fight using God's perception of you!

We abide in all that God says to us. We become it and we remain in it. We have to look like the prophecies we have received. We must exhibit a lifestyle in line with the revealed Word of God. What is proclaimed in prophecy stands on what has been published in Scripture. Prophecy compels us to adhere to the Christ of the Word. Our identity can only be established by abiding in the truth of how God perceives us in Scripture. Personal prophecy is a part of that perception, but Scripture is the whole. To lose sight of our identity indicates that we have stopped abiding in it. We are accountable for our abiding as well as our identity.

In the early stages of mentoring someone, seventy-five percent of the conversation is about establishing an identity in Christ. In the latter stages of mentoring, twenty-five percent must involve checking a person's ability to abide in that identity. Abiding is the platform for self-control to emerge. If an individual has no self-control, they will fold under pressure. If a disciple has not learned to abide in what they have seen, known, and experienced, they cannot mature. When we have to keep relaying the foundations of true spirituality (Hebrews 6:1-3), then we know that we are still

> God is not available to a casual seeker

dealing with children. When we see the flesh in evidence, we are dealing with babies, not mature people (1 Corinthians 3:1-3). When people are not able to process deep truth (solid food), we are dealing with children. When the world is in our actions, we are not abiding in anything worthwhile, and we have hit a ceiling in our own development.

Breakthrough must have follow-through. Abiding in Christ is the key to maturity. Without it, we have no real place of significance. The promises of God in our development are to teach us to abide in the Lord Jesus Christ.

The Importance of Brokenness

The length of the process is determined to some extent by the outcome, and the speed of the process is dictated by the partnership we develop with the Holy Spirit and the people He puts around us. For example, if we want to become a home/small group leader, the process may take one to two years. We will need some formal training in leadership, communication and people development skills, plus a period of time assisting a current small group leader and practicing what we have seen and learned.

If we want to be a prophet, the training is much longer and far more expansive. With access to a good mentor, excellent training and the appropriate environment, the training may take around twelve to sixteen years (assuming that acceleration occurs). A prophet is a high definition, relational ministry with the Lord. If we want to be His mouthpiece, we must be fully engaged with His heartbeat. Prophets are not casual people, but deeply intentional. The flesh has to be removed and natural strength must be broken. It takes serious time to develop the necessary level of patience, gentleness, humility and grace. Anger, frustration, and dissatisfaction must give way to consistent contentment, joy, and encouragement.

Stress must become rest. Anxiety needs to be replaced by peace. The process of becoming Christ-like in this most demanding public office can be hard if we do not love the learning. Such a long-term process is broken up into a series of times and seasons where we learn to walk in a variety of ways before the Lord. Our internal development becomes a part of our presentational style.

The motive behind a high level of accountability is that we want more of God and are prepared to pay any price to know Him! The heart cry of accountability is our prayer to the Lord that is full of desire. David was a man after God's heart and pursued the Lord constantly. His prayer in Psalm 139:23-24 shows his heart:

> *"Search me, o God, and know my heart; try me and know my anxious thoughts; and see if there be any hurtful way in me, and lead me in the everlasting way."*

Throughout the whole notion of God's relationship with man, there is the idea that all progress into the deep places of God can only be reached by a searching and a testing of our hearts and minds. God is not available to a casual seeker. *"You will find Me when you look for Me with all your heart." "I will refine them by the process of affliction, to remove the dross. I will test them."* (Jeremiah 9:7; 17:10; Zechariah 13:9; 2 Thessalonians 2:4)

Walking in the Way is always a process. We are always subject to change, so we need a joyful mindset about it. A mindset that enjoys the journey will always travel well. Most of the time the process is sweet, fun, and exciting. We get to see God in all His beauty. This is vital or adoration is not possible. Then there are moments where the process is tough, relentless, and heartbreaking. We learn to bow down and kiss the hand that hurts.

> *"Beloved, do not be surprised at the fiery ordeal among you, which comes upon you for your testing, as though some strange thing were happening to you."* (1 Peter 4:12)

It is at times like this where we discover the true nature of the Comforter. Only God can bring us comfort from the rod. If we take comfort from elsewhere we cannot grow as much as He would like. The righteous God tests our hearts and minds (Psalm 7:9). Some of the process that we engage upon is not concerned with just change, and the discovery of who God is for us.

The Lord must bring us face to face with what we are like without the Christ. We must learn how stubborn and willful we are as we get introduced to the worst parts of our sin habit. God will not do this without permission. Somewhere in our past, our heart became so full of love and longing for the Lord that we gave Him permission to do whatever He wanted in our lives, in order that we might be changed. Initially nothing happened; but trust me, the prayer was filed away, waiting for the right moment to be answered.

We get to a point in the process where something in us has to break before we can move on to the next level of relationship and anointing. There may be hardness in us because of previous hardships or bitter experience. There may be a besetting sin that constantly overcomes our desire for righteousness. We may have poor attitudes or a victim spirit. It could be that we must be humbled, not because we have an excess of pride, but because of what the Lord is calling us up to in life and ministry. Humility is more necessary when we examine the higher the calling.

There are times in the process of life when God puts His finger on something and demands your death. It is not a request. It is a command. We look into His face and He is no longer smiling. There is a different look on His face. We realize that we are looking at His holiness, His righteousness, and His awesome purity. He points to the Cross. We see the things in ourselves that we hate and despise. Then we discover something truly awful about ourselves. We want to keep and hold onto it.

The struggle makes no sense until we realize that it is not about sin. It is about the will that is behind it. The sin just represents the power of our own independence. The part of our life that we did not know we were holding back is now rising up within and we realize that it has been killing us for some time! It is the one thing that prevents us, at this time, from fully experiencing the beauty of true fellowship with God.

This power must be broken, once and for all time. The flesh is too bad to be cleansed; it must be crucified. The Father has to destroy all resistance to His nature. He is relentless, but compassionate. He is ferocious, but loving. He is present to bring humility to bear. We will be humbled or humiliated. Some of these dealings become public. We are savaged by the enemy and by legalistic people with no heart for grace. Well-meaning Christians will join in our demise because they are offended on God's behalf or they simply want to make a moral stand or have their voice heard by many.

People will comment, stories will be told about us, blogs will be produced. People who are quick to judge seldom understand process and almost certainly do not understand the depths of brokenness. They see the problem; they do not look for the process. People withdraw from us. We discover who our true friends are, which although rewarding, eventually is initially incredibly painful.

There is a line in a great Bob Seger song, "Against the Wind," where he writes about being "surrounded by strangers I thought were my friends." I have known that level of bitter betrayal, where people do the expedient thing and wash their hands of you. Everything we have done is put to the torch (1 Corinthians 3:13).

In my case, people who wanted what I had, took a hand in exposing and humiliating whatever they could find (whether it was true or not), just to get their hands on the ministry. If God does not own the getting of something, then He cannot own the having of it.

There is nothing to be said or done. There is no appropriate defense. Sometimes we just have to stand and get fleeced (Isaiah 54:7). If we rail against the injustice, it prolongs the process. If we open our mouth there is a good chance that we will become bitter rather than better. We are going to be misunderstood, misinterpreted and misjudged. If we do not defend ourselves, we cannot attack anyone. If I meet an accusation with an accusation, then I do the work of the accuser.

We are assaulted by anger, grief, resentment, self pity, defensiveness, humiliation, and rejection. It is galling, every bit of it. There is no hiding place. All the time, God never leaves us. He stands by us, but we do not know the reality of His Presence. In one of the most traumatic seasons of brokenness in my life, I wrote a poem entitled *Inward Journey*. It is the story of my journey from 1976-1993. In one verse I wrote about being "vile with introspective madness, beaten, sad, and wild."

I remember the patience of the Father as He peeled away the layers of my own deception, self-interest, ego and pride. Until one day I could not run anymore. I had no strength left to struggle with Him. I looked around at all the mess and came to my senses. I could not stand what I looked like. I remember asking God to kill me, not realizing that He had. I could not apologize enough. I confessed to everything. It was there, in the midst of my nothingness that I felt the kiss of God. The Comforter came and we cried together — I cried for the grief that I had caused Him, and the Holy Spirit wept for joy because now I was truly His. There were other times of brokenness, but I went through them in a different manner.

Breakthrough comes when we recognize it all as the hand of God. Sometimes He hurts us, other times He allows other people to wound us. It does not matter anymore. When we learn wisdom, there is no more need for vengeance. Joseph, betrayed by His brothers, came to understand that it was the hand and purpose of God.

The Promises of God and Our Development

"Then Joseph said to his brothers, 'Please come closer to me.' And they came closer. And he said, 'I am your brother Joseph, whom you sold into Egypt. Now do not be grieved or angry with yourselves, because you sold me here, for God sent me before you to preserve life. For the famine has been in the land these two years and there are still five years in which there will be neither plowing nor harvesting. God sent me before you to preserve for you a remnant in the earth, and to keep you alive by a great deliverance. Now, therefore, it was not you who sent me here, but God; and He has made me a father to Pharaoh and lord of all his household and ruler over all the land of Egypt.'" (Genesis 45:4-8)

It was not you, but God. How we respond in a time of brokenness will determined the level of our anointing and Presence in the next season. Accountability means that we can give ourselves an edge that guarantees growth. This I can say with complete confidence: God will feel everything we feel. When we cry, He will cry. When we laugh, so will He. When He laughs, so will we.

We pay a price to walk with God in the high places. The price of sin was not ours to pay; it has been paid in full. We pay the price of ownership, in that we can never own anything ever again. We become a steward now of all that He has given us.

We have no possessions. Our time, work, career or ministry belongs to the One. Our relationships are lived through Him. Our mind, emotions, words, and actions are all His. Everything belongs to Him. We are gloriously sons and bond-slaves together. We only say what He is saying. We only do what He is doing. We have settled the question of ownership. It is no longer I who live, but Christ who lives in me. We go where we are told, we live where He commands. Everything is subject to His will, not ours (Matthew 6:10). We learn the joy of dependency and the sacrifice that may come with that position. We agree with Paul's assessment of our circumstances:

"But whatever things were gain to me, those things I have counted as loss for the sake of Christ. More than that, I count all things to be loss in view of the surpassing value of knowing Christ Jesus my Lord, for whom I have suffered the loss of all things, and count them but rubbish so that I may gain Christ, and may be found in Him, not having a righteousness of my own derived from the Law, but that which is through faith in Christ, the righteousness which comes from God on the basis of faith, that I may know Him and the power of His resurrection." (Philippians 3:7-10)

Brokenness takes us to a far more powerful place of value and relationship. Death works life. In the time of being broken, we discover a level of fellowship with God that takes us out of the grip of the enemy by taking us firmly into the secret place of abiding.

The Promises of God and our Development

Reflections, Exercises and Assignments

The following exercises are designed with this particular chapter in mind. Please work through them carefully before going on to the next chapter. Take time to reflect on your life journey as well as your prophetic development. Learn to work well with the Holy Spirit and people that God has put around you so that you will grow in grace, humility and wisdom in the ways of God.

Graham Cooke.

What Constitutes Maturity?

It is so vital that prophetic people know the difference between knowledge and true knowledge. Study is great but knowledge that does not lead to experience will not empower us to walk with God as He desires. We must understand, agree, and consciously align ourselves with God's perception, so that we can experience our journey into freedom rather than just give mental assent to it. A life focused on righteousness will inherit everything and establish our testimony in the goodness of God.

- A joyful self-examination will connect us with the next stage of our identity and God's intention. It helps us to discern the new word of the Lord and follow through on it. Our capacity to feed on God's faithfulness to us is very important.

- Our experience of God's nature enables favor to be tied into the new creation, not the old. The Holy Spirit always acts in line with who Jesus is for us! In this way we know by experience that all circumstances must reveal our true identity. Therefore, we can use prophecy to challenge our circumstances.

- Our maturity involves engaging our inner man with the reality of Christ within. That means we must develop new ways of thinking that release joy. It involves cultivating a sense of majesty through Jesus and learning the ways of rest and peace. This process is centered on our knowing the disposition of the Holy Spirit toward us.

- Like Jesus, we are becoming the GOOD NEWS in word and deed. New Covenant prophecy mentors people in grace and empowers them to become good disciples in their lifestyle.

- Prophecy is about the presence and the practice of compassion. It requires a humble, patient heart to be able to communicate a deep sense of love alongside the truth. When we practice the likeness of Christ in a genuine way we can put value into the lives of people so that we can be an inspiration to them.

- In order to develop your assignment in ministry you must be able to call up your identity when under pressure. We move our identity into destiny when we establish personal strategies for our development. This is a major part of knowing your authority and jurisdiction in the Spirit and how to reflect that joyfully to the people around you.

- We turn every obstacle into our advantage as we live in the delight of the Father. All times of testing are extremely beneficial to us as we seize the opportunity God gives us in a positive or negative circumstance.

- Abiding in what we see in Christ is the key to growth. Brokenness reveals the depths of God's love and abiding helps us to focus on becoming the Beloved.

- Abiding is the platform for self-control to emerge so that we develop the relationship to become a steward, not an owner, of all that God would give us.

What Constitutes Immaturity?

Knowledge without experience prevents transformation. It is another version of hearing without doing the word God gave us. It means that we repeat the same cycles of learning without changing. We develop an over-dependence upon logic and reason at the expense of wisdom and faith. When we are disturbed by the external world we become unfamiliar with our next upgrade in the Spirit.

- Immaturity pays no attention to the problems incurred by disobedience. It is caused by complacency in our spiritual walk, where a lack of joy only increases our incompetence in life and ministry. When we have an outlook that is present/past we are cultivating a thought life incompatible with God's perception.

- Failure to enjoy our new nature in Christ will allow circumstances to challenge our identity. We learn to live without good cheer! It enables negative situations to downgrade our promises and the result is that we try to change our own behavior rather than conform to Christ.

- Adolescent spirituality occurs when we remain aligned with negative emotions of fear, anxiety and unrest. We allow impatience and intolerance to rule in our heart. We maintain a victim mindset and a slave mentality because we are not wholehearted toward the Lord. Difficulties make us bitter rather than better, and we are empowered in our negativity toward others.

- When there is an absence of kindness and mercy, then people around us do not feel safe or loved. A deficiency in our humility will cause us to speak truth without any real loving-kindness.

- Adolescent prophetic ministry seeks the detriment of people, not their blessing. The enemy feeds off every negative that we manifest. Our natural, carnal strengths cannot consistently nurture the people around us.

- When we choose expediency rather than integrity, we become pharisaical in behavior. We allow negativity to overwhelm our heart. We blame-shift and fault-find. We only think of ourselves, our needs and our position. We take no responsibility for our negative anger.

- Adolescent prophetic people rely purely on spontaneity regarding their gifting and call. A vision without a plan is just wishful thinking. Not having a favorable, confident expectation of goodness leads us into having unclaimed upgrades in life.

- Disempowerment is our choice. Self-pity destroys destiny. Negativity slows down our development. Knowledge without experience produces mediocrity, where we lose sight of our identity. People do not drift to the top of a mountain. They have to make plans to go up into a high place.

AN ASSIGNMENT

Think of a person in your life at this time that is struggling to understand events and circumstances around them, but are also not perceiving what God is doing in their life currently.

Read Jeremiah 33:3

Many people lose sight of God in times of difficulty. They become oppressed by their situation, weighed down by stress and lack of confidence. Praise is often the first casualty, followed later by prayer. They feel that they are in limbo and lack the strength to move forward. These are classic signs of oppression and enemy attack.

In your presentation of this word you must put a stop to what the enemy is doing. You must open this person up to all the possibilities of what God will say and do.

You must create a certainty, a confidence and a conviction that God is ready to answer their call. As they call out with joy, power and persistence, an answer will come. The answer will be bigger than they imagine, because it will contain revelation, wisdom and insight that will cause them to come into a different place in the Spirit.

1. Meditate on this Scripture. Allow powerful thoughts to take hold of you. They will come to you as words and phrases. Write them down.

2. Allow your own heart to be touched by the Lord. Feel the emotion that He wants to release to this person. God gave us emotions so that we could feel His Presence. What are they? How would you speak to the individual in a way that would inspire them?

The Promises of God and Our Development

3. What promises is God making to this person, both general and specific? Write them down.

4. Write out a prophetic word that encompasses all these attributes. Speak it over them and give them the written prophecy. Mail it to them, if they live far away.

5. What happened in you during this assignment? What deposit has been left in your own heart? What has changed between you and the Lord as a result of this assignment?

KINDNESS — FRUIT OF THE SPIRIT

I have said this many times, but it bears repeating: God is the kindest Person I have ever met. Fifteen years ago, God began to give me a revelation of His kindness. I believe God wants to show each one of us the panorama of His nature. He wants to show us everything, but there is one aspect of His character that He wants to be ours in particular. This is our doorway into His presence. I love the compassion, mercy, integrity and grace of God, but my personal access point to Him is always His kindness.

God has been relentlessly kind to me these past fifteen years — day in, day out, month in, month out, year in, year out. Every day, the kindness of God has been in my face; I can't get away from it. I can't remember a day in years where there hasn't been some word of God, some act of kindness, to help me. His kindness is relentless. I've come to such a place of dependence on the kindness of God that I have an expectation for it every day. Something kind is going to happen to me. I wake up, I bounce out of bed, and I wonder what the kindness will be today. It is my image of who He is. That kindness He has shown me makes me want to be kind and generous to others. It carries forward. God exudes kindness. It is the natural by-product of His existence.

Reflections, Exercises and Assignments

Expressing God's kindness to others is a discipline like any other spiritual practice. We can look for opportunities to be kind to the people around us. Strangers and friends: both deserve to experience the kindness of God. What can you do this week to express kindness to someone? How can you help your neighbor? What can you do to bring a smile to someone's face?

Here are just a few suggestions of ways to express kindness to someone else:

- Send a thank-you letter to a former teacher or pastor and let them know the difference they made in your life.

- Ask an older person to tell you a story about his or her youth.

- Send a gift anonymously to a friend.

- Praise the work or attitude of a coworker to someone else in your work place.

- Mow someone's lawn.

- Wash someone's car.

- As you walk through your neighborhood, pick up any litter you see.

- Make an anonymous donation to a local charity.

- Organize your friends to gather food or used clothing and give it to homeless shelters.

- Offer to babysit for a friend's children so they can take a break from parenting.

Think about the people around you and also those with whom you see on a semi-regular basis. Kindness is an intentional behavior, not just a random act. What can you do to help or bless another, without drawing attention to yourself?

We do not perform acts of kindness to be seen by people. We do them because we are celebrating who God is for us. All the fruits of the Spirit must be relentlessly practiced as a main part of our lifestyle in the Lord. We decide who we want to be and how we want to show up in life for Jesus sake. It is our personal desire to glorify Him that fuels our passion to live in His image.

Kindness should not be event-driven, but a lifestyle necessity. When we practice the fruit of the Spirit relentlessly, we provide an unconscious inspiration that influences other people to discover who God really is for them. Enjoy life and celebrate Jesus by living the life that draws attention to His beauty and character. To love God's nature is a good thing. To allow yourself to be made in that image is better.

CASE STUDY

Matching prophetic delivery with content

The delivery of a prophetic word must match its context. The vision that we perceive over someone requires good interpretation in the Spirit, not just a reasonable explanation in the natural.

The vision and subsequent prophetic interpretation was given during a prophetic school in the UK. The name of the individual has been changed for reason of privacy. In this exercise, read the prophetic word and answer the questions.

Chamal, I see a picture of a little girl in a sleeveless dress, shorts and trainers, standing in the rain. She is soaked; her hair is plastered to her head. She is on a path out in the countryside. Her eyes are open and curious. Her mouth has the beginning of a smile. Her arms are up in line with her head. Her fingers are outstretched.

The Lord is saying that you need no other protection but Him. Always lift your face toward Heaven. Always stand in the place of intimate vulnerability before His goodness. Love the rain of the Spirit. It brings life. It creates growth. Walk in it with your head held high.

Desire always to be soaking in My love, My goodness, My kindness and My pleasure in you. As you lift your hands in worship, My Presence shall fill you again and again. Take advantage of the soaking times that I bring into your life. They are to teach you to abide and access the next part of your identity.

In the world, rain represents adversity, so I give you power over hardships, difficulties and adverse circumstances. Worship is a key for you. Give yourself continuously to rejoicing, thanksgiving and praise. You are a woman of intimacy and Presence.

When life looks like it could overwhelm you, I give you permission to stand before Me as a much loved child. In times of stress, this is your place before Me. It is your fallback position when the enemy and difficult people are active against you. Be a trusting child in My Presence. Give thanks, trust Me, and then ask your questions. As a much loved child, expect My Comforter, receive My blessing, find new strength. Love the rain. Love the rain!

Showers of blessing will follow you all your life. In all the dry places that you find yourself, pray for rain! Ask Me to pour out My Spirit and My

Presence. Rain is in your very footprints. You will know significant out-pourings of My Spirit in your life. Rain follows you! You will see many people filled with the Holy Spirit as you pray for them.

Places will come alive to Heaven because you will bring the rain. Show-ers of blessing will follow you all the days of your life. Never give in to dryness. Never settle for measure. I will always pour something out over you and to those around you.

You are My child of the rain. You are My daughter of the Outpouring.

Answer the following questions:

1. Name each particular focus that the Father has for Chamal.

2. What is the Father's overall purpose for Chamal?

3. What would be the best way to deliver this prophecy? What tone of voice would be best to use?

4. After delivering this word, what would you pray over her?

5. What specific emotion would you want Chamal to experience at this time?

LECTIO DIVINA

Lectio Divina (Latin for divine reading) is an ancient way of reading the Bible — allowing a quiet and contemplative way of coming to God's Word. Lectio Divina opens the pulse of the Scripture, helping readers dig far deeper into the Word than normally happens in a quick glance-over.

In this exercise, we will look at a portion of Scripture and use a modified Lectio Divina technique to engage it. This technique can be used on any piece of Scripture; I highly recommend using it for key Bible passages that the Lord has highlighted for you and for anything you think might be an inheritance word for your life (see the Crafted Prayer Interactive Journal for more on inheritance words).

Read the Scripture:

Therefore the LORD longs to be gracious to you, and therefore He waits on high to have compassion on you. For the LORD is a God of justice; How blessed are all those who long for Him.

O people in Zion, inhabitant in Jerusalem, you will weep no longer. He will surely be gracious to you at the sound of your cry; when He hears it, He will answer you.

Although the Lord has given you bread of privation and water of oppression, He, your Teacher will no longer hide Himself, but your eyes will behold your Teacher.

Your ears will hear a word behind you, "This is the way, walk in it," whenever you turn to the right or to the left.

And you will defile your graven images overlaid with silver, and your molten images plated with gold. You will scatter them as an impure thing, and say to them, "Be gone!"

Then He will give you rain for the seed which you will sow in the ground, and bread from the yield of the ground, and it will be rich and plenteous; on that day your livestock will graze in a roomy pasture.

Also the oxen and the donkeys which work the ground will eat salted fodder, which has been winnowed with shovel and fork.

On every lofty mountain and on every high hill there will be streams running with water on the day of the great slaughter, when the towers fall.

The light of the moon will be as the light of the sun, and the light of the sun will be seven times brighter, like the light of seven days, on the day the LORD binds up the fracture of His people and heals the bruise He has inflicted (Isaiah 30:18-26)

Reflections, Exercises and Assignments

1. Find a place of stillness before God. Embrace His peace. Chase the nattering thoughts out of your mind. Calm your body. Breathe slowly. Inhale. Exhale. Inhale. Exhale. Clear yourself of the distractions of life. Whisper the word, "Stillness." Take your time. When you find that rest in the Lord, enjoy it. Worship Him in it. Be with Him there.

2. Read the passage twice more. Allow its words to become familiar to you. Investigate Isaiah's prophetic words and promises. What image does it bring to your spirit? What do you see? Become a part of it. What phrases or words especially resonate with you? Meditate especially on those shreds of revelation. Write those pieces down in your journal.

3. Read the passage twice again. Like waves crashing onto a shore, let the words of Scripture crash onto your spirit. What excites you? What scares you? What exhilarates you about this revelation of the nature of God? What are you discerning? What are you feeling? What are you hearing? Again, write it all down in your journal.

4. Write the theme of this passage in your journal.

5. Does this passage rekindle any memories or experiences? Does it remind you of any prophetic words you have given or received? Write those down as well.

6. What is the Holy Spirit saying to you through this Scripture? Investigate it with Him — picture the two of you walking through it together. Write those words in your journal.

7. Read the passage two final times. Meditate on it. Is there something God wants you to do? Is there something He is calling you to? Write it down.

8. Pray silently. Tell God what this passage is saying to you. Tell Him what you are thinking about. Write down your conversation together. Picture yourself and the Holy Spirit as two old friends in a coffee shop, chatting about what God is doing.

9. Finally, pray and thank God for His relationship with you. Come back to the passage once a week for the next three months. Read it and let more revelation flow into you. If you feel compelled to, craft a prayer based on this passage for yourself, your family, your friends or your church. Pray that prayer until you feel God has birthed it in you.

194

Notes

Notes

MODULE THREE

PROPHECY ELIMINATES
NEGATIVITY

Prophecy Eliminates Negativity

WHAT YOU WILL LEARN IN THIS SEGMENT:

- That God loves a failure

- That failure is a part of our learning cycle

- Living within the culture of the New Covenant

- The difference between judgment and justice

- How to empower people to overcome negative experiences and influences

- Bringing Good News to the afflicted and heartbroken

- Opening prison doors with the prophetic word

- That God is wonderfully affirming

- Discover what a new creation actually means

- Connecting people to the nature of God

- The meaning and the purpose of Romans 7

Prophecy Eliminates Negativity

WHAT YOU WILL LEARN IN THIS SEGMENT:

- The work of the Holy Spirit in the finished work of Christ

- How important admonition is in discipleship

- The difference between Kingdom and worldly shame

- There is no transformation without true repentance

- The key to transformation is identity

- To admonish is to seek someone's highest good

- The five elements of prophetic witness to the Spirit

- Discern the descriptive components of a prophecy and how to align ourselves with them

- The importance of impartation and process in your development

- Knowing how to contend for prophetic fulfillment

Prophecy Eliminates Negativity

Prophecy Eliminates Negativity

Making the Most of Failure

WHAT WE THINK ABOUT GOD is the single most important thing in the world. How we perceive Him will dictate how we live our life. How we see ourselves in relation to Him will orchestrate all that we are and do in this world.

We live in a success-driven world. So, in particular, see-ing any failure in relation to the heart of God is absolutely vital. God is love and the nature of that love must be the driving force behind everything that we do or attempt.

> *Failure does not demean God*

God is not human. He is the sum of everything. He is not just the Creator of the world. He is the Creator of all things, including love. He does all things well, including love. His standard for everything is excellence. The benchmark for success in the Kingdom of God is so high no one can reach it without His input. And yet He chooses mostly failures to represent Him.

> *"For you see your calling, brethren, that not many wise according to the flesh, not many mighty, not many noble, are called. But God has chosen the foolish things of this world to shame the wise, and God has chosen the weak things of the world to put to shame the things which are mighty; and the base things of the world and the things which are despised God has chosen, and the things which are not, to bring to nothing the things that are, so that no flesh should glory in His presence. But of Him you are in Christ Jesus, who became for us wisdom from God and righteousness and sanctification and redemption that, as it is written, 'He who glories, let him glory in the Lord.'"* (1 Corinthians 1:26-31)

It's official. God loves a failure! He did not want the beauty of His nature and the glory of His Kingdom solely to be represented by the great, the good and the clever. He did not want a Who's Who of humanity to portray His own magnificence.

He does not need to be seen in the right places with the right people. Jesus was criticized viciously for hanging out with the very people society detested. He chose to become despised and rejected. God does not have an image problem.

He chose people who had a history of failure. He picked people who had a history of not learning and who repeated their mistakes continuously.

God chose people who are despised as being stupid by people who should know better. He accepted people who would require lots of training just to be normal, let alone successful.

He chose them because He wanted to love them in such a way that they would always be safe and whole, whether they were successful or not. He chose them so that His love for them could heal them of their foolishness. He has a wonderful capacity to enjoy us in our weaknesses. He has a plan to make us successful through using failure for us and not against us. Failure does not demean the Father. His character and identity are so wonderfully secure that He is not afraid to know us, bless us and stand up for us. Whether we are doing well or badly, our identity is always in Jesus.

We are in Christ and He is in us. The Father has a plan for our personality as much as He has a design for changing our character — to make us more like Himself. A big part of that plan therefore is to love us in exactly the same way that He loves Jesus. We are not loved only because we succeed in Christ. We are loved fully because we are in Him. God loved us powerfully when we were lost in sin.

Our love for God is seriously upgraded when we realize that our mistakes are already covered. No matter how well or badly our life is going, we learn to live under the smile of God. Know that in the love of God we cannot fail; we can only make mistakes and every mistake has already been covered by the Cross.

Where were you when Jesus died? You had no existence. All our sins and mistakes were in the future, and they were covered by that one incredible act of sacrificial love. All our past, present and future sins and mistakes have already been covered. Our future has been secured in the love of God. Shame is not on God's agenda for us. He allows us the wonder and joy of repentance; literally "to think again," to think differently, and to become what we think about.

We overcome failure when we discover that God wants us to love the learning that exists in every situation. All forms of accountability are about loving the learning that is present in every circumstance. That learning produces the fruit of self-control which in turn guarantees lasting change.

God knows that when we do things for the first time we learn how not to do them. Loving the learning in every situation enables us to become wise and also beloved. Wise, because we learn from our mistakes and grow; beloved, because our sense of acceptance comes from being in Christ and not from our ability or performance. Therefore, if we fail at something we can still grow in the love of God. The joy of repentance and the beauty of God's unchanging nature guarantees forgiveness and acceptance.

We overcome failure when we realize that God is not even remotely embarrassed by our weaknesses. He defends us to all our detractors. He is not ashamed to call us brethren. We are in Christ and cannot be condemned (Romans 8). He is the One who loves us the best, knows us the best. God does not get disillusioned with us because He has no illusions in the first place!

We overcome failure when we allow ourselves to be comforted. Our mentor is the Holy Spirit who helps us to laugh at ourselves. He is the Comforter sent to lead us into all truth. When we are embarrassed at the truth of our current mindset or behavior, He comforts us so that we are not paranoid about screwing up. Then He helps us with the learning. Every test is repeatable. We cannot fail the tests of God because we get to take them again… and again… and again, until we pass. Even in the consequences of our actions, the love of God reaches out to cover, protect and nurture us in our woundedness.

The biggest lesson I get to learn is that God loves me for me — not for what I can do. God's love helps us to relax about ourselves. The grace of God is given to us to enable us to feel loved when we mess up. God's grace enables us to feel good about God and therefore to have mercy on ourselves and others. We are a work in progress. No one condemns the artist of an unfinished picture. Instead we look at what is there and we picture what it could become. We wonder, we imagine and we are excited by the possibilities.

In my weakness I am lovely to God. It's the sheer beauty of God that sets me free to be loved outrageously. He allows us to fail when He could have prevented it — maybe because He wants us to see how much we are loved when we can't do anything right. He gives us freedom to fail and His intention is to show us that we are still His beloved. His love for us is not based on how well we do. We desire excellence because He is excellent. No wonder David said, *"One thing I ask, that I may dwell in the house of the Lord all the days of my life. To behold the beauty of the Lord and to (think about Him and all that He is) meditate in His temple."* (Psalm 27:4)

In failure, we understand how lovely we are to the Lord. That is what empowers us to overcome failure as a negative construct. We fail badly when we imagine that failure should not be part of our inheritance or when we believe that failure is not a part of God's plan. Does God cause us to fail? No. Does He allow us to fail? Obviously. Does He use our failure to improve our relationship with Him? Everything God does is relational. Every circumstance can be turned around so that we discover the height, depth, length and breadth of God's love.

> *Every failure carries a do-over!*

When we hit the heights of achievement, God's love is present. When we hit the depths of despair, sin and ugliness, His love covers everything we hate about ourselves. In the pit of depression, God's loving-kindness builds a stairway to recovery. No pit is so deep He is not deeper still. His love is high enough to lift us above everything, deep enough to rescue anyone from anything, long enough to last for eternity, and broad enough to cover every failure.

We fail badly when we choose not to look into the face of Jesus. In failure, God always moves closer to us. People distance themselves from failure and failures. Not so with God. His heart beats for us. He has given us a Comforter so that we can feel His heartbeat. In recent times I have gone through some of the most painful things in my life, but I have discovered the Comforter afresh.

My failures do not haunt me because the Holy Spirit has exorcised the ghost of shame and dishonor. I am comforted. I am learning. I am the beloved of God. My name is Graham and I am a man greatly beloved of God.

He does hide from us occasionally, but that is to draw us into His realm. He manifests Himself to us when He invades our time-space world. When He hides, it is to teach us wisdom by revelation. God's hiddenness is always about us discovering deep truth. (For further information see *Hiddenness and Manifestation* from the *Being with God* series).

Failure is not so much falling down as it is refusing to get up once we have fallen. We fail badly when we imagine that God is annoyed by our failings and will punish us or make us pay for messing up.

In the process of discipling us, God has budgeted for our failure. Our failure cannot diminish the Kingdom, therefore it cannot diminish us. In failure, the Father budgets to be to us exactly what we need at that precise moment. I AM is with us. Intentional love is present and it is more lavish than we can imagine. His love can be so extravagant that it picks us up and makes us want to try again.

God's glory is not enhanced by our success, nor can it be tarnished by our failure. God is simply above all of that. What if most of God's glory is derived from people who are astonished and amazed to be loved so fully in the face of their own inabilities and weaknesses? What if it is part of our own glory in the Lord for us to be loved so wonderfully when we are at our most brainless and ignorant?

My own failures are many. My capacity for weakness on days seems undiminished. I am an embarrassment to myself and yet I am loved so wonderfully. There is perhaps one difference that my experiences with God have given me. I no longer weep tears of shame; I cry tears of joy and wonder. I am amazed by God and His power to love me. He makes all things work together for good. I'm not much of a challenge to His genius and creativity.

We can discover God just as much in failure as we can in success because God never changes. He is the same whether we succeed or fail. We will all fail at times; we must learn to bounce back more successfully. God's love makes us free to fail. Overcome failure in a way that makes you whole and makes the Lord smile!

Prophecy Eliminates Negativity

Misrepresenting the Kingdom

The role of the Church in the world is to have a radiant idea of God's nature and a radiant idea of the Kingdom of Heaven coming to the earth.

We represent all that is wonderful about the person of God and His willingness to forgive, redeem and restore. Our very lives are a description of His goodness. Our testimony reveals His beauty and loving-kindness. We are the New Testament, not written on paper or stamped onto stone blocks, but a revelation of God's love lived out before men.

Yet our communities are full of people who distrust God and disavow His love. There is a hatred of church and organized religion (which they see as the same thing) and a suspicion of Christians.

The obsession of the Church with sin and judgment has created a deeply rooted animosity in our communities toward the Gospel. We have much hardness to overcome initially before we can plant seeds of love and truth. The Gospel calls people to repentance — literally, to think again about God and turn toward Him. The image that we portray about God prevents repentance from taking place. We cannot threaten people into receiving good news. We cannot proclaim the anger and determination of God to punish people and think that we can intimidate them into faith.

If anyone told me about a person who was angry, intolerant, negative, with a history of punishing people for wrongdoing, and then invited me to become a member of his family, I would definitely decline the offer.

Fortunately, that is not the Gospel. There is no good news in negativity. Christians who act like that misrepresent the essential nature of God and the relevance of the sacrifice of Jesus. In Christ, the Father can now forgo wrath. He is satisfied with the blood of Jesus. We tread underfoot the Cross of Christ when we represent God as angry. We are saying that the blood of Jesus does not work effectively.

One of the root causes of the malaise in our culture is that many Christians have not had a real, ongoing encounter with the nature of God. They require a relational upgrade.

Many people have a distorted image of God's true nature, which can only be corrected by an upgrade in our experience of His grace, marvelous love, goodness and kindness. We are ambassadors of the King of love, and a Kingdom so radiant with beauty, our faces shine upon contact.

In this Kingdom, love and goodness are huge factors in our relationship with the Lord. Goodness is at the heart of all revelatory gifting. *"But to each one is given the manifestation of the Spirit are given for the common good"* (1 Corinthians 12:7). Everything we do is to pursue love and develop the prophetic gift, especially so that people are edified, encouraged and comforted as they require in the course of life (1 Corinthians 14:1-3).

We cannot escape the culture of the New Covenant. Neither can we operate from an inferior covenant when a new one is in place. John the Baptist was the last of the Old Covenant prophets who bowed the knee to Jesus, who is a New Covenant Prophet, Priest and King. He is the model for New Covenant prophetic gifting which represents the image of the Father and acts in line with the Kingdom principles laid down by Jesus in His ministry. To prophesy in the style and context of the Old Covenant is now illegal behavior. John came to prepare the way for an entirely different kind of prophet. Jesus came saying, *"You have heard it said* (Old Covenant), *but now I say to you* (New Covenant)."

> **Negativity saves no one**

As a prophetic devotional, read The Sermon on the Mount in chapters 5-7 of Matthew. The ministry of Jesus caused consternation and controversy because He was pulling a culture out of its Old Testament thinking and behavior into a new relationship with God.

We have some similar difficulties today where some churches are quick to judge and condemn others because they themselves are unfamiliar with the Gospel of reconciliation and redemption. The world has been reconciled to God from His end.

Through Jesus, the Father has reconciled all things to Himself (Colossians 1:20). While we were sinners, Christ died for us. When we were still enemies, we were reconciled to God through the death of His Son. Jesus made Himself available for judgment on our behalf (Romans 5:6-10).

To reconcile (*Apokatallasso*) means to change from one condition to another so as to remove all enmity and leave no impediment to unity and peace. God does not change! Removing His wrath does not contravene His immutability. He always acts according to His unchanging righteousness and holiness. His love, grace, mercy, goodness, patience, loving-kindness and joy are unchanging also! He is immutable in all aspects of His nature and character. The sacrifice of Jesus satisfies the Father so completely that wrath and judgment are suspended in this life. There is no judgment but there is still justice! People will still reap what they sow. We can appeal to God for the exposure of wickedness and evil deeds. We can pray for the light to shine on the unfruitful works of darkness. We can use our authority in Christ to cast out devils and come against spiritual wickedness in high places.

> **We judge the enemy, not people**

The Holy Spirit convicts the world of judgment by disclosing that the ruler of this world has been judged on their behalf (John 16:11). We judge the demonic, not people, in this present world.

On the Day of Judgment they come back into play. Scripture is clear: *"Therefore, do not go on passing judgment before the time, but wait until the Lord returns. He will bring to light the things hidden in darkness and disclose the motives of men's hearts. Then each man's praise will come to him from God."* (1 Corinthians 4:5)

Our battle is not against people (flesh and blood) but against spiritual powers. In a sin-sick world where evil and wickedness are rampant, we fight the
power that is behind it, not the people deceived by it. We determine what is
enemy oppression and the spiritual bondage of possession, and we take authority over the enemy in order to set captives free.

How much warfare does it take to bring freedom? What are the weapons of
our warfare? If we overcome evil with good (Romans 12:21), then goodness is a
weapon. If it is the kindness of God that leads people to repentance (Romans
2:4), then surely kindness must be a weapon. If God so loved the world that He
gave His only begotten Son (John 3:16), then love is a weapon. If we are bringing GLAD TIDINGS of GREAT JOY to the world, then joy is a weapon.

The issue in any locality is how do we cast out the devil and bring freedom
to this community? Our assessment of the situation must involve this radiant
idea. How much goodness and kindness needs to be released so that this community can taste and see that the Lord is good?

Jesus went about doing good and healing all who were oppressed by the
devil (Acts 10:38). Our language to all people must reflect the heart of God. He
has committed to us the Gospel of Reconciliation. The word is out. A price has
been paid. There is no longer any enmity between God and man. All men have
the potential to be saved, they are pre-Christians. The Way is open and clear
from God's side. Favor is now possible because of God's goodness and kindness.

*"God was in Christ, reconciling the world to Himself, not counting their tres-
passes against them, and He has committed to us the word of reconciliation."*
2 Corinthians 5:14-21 is breathtaking in its beauty and its Heavenly approach
to the world in which we live.

Reconciliation is the good news of the removal of wrath in this life and
the very real possibility of redemption. Reconciliation is God making the first
move in Christ toward humanity. Redemption is our response. Reconciliation
puts man into a state of receptivity to the Gospel of atonement. Reconciliation
is the process of goodness and kindness leading to repentance and redemption.
Reconciliation stresses the promise of atonement.

Reconciliation and Redemption are the way to God. People step onto the
way in reconciliation and step into redemption when repentance becomes salvation. The journey does not stop at redemption, but goes
on into relationship, fullness and being made in the image
of God.

> God is diligent
> to love

Reconciliation is the process that empowers people to
come to Redemption. People are awakened to love and all the possibilities of
goodness and kindness that reveal God's loving nature.

When the Church has a distorted image of the nature of God it is always
people who suffer. By presenting God as angry, judgmental and condemning,
the Church has robbed the world of reconciliation as a process to discover God.

They are now blind and defenseless against a malignant enemy who loves to steal, kill and destroy.

We are ambassadors of reconciliation, representatives of Heaven. The GOOD NEWS is that each geographical location has numerous ambassadors who represent God's intentionality. Each location has several embassies where people can go to a King who would say yes to them belonging permanently and forever.

Love empowers repentance

To reconcile means to restore and bring back to relationship. It means to bring to agreement, call together and render favorable. God is disposed to be gracious. He is full of promise and favorably inclined. What we saw Jesus do in a pre-Christian, pre-redemptive society, we can do in a post-reconciliation, redemptive community. We are the GOOD NEWS!

If we see ourselves as ambassadors of Good News, what is our proclamation? What image are we giving of the Kingdom we represent? Our voice is critical in the earth. There are lots of voices and ours must become the most significant. It is crucial that our voice matches God's heart for all people. The Gospel is glad tidings of great joy.

A prophet has to be good news — even if that news is to repent. Our language toward people is vital. The testimony of Jesus (in our lives) is the spirit of prophecy (Revelation 19:10). What Jesus is to us, we become to others. We can only reveal what God has made real. When we are Christ-like, people discover Christ.

The world is desperate to know God. People are hungry for love and significance. People want to belong to and believe in a God of outstanding grace, love, and kindness. People long for the security of a daily trust and confidence in a higher power. Many people are broken, destroyed and discarded. Speaking of an angry, vengeful God only reinforces every abusive relationship they have ever suffered.

Our message to the world cannot be double-minded. It must have a focused heart view. We are soul winners, not people destroyers. We do not put people down, we raise them up.

If this is true of our relationships in the pre-Christian community, how much more true is it of our fellowship in the household of God?

Prophecy Connects People To the Father

Everyone in the world wants to live a life that has worth, value, and significance. No one sets out on their life adventure intending to fail. Behind every person's failure there is an individual needing to connect with something more. People are looking for attachment. They want relevance in terms of who they are, who they associate with in the course of their journey and what they achieve in the business of life and living.

Only the Father can provide ultimate significance that satisfies every aspect of our longing to be more. He seeks a relationship with us that enables His vision of us to be realized in our own hearts. His great heart is full of positives about us. He puts us into the most wonderful place imaginable. He puts us in Christ. All things are possible to us because the Father has connected us to Himself in and through Jesus.

> *We are strategically placed in Christ*

Prophecy not only reminds us of that connection but also seeks to enhance the relationship at every opportunity. Good relationships occur because we are intent on helping one another become better. Friendships that seek positive increase for others are to be treasured. A positive increase occurs when we support the learning and development of another without controlling it. We can tell people what to do. We can use sanctions to enforce particular growth. We can register disapproval and frustration at lack of progress in order to push people forward. There is, however, no substitute for loving, firm, patient and joyful support for people that empower them to think, plan and purposefully connect with their real identity.

Prophecy is a part of that context. The Father is wonderfully affirming of us because He sees us through the lens of Jesus. If we are to succeed with people, we must view them from Heaven's perspective. The Father has strategically placed us in Christ so that Heaven can relate to the new life of Jesus in us. The Father is obviously connected to Jesus. Having put Jesus in us and us into Jesus, He is now connected to us in a major way. Our old nature is dead, crucified in Christ. We no longer have a sin nature; it died on the Cross. We are not crucifying the old nature; the Father has already done that in Christ. We are crucifying the flesh which is our old mindsets, our learned behavior, and our poor choices. We are killing off our old habits by positively learning to abide in our new nature.

Too many people are preoccupied with the bad things in life. This puts us more under the influence of the enemy than it does the Holy Spirit. The Holy Spirit deals with our negatives by empowering us to walk in "newness of life." We are dead to sin and alive to God. We kill the flesh with the strength of our abounding life in Christ. Our very alertness to the Spirit compels us to overcome our own deficiency. We never focus on a negative, it is already dead. Baptism was our funeral. Focusing on our own negatives is like continuously resurrecting a corpse! We are alive to God. We have His energy, abundance and zest for life. We are learning to overflow, to be vigorous and vital. The Holy Spirit is brilliant in this regard. He is the best personal trainer in Heaven. He is animated, cheerful, passionate and always ready to empower us to develop in the likeness of Jesus.

Life in the Spirit is always about displacement. When the Father puts His finger on a part of our life that needs upgrading, He is pointing out the site of our next miracle. If the Father has put to death the old nature, why should He deal with it as though it is still alive? That would demonstrate that He had no confidence in the power of the Cross.

If our old nature is dead in Christ then we are only dealing with the residue of its previous effect. The flesh is our bad habits, which need to be adjusted to become new mindsets, empowered behavior and better, more powerful choices. Underneath the flesh is our new nature in Christ which needs to rise up within and displace the old. When God points to a deficiency it is to draw attention to what has already replaced it in Christ. He has dealt with sin once and for all in Christ. Now He is dealing with righteousness, the process of sanctification, and the wisdom of life in the Spirit that upholds and guarantees redemption (1 Corinthians 1:30).

> *The Holy Spirit is the best trainer in Heaven!*

The focus of our life is no longer the wearying, incessant struggle against sin. It is the joyous involvement with life and being alive to God! There is no need for a "fix what's wrong and do what's right" approach. We are the righteousness of God in Christ (2 Corinthians 5:21), which is solely achieved by Jesus taking our place on the Cross.

God is not dealing with sin. He has dealt with it and destroyed it on the Cross. Now, all who come to Him through Jesus are placed in Jesus so that they can walk in newness of life by the power of the Holy Spirit. We are now a new creation, all the old things have passed away and behold, new things have come (2 Corinthians 5:17-18). All these new things are established in us by the Holy Spirit, who takes the things of Jesus and makes them real to us (John 16:15).

It was not God's intention to return us to the state that Adam enjoyed, pre-temptation, in the Garden of Eden. That was the first Adam around whom was developed a covenant in the law that was focused on continuous repentance, atonement and sacrifice for sin.

Jesus is the Second Adam who came to birth an entirely different race of people — literally a new creation. The first Adam was a living "soul"; the Second Adam, a life-giving "spirit." They are chalk and cheese. Adam mark one, lived through his soul where he was subject to external influence in his thinking, feeling and choosing. The soul is made up of our mind, emotions and will, which can all be elevated or subjugated.

However, we are born again of the Spirit, which is a higher order of being. We are now connected to Heaven through a life-giving Spirit, which is Jesus, the Second Adam.

The first man and the Old Covenant were earthly and natural in their relationship with God. They depended on death, blood and sacrifice to be continually made for atonement. Natural man could have the Spirit of God come upon them, but not reside in them.

The second creation is born from above by the Spirit. They are supernatural in their relationship with God because they live from Heaven to earth in their spirituality. All the old things have passed away and everything has become new. Now we recognize no one after the flesh. That means

God is dealing with our righteousness

that we relate to one another based upon our new nature, not the old. God is dealing solely with our new nature. He does not relate to us according to our flesh. He is constantly presenting to us, who Jesus is for us. The Holy Spirit discloses Christ in us, the confident expectation of glory.

In the old way, man lived toward God, for God. In the new creation, we live from God, with God. When we awaken to righteousness, we do not sin (1 Corinthians 15:34). We are the righteousness of God in Christ (2 Corinthians 5:21), ambassadors of a Covenant so powerful it will change the world. Hell cannot prevail against a Church that truly knows by experience the full nature of God (Matthew 16:18). The rock of the Church is a true revelation of Jesus Christ as Lord over all things for all time. He is not just the God of Salvation; He is the Lord of Life. To be saved is wonderful; but that is the beginning, not the outcome. The outcome of salvation is encounters and ongoing experiences of God that are so sublime they propel us into an engagement with Heaven on earth. We simply must taste the power of Christ within. It is the power of the age to come. We are a new creation in Christ. That means that Jesus gave life to a whole new race of people that have never been seen in the earth before.

Prior to Christ, man was a living soul, subject to external pressures, finding their way to God through sacrifice and atonement, living by a set of rules known as the Law. Now in Christ we have no more responsibility for sacrifice; Christ has removed that in Himself. We cannot move toward God by our performance as believers in obedience to a set of rules or a code of conduct.

In the New Covenant it is Christ in us which is the confident expectation of glory (Colossians 1:27). The issue now is what are we going to do with Christ within? Before the Cross, such possibilities never existed! Now in Jesus a whole new people group has emerged in every tribe and nation in the earth. We are the people of Heaven living among the peoples of the earth. We are subject to a different lifestyle with amazing possibilities.

We are servants of righteousness because God only works to empower His righteousness in us through Christ within (Romans 6:18). This wonderful standing totally counteracts the effects and pernicious hold of sin. This is where prophecy is brilliant. All true prophecy totally supports the theology of Christ within, the confident expectation of glory. Why deal with sin when the old nature is dead? When we deal with our righteousness in Christ it

A positive will always kill a negative

has the power to kill off (crucify) the bad habits of the flesh.

We always deal with a negative by reinforcing a positive. "Christ within" is the backbone of prophecy. Our testimony of who Jesus is for us is the very essence of the prophetic (Revelation 19:10).

Prophecy Connects People To the Father

Prophecy connects us to the very heart of God. It connects us to the GOOD NEWS of Heaven. We cannot promote transformation if our attention has been taken by a negative. If we are focused on the problems we see in people, our prophetic output can be clouded by a negative. It is so important for prophetic people to be marinated in the nature of God. We need to be both highly flavored and contextually softened by His Presence in our hearts.

> *Prophecy connects us with the GOOD NEWS!*

Obviously God does exhort, rebuke, and admonish, but always in the context of learning, becoming more and growing (more of that in another segment). God does not punish us; He did that to Jesus. The Father develops us in such a wonderful way that even chastisement makes us feel extraordinarily loved *"For those whom the Lord loves He disciplines, and He scourges every son whom He receives"* (Hebrews 12:6). If one of the purposes of chastisement is the expression of love, then how we discipline people must primarily satisfy the heart of God. Chastisement as a further revelation of God's love must therefore be the goal of every leader, every mentor and every parent. The Father loves to reveal Himself. That was the purpose of Jesus: *"He who has seen Me has seen the Father"* (John 14:9). The joy of the Holy Spirit is to reveal Jesus whom He adores.

Prophecy is part of that revelatory process, giving people a taste of what God is truly like. God is not a repair man; He is a restorer. He makes all things new. He is delighted with Christ and in choosing to put us into that place of delight, He can now choose to be delighted with us. His delight cannot be impaired by our struggle. The Father's focus is Jesus. He sees us through that lens. He sees Jesus in everything in us. He is intimately acquainted with us in Christ. We are connected through Jesus! Prophecy maintains that relationship and empowers it to go higher, further and deeper.

God is not trying to fix us. He wants to resource us! He has given us a new nature which overcomes our bad habits, poor mindsets, and unproductive learned behaviors. He points to Jesus as our place of acceptance (Ephesians 1:6). We are learning to live from God, not toward Him. We are enjoying being with God, not looking for His Presence. He never leaves us nor forsakes us. So clearly, seeking the Lord has to be concerned with something more than just looking for Him.

Obviously if we move away from an ongoing experience of His Presence, then we must wholeheartedly seek to put that right and move back into the place of His delight. However, when we are actively enjoying being with Him and living from Him, then seeking Him can only involve a greater discovery of who He is and what He wants to be for us. Life in the Spirit is incremental. We are moving into new levels and higher dimensions of involvement with Christ in Heavenly places (Ephesians 2:6).

Prophecy Eliminates Negativity

Life in Christ is always about guarantees. "Ask and you will receive." There is no hesitancy in the heart of the Father. He is not reluctant to bless us. "Seek and you will find." He is wonderful and extravagant in His giving. He loves to provide. He loves us to discover His goodness. "Knock and it shall be opened to you." Life is an ongoing encounter with goodness. It is an ever increasing experience of God's permission. Everything is "yes and Amen" in Christ (2 Corinthians 1:20).

Seeking is concerned with the discovery of all that the Father has placed us into in Christ. It is the joyful exposure of Christ living in us and making all things possible. When we seek God internally, we find our truest self in Him. People who spend too much time and energy on the flesh seldom discover the wonder of Christ within, and the expectation of goodness prevailing that combines with that revelatory experience.

> *Salvation is the starting line*

Grace does not need to expose the bad in order to be appreciated. Grace receives more value by glorifying Jesus in us. The riches of His grace (Ephesians 1:17) are immeasurably tied in to the riches of the glory of His inheritance in the saints (Ephesians 1:18). The goal of prophecy is to connect people with the heart of the Father, the Presence of Jesus within, the empowering Presence of the Holy Spirit to lead us into all truth and the ongoing experience that goes with a true knowledge of Christ.

The Father has put something into us that is glorious — it is Christ within. Our goal in prophecy is to build people into that fullness of encounter. We are gladly exposing people to the reality of being in Christ and empowering them to live from that place of delight.

Speaking the truth in love is totally concerned with people growing up into all things in Christ (Ephesians 4:15). There is a huge difference between that which is true about a person's sin habits and that which is the Truth about their new nature in Christ.

> *"Therefore from now on we recognize no one according to the flesh; even though we have known Christ according to the flesh, yet now we know Him in this way no longer. Therefore if anyone is in Christ, he is a new creation; the old things have passed away; behold, new things have come. Now all these things are from God, who reconciled us to Himself through Christ and gave us the ministry of reconciliation." (2 Corinthians 5:16-18)*

The Truth is a person: Jesus Christ. Therefore, everything we say to people should emphatically upgrade their relationship with the Lord Jesus so that they are growing up into everything that He is for them. Truth is relational; it connects us to how the Father sees us in Christ. Truth empowers us to become like Jesus.

It may be true that a person has a bad temper but the Truth is that the Father has already done something about that in Christ.

The Truth sets us free to become Christ-like. When we look at people's poor choices outside of Christ and relate to that behavior **then** we are dealing with the flesh, not the spirit. What is true relates to the flesh in this context. The Truth relates to who Jesus is for us. It is for freedom that Christ has set us free (Galatians 5:1).

We do not regard anyone after the flesh. If this is true in regard to Jesus it must be equally true in the context of our new nature in Him. Those who knew Jesus as the Son of Man (pre-resurrection) and who walked alongside Him, must now relate to Him as the Son of God who lives in them. It is a breathtaking new relationship!

When we speak the Truth in love we are reminding, teaching and exhorting people about who they are in Christ. We are reinforcing their true identity in the Spirit. We are not calling them out because of their inappropriate old behavior; we are calling them up to the Truth of who they really are in Jesus.

In Christ we are a new creation. All the old things have passed away — he that is dead is free (Romans 6:7), and all things have become (past tense) **new**! Speaking the Truth therefore must relate to the new things of our identity in Jesus. Lovingly tell people who they are in Him.

Salvation is not the finishing point. It is the starting line, the entry point to a whole new territory in experience of God. It is the promised land of Christ within. We must enter it and overcome all that is present which aligns itself against God's loving-kindness. We can enjoy the fruits of the land while taking down any internal fortresses or tackling giants. God is with us and goes before us. We fight from victory, not toward it. Living from Christ makes it easier to break through. Jesus has already conquered. Someone who is more than a conqueror is a person who joyfully occupies and enjoys the territory that has been established.

In prophecy we can take ground within ourselves and seal our possessions in the Lord Jesus Christ. Prophecy provides an amazing, immediate, in-the-moment connection that moves us into a higher place in God, or re-connects us with our place of delight in Christ.

Prophecy Attacks Distortions

The world always gives us negative information. In order to sell certain products, advertising must first make us discontent. It may create fear. It may attack the roots of our self-esteem, promoting dissatisfaction.

For many people the environment they grew up in can clash with their positivity. Upbringing, poor education and limited prospects grind people down into a self-image that is presumed because it has been relentlessly imposed.

Poor role models have a powerful impact on people's mindsets. Our soul can become distorted with negative personal perceptions. On my first day of class at my senior high school, my teacher informed me that I was no good and a troublemaker. He knew my brothers. At that point I had not said or done anything. Throughout my high school period he was relentless in his aversion and condemnation. The Biblical version of prejudice is, *"Can any good thing come out of Nazareth?"* spoken by Nathaniel concerning Jesus (John 1:46).

Most people on reaching adulthood will possibly have been betrayed, let down or humiliated on any number of occasions. We will all have tasted someone's negativity at some point. Some people's exposure to suspicion, mistrust and cynicism will be so severe it will lead them into being self-critical and oppressed.

Others will be so severely emotionally and mentally traumatized by abusive people that they will think themselves utterly worthless and deserving of poor treatment by other people. At the least, people may have real problems with self-acceptance and receiving praise. At the worst they may seek to harm themselves physically through cutting themselves, burning their own flesh or bruising their own body. People feel unattractive and develop an emotional disorder characterized by an obsessive desire to lose weight by refusing to eat. Alternatively, other people will have bouts of overeating and oscillate between fasting or self-induced vomiting as a way of purging food from their bodies. There is a social networking site for beautiful people with over half a million members worldwide. Apparently it axed over 5,000 members for putting on a few extra pounds over the Christmas period. This site has a strict ban on ugly people. People upload photographs of themselves to see if they qualify. Once accepted, people have to keep updated images of themselves. Vigilant members noticed those with extra weight.

When challenged on this issue their response was, "Our members demand the highest standard of beauty be upheld. Letting fatties roam the site is a direct threat to our business."

Apparently members who become festive fatties can reapply once they have lost weight. People are rated by the opposite sex on whether they are hot, merely OK, or have an "ugh" factor.

Exclusivity is repulsive to the Gospel, which is inclusive and accepting of people. Real relationships go way beyond the external look of people. Beauty is not skin deep.

> *Most people have real distortions regarding themselves and God*

It is ironic that this shallow behavior has a shelf life that guarantees exclusion at some point. Like pack animals they will turn on one another at the first sign of aging.

Millions of people are on medication just to help them get through another day of inner turmoil and mental, emotional distress. In times of acute stress and anxiety, people have a tape message playing in their head where they replay hurtful words and negative information about themselves. Everyone hears voices inside themselves to a greater or lesser extent. Everyone needs to know the inner voice of Jesus (John 10:3-5; 16:27). The voice of the Lord must never be an echo. It needs to be clear and distinct in the heart of every believer.

People have a DVD player in their head that relays images of past–present situations where they have been used, abused or even humiliated. Their self-perception can become so warped that they look for verbal abuse in every conversation. The slightest gesture can be a slight to them. They expect rejection to such a degree that their own approach to people and subsequent behavior almost guarantees that possibility.

That is the extreme shortened version of the damage, devastation, and desolation that the enemy has inflicted on the lives of people we live among. The enemy is a malevolent, malignant being that loves pain and destruction. Jesus came to destroy the works of the devil (1 John 3:8). He went about doing good and healing all who were oppressed by the devil (Acts 10:38). The gift of prophecy is a part of that healing process.

Prophecy is designed to edify, exhort and comfort people in their time of need. The devil may put people down but the prophetic raises them up. It deliberately creates an alternative message to the one currently playing in the minds of people. It constantly upgrades that message to ensure that people live by every word that God proclaims over them.

> The true
> prophetic edifies

People have been heavily influenced by the world, the flesh and the devil. Those voices have been common to all mankind. To ensure transformation of the inner man we must impact people with the voices of the Kingdom. People need to hear about who they are in Jesus. They need to understand how the Father sees them. They must be taught to live by those voices that proclaim good news to their hearts.

Jesus came to bring good news to the afflicted (Isaiah 61:1-4) and to heal those whose hearts have been broken by grief, trauma and abuse. He came to restore favor. He came to proclaim liberty and freedom to people. This is a double emphasis that carries with it a powerful sense of urgency. It denotes an intention to move rapidly, to expedite freedom and release from captivity as fast as possible. Prophecy is a "quick release from oppression" gift. That is why the prophetic and the pastoral should combine in moments of dealing with oppression.

The prophetic raises people up out of their devastation and seeks to rebuild what has been ruined and to bring health and wholeness to those who are desolate. The Lord hates bondage and oppression. His heart is to respond quickly to people in subjection to wickedness.

When prophetic people move in anger and judgment they aid the purpose of the enemy and fail to demonstrate a compassionate God. *"This you know, my beloved brethren. But everyone must be quick to hear, slow to speak and slow to anger; for the anger of man does not achieve the righteousness of God"* (James 1:19-20). The Spirit of the Lord is with us to set people free. We are anointed to bring an end to oppression and slavery. Prophecy restores favor. It is the dispensation of blessing, grace, benevolence and kindness. Prophecy comes to people's aid with words of encouragement that cause them to develop self-esteem. It restores people's dignity and self-respect.

Our speech must always contain grace. In this way we preserve the purposes of God which are freedom and liberty (Colossians 4:6). It is for freedom that Christ has set us free. Our spirit has been born-again from above so that we can represent Heaven, not earth, in our choice of words. *"Let no unwholesome word proceed from your mouth, but only such a word as is good for edification according to the need of the moment, so that it will give grace to those who hear"* (Ephesians 4:29).

The true prophetic edifies; the false prophetic condemns. The real prophetic builds people up in their search for God and in the establishing of empowering Presence (grace). Prophecy must increase grace and improve the possibility of freedom. An increase of grace upgrades our perception of where we are currently in the compassion of God.

Unless people put away anger, wrath, malice, slander, and abusive speech from their mouth, they cannot represent God's essential goodness (Colossians 3:8). The prophetic is tainted by a lack of discipline. Such behavior is a demonstration of crass immaturity. Pursue the edification of another human being (Romans 14:19) and the purposes of God will be fulfilled. As people who live within the beautiful surroundings of the Father's heart, we dwell in the place of purity, loveliness, and excellence so that out of our mouth come words of good repute and worthy of praise (Philippians 4:8).

Two passages of Scripture that accurately illustrate the importance of the prophetic in destroying the works of the devil are Jeremiah 1:9-10 and 2 Corinthians 10:3-8:

> *"Then the LORD stretched out His hand and touched my mouth, and the LORD said to me, 'Behold, I have put My words in your mouth. See, I have appointed you this day over the nations and over the kingdoms, to pluck up and to break down, to destroy and to overthrow, to build and to plant.'"* (Jeremiah 1:9-10)

The prophetic gift is incredibly destructive toward the enemy. It contains four negative weapons to pluck up, break down, destroy and overthrow the activities of the enemy in the lives of people. It contains two wonderfully positive weapons that build people up in faith and plants them firmly in the heart and purpose of God.

The prophet is vigilant against the enemy. A true prophet loves freedom above all else. Our anointing is to break the yoke of oppression wherever we find it. The two positive weapons to aid man are much more powerful than the four weapons used against the enemy. God saves His best for people.

To **pluck up** involves the action of weeding out what the enemy has sown in the hearts of people. Those seeds can grow into areas of perception that can cause a fear that cripples a person's life.

> *A prophet is vigilant against the enemy*

"The old life has passed away; God has given you a new life. Your anointing empowers you to bind anything from your old life that seeks to affect the new. That includes any genetic disorders…" The scene is a meeting in the north of England in 1983. I was prophesying over a middle–aged man. I don't know why I said the last five words, but as I spoke them, the man fell to his knees and began to cry out praise and thanks. A woman and two teenage children jumped out of their seats and began to cry out in joy. Numerous others punched the air in delight. I am standing there, open-mouthed with a bemused look on my face, thinking, "What? What did I say? What just happened?"

People were cheering and clapping each other on the back. Several men had mobbed the guy I was ministering to and were all in a heap on the floor. When we restored a semblance of order to this joyful melee, I discovered the reason for the outbreak of rejoicing.

The man had a heart defect and was suffering chest pains, numbness and other side effects. He was on the list for a transplant, but no suitable donor could be found. His grandfather and father had both died at forty-two from the same condition. This guy was forty-one years old. Over the years I have been in this exact situation, numerous times with both men and women. It seems genetic disorders are becoming increasingly common.

The man was extremely fearful of the next year of his life being his last. The enemy had sown such seeds of doubt, fear and unbelief in his heart that he had become, in the words of his wife, "massively pessimistic." Nothing could get through to him. Scripture was not believed and prayer did not help. The enemy had filled his head and heart with a conviction that death was imminent and nothing could prevent it."

Prophecy broke through where nothing else could. The impact of those five words was so powerful to him that all his negativity was plucked up and out of his conscious thinking. His heart opened and hope with faith rushed in. We took action immediately with the proceeding word. He lived.

Prophecy also **breaks down** negative mindsets and walls of poor self–esteem. It interrupts patterns of thinking and behavior that are destructive. Where people have been systematically abused, a brick wall has been erected that is built to keep people out.

Behind that wall people can be cold, unfeeling, or mistrustful, wary — even cynical or indifferent. Without Jesus people's attempt to save themselves in life can take many forms.

When praying for a guy in his early thirties, it was apparent that he was shut down in his personality. He would not look at me. His whole demeanor was based on a strong feeling of self-revulsion. He had no sense of self-worth. He had undergone numerous psychiatric evaluations and received much specialized counseling, but was unmoved.

When praying, I had a vision of a six-year-old boy on his birthday. His father had lovingly and painstakingly designed and built a beautiful kite. Father and son were extremely close, a hugely affectionate relationship. His father had worked on the kite in the garage every evening for several months. They were part of a local kite flying club. The kite was a masterpiece of aerodynamic design. The boy was thrilled, the father proud as he watched his son unpack the gift. They assembled it and enthusiastically prepared to fly it imme-

Prophecy is a breakthrough gift

diately. Kite in hand, the boy ran to the front door, tripped over his own feet, fell, and demolished the present. He was appalled. His father, speechless with rage, struck him across the face. His birthday destroyed, he was sent to his room for the rest of the day.

His father never spoke to him again beyond the absolute necessities of communication. The boy was frozen out as his father lavished attention on his siblings. No matter what the son did, he never regained the affection of his dad. Years of silent recrimination eroded his confidence and self-worth, till eventually he shut down.

As I am seeing those things unfolding the Father is touching my heart with compassion for this man. As I shared the picture with him, he lifted his head and stared at me. The look on his face turned from one devoid of emotion to blank despair. His eyes filled with tears. He began to shake. He broke down and wept. Actually, wailed would be a better description. Something broke in him and healing began. I held him for quite a while and spoke prophetically into his ear as he wept. It was recorded. I learned later that he returned to counseling and received further breakthroughs. The enemy loves to incarcerate us in our own misery; prophecy breaks down the walls that have imprisoned us.

Jesus went about doing good and healing all who were oppressed of the devil (Acts 10:38). He came to **destroy** the works of the destroyer (1 John 3:8). Prophecy is a part of Heaven's destructive power against the evil one. Oppression can be the result of occult activity in our family line. We may have been under the control of oppressive, domineering people. I have seen many people who live under astonishing bullying, harassing, and menacing people.

In an event in South Africa, I felt compassion rise up in me when praying for a young woman. She was weeping in the arms of a female member of the team. I felt the Holy Spirit indicate that I should use my hand as a sword and pass it over her body. The prophetic word I received was that God is cutting her off from an occult presence in her family line. She screamed and was delivered of an evil spirit. Later, we learned that her grandmother was a witch.

In Christ we get to destroy the power of the enemy wherever we find it. In His Presence and His name we are given authority over all the power of the enemy (Luke 10:17-20; Mark 16:15-18). The Gospel is GOOD NEWS for humanity and bad news to the enemy. Prophecy is a key gift in the destructive process of binding and loosing.

Prophecy **overthrows** the rule of the enemy and replaces it with the reign of Jesus. I have seen plenty of people rescued from the occult and come under the reign of the Lord Jesus. The Holy Spirit is hugely involved in and around the new age movement, intent on redemption, healing, deliverance and bringing freedom.

There are many ministries that have a specific and dynamic role on the front line of the clash between two kingdoms. One of my personal favorites that I have the privilege to speak into and support financially is New Earth Tribe, which is based in Byron Bay, Australia. Byron Bay is a major new age center with over one million backpackers annually visiting the town. It is a vibrant, healthy, happy, intentional band of warriors — many who have been saved out of extreme occult bondage and involvement.

> *Prophecy is a frontline gift in the clash between two kingdoms*

They minister at new age festivals from the main stage with words of knowledge, prophecy, healing and signs and wonders. They are well received by new-agers who are seeking after truth and spiritual encounter. Phil and Maria Mason, who lead The Tribe, are patient, enthusiastic, and powerful in their approach to sharing the Lordship of Christ. Backed up by a stalwart team and an excellent spiritual community, their mission is to overthrow the evil one and establish lordship.

Phil is one of the best speakers in the world on how to understand, infiltrate and overcome postmodernism. They run the Deep End School of Post-modern Ministry: an exciting, joyful, compassionate bunch of extravagant worshippers who adore Jesus and love to partner with the Holy Spirit. They are a fabulous bunch of people, beholden to the Father, who are a joy to be with in fellowship (www.newearthtribe.com). I love the way the Holy Spirit ministers to the new age movement. It is clearly not the same approach that He would use with conservative evangelicals, charismatic believers, tribal nations or eastern mystics. That is the beauty of the Holy Spirit. He can position Himself so effortlessly in the hearts of man, making the Gospel come alive irrespective of culture, tradition or spiritual experience.

The Tribe is not for everyone; and indeed they have no aspirations to be that broad in their approach to life and spirituality. I love the way they use the gift of prophecy to open people up to the claims of Jesus. They are intent on overthrowing the enemy and prophecy is one of their weapons.

Mercy triumphs over judgment (James 2:13), and as we allow ourselves to become more intimately acquainted with God's heart, His compassion fills us to overflowing. All spiritual gifts are to be used for the common good of people (1 Corinthians 12:7); specifically to build and to plant (Jeremiah 1:9-10).

Building people up is one of the chief requirements of prophecy. Edification of people is of the utmost importance to the Holy Spirit (1 Corinthians 14:3-5, 12, 17, 26; Romans 14:19). Prophecy is a wonderful gift of encouragement, release, comfort and exhortation. It inspires, persuades, admonishes for good, entreats and arouses people to a deeper place of faith, passion and relationship with God. It raises people to new heights of ongoing fellowship with the Lord. It increases trust and fresh expectation. It awakens people to passionate encounter with the Lord Jesus Christ. It challenges a negative lifestyle with joyful possibility in Christ. It kindles desire and provokes a deeper reality of God's loving-kindness. Prophecy stimulates growth and promotes much-needed change. It awakens us to a new level of identity and destiny.

Prophecy plants us deep into the soil of God's affection. We are imbedded into love, joy and peace. Prophecy empowers us to abide, dwell, and remain in the place of encounter and ongoing experience. The Holy Spirit oversees our growth in Christ. He loves to plant us in the next place of growth and development that will ensure we bear fruit in abundance. Prophecy can plant us firmly in the place of focused, intentional and powerful determination. Prophecy touches our backbone and stiffens our spine. We receive courage and are strengthened to overcome and destroy all negative situations. When we build people up and plant them deep, we are dealing with extremes of height and depth with regard to God's faithfulness and consistency.

Prophecy Removes the Struggle

We live by every word proceeding from God's mouth. We are people of proclamation. The Good News is the truth, not just about becoming saved, thanks to the Lord Jesus; it is also about developing a relationship with Him that empowers us to live the life of Christ within.

Salvation is the starting point, not the end result. It is the entry point into a life of fullness and not measure. It is a life that takes us into the high places of trust and faith. We are delivered from doubt, unbelief, toil and struggle. If Christ is as powerful as we believe, then our internal spirituality must surely go to heights of experience in Him that enable us to live above all that the world, the flesh and the devil can throw at us.

Scripture is the foundation for encounter and ongoing experience. We are learning to grow in grace and truth. We are developing in the Holy Spirit; a walk with God that empowers us to grow up in Christ in all things. Everything is connected to our growth in Christ. We are developing new mindsets, better habits and righteous learning experiences as we encounter the joy of walking in the Spirit.

In particular we are developing a lifestyle in Jesus that is not present–past, but is working in the present toward a powerful future. In this walk we are most dependent upon the truth concerning our past and our future. The present must have a sound relationship with the Spirit of wisdom and revelation.

> *Christ uses the Cross to free us from our past*

The last words of Jesus were, *"It is finished"* (John 19:30). What is the "it" that so consumed Jesus in the moment of His agony and separation from the Father?

The "it" is judgment, sacrifice, death, religious bondage, sin, the curse upon Adam and Eve, sickness, fear, bondage to the world, poverty, any form of mental or emotional disorder, anything that would separate us from the ongoing experience of the love of God.

Prophecy cannot remove our struggle if our whole approach to God is not fully centered on the revealed word of Scripture. How we interpret Romans chapters 6-8 is one of the most important foundations of our whole life and walk. This is some of the most important theology in all of the Word of God. It is so vital for us to understand the work of the Cross in our lives: what it did, how it applies and how we make practical application of that in the course of life.

The purpose of the Cross was not just to forgive us our sins but to crucify the sin nature. There is a huge difference in terms of which side of the Cross people choose to live. If we only believe that it was about the forgiveness of sins then we will stop short of an ongoing walk with God that truly represents the Kingdom of Heaven. Every time we default we will go back to the Cross for forgiveness because we only view the Cross in terms of our present–past experience. We will continue in our shortcomings because we do not know anything different, but we will not personally change. One side of the Cross is about forgiveness and cleansing because of our personal struggles. The other side of the Cross is about freedom and glory because we are learning to be partakers of His divine nature (2 Peter 1:1-4).

> *The Holy Spirit uses the Cross to establish freedom for the present–future*

The Cross actually crucifies our sin nature so that we can partake of resurrection power. We can learn to be empowered with the same Holy Spirit that filled Jesus. The purpose of the Cross is to provide a salvation that takes us into the realm of becoming like Jesus. Making man in His image has always been the goal of the Father.

Everything Jesus has, we can have. Everything that He did, we can do (John 14:12). The same fullness that is at work in Him is also available to us. As He is, so are we in this world (1 John 4:17). The same power, purity and passion of Christ are open to us because He is in us and we are in Him. The same authority and resurrection power is available to us through the Cross.

The fullness of the Gospel of the Kingdom is that Jesus Christ did not just die for our sins, but He died to crucify our sin nature so that we could receive resurrection power, not just when we die, but now in our mortal bodies (Romans 8:11). The indwelling Spirit provides the wisdom, revelation and power to enable us not to be subject to a lower form of spirituality.

This is what prophecy will remind us of as we work out our own salvation with respect and awe. Scripture and prophecy both call us up to a dynamic partnership. It is God who works in us for His own pleasure (Philippians 2:13). He delights to be involved with us in every aspect of our ongoing experience of redemption.

Before the Cross it was our nature to sin. When Jesus died, however, we died with Him. We were buried with Him. Our old nature is gone. We were raised with Him so that we can now walk in newness of life. We are fully united with Jesus in every aspect of our nature. Our old nature is destroyed and we now have a new nature. He who is dead is freed from sin. Because of our belief that the old nature has passed away, we are free to become a new creation, free to live with Jesus in a new and living way. We joyfully consider ourselves dead to sin and fully alive to God in our position in Jesus (Romans 6:3-11).

It is no longer we who live but Christ who lives in us, and the life which we now live we live by faith in the One who loves us and gave Himself for us (Galatians 2:20). We are dead and our life is hid with Christ in God (Colossians 3:3). Jesus is made unto us wisdom, sanctification, righteousness and redemption (1 Corinthians 1:30).

What we have to overcome, conquer, and crucify in partnership with the Holy Spirit is our flesh. This is our bad habits, poor mindsets, learned behaviors and the memory muscles of a previous way of life that was focused on sin and self. We eliminate the flesh by drawing on the righteousness of Jesus that resides within our own spirit. As we learn to be alive to God, our inward focus becomes our outward behavior. We do not become a new person by changing our behavior in our own strength. Instead, we discover the person that we already are in Christ and behave accordingly. Prophecy tells us who we are in Christ! It reminds us of our new nature.

The Holy Spirit reminds us of who we are in Jesus. Prophecy edifies us in the truth of the Gospel. It presents the eternal facts of life in a way that empowers us within. The Father gives us a hunger and a thirst for righteousness. He does not concentrate on sin. He is focused on righteousness. In putting us into Christ and Christ in us, He challenges us to discover our real identity in His Beloved Son.

> The flesh is the residue of our former life, not the substance of it

We do not own the struggle with sin. We own the freedom of righteousness. We are learning to put on Jesus. We are learning Christ, God's way. In reference to our former life, we are laying aside the old self. We are not dealing with our sin nature, only the old habits that linger in our memory and mindset. We are being renewed in the spirit of our mind so that we joyfully experience our new and true self. This is the likeness of Christ that has been created in the beauty of righteousness and the holiness of truth (Ephesians 4:20-24).

This is the Truth that sets us free. We must view Romans 7 in the context of what has preceded in chapter 6 and what follows in chapter 8. Our struggle is not against sin. It is for freedom. We begin every day with victory, not defeat. Our starting point in salvation is our identification with the death, burial, and resurrection of the Lord Jesus and our glorious inclusion in that process. We always know, through the Holy Spirit, where we are in relation to the finished work of Christ regarding our past. The Father also loves to give us full assurance in relation to the work of the Holy Spirit with regard to our present and future.

Righteousness is not just about having right standing with God in regard to sin. It is also a huge part of our living the life in Christ that God has set aside for us. The key to this lived-out righteousness is a celebration of the life of Christ within and a joyful partnership with the Holy Spirit as we walk in the Spirit in newness of life.

The whole point of Romans 6:1-7:6 is the concern that we are fully identified with Christ in all that He has accomplished. We are released from our old nature and also the law; the system of rules of conduct and performance, initiated by God and overdeveloped by man. Our performance as believers cannot gain us any better position before God. We are granted our acceptance in the Beloved as a pure gift of grace. In order for us to move on in our experiences of God, we must love the grace that underpins our life, saturates our heart, and surrounds us like a fragrant cloud. To live fully exposed to grace is one of the most fulfilling of all life's experiences.

The whole point of Romans 8:1-30 is the role of the everlasting Holy Spirit, in all that He does in working out the righteousness of Christ in the life of the believer. The Presence of the Spirit is brought forward at the end of Romans 7:6:

> *"But now we have been released from the law* (man's religious performance), *having died to that by which we were bound, so that we serve in newness of the Spirit and not in oldness of the letter."*

The place of the Holy Spirit is established as the necessary support for us to become the righteousness of Christ. Jesus is brought forward at the beginning of the role of the Holy Spirit (Romans 8:1-31) as the prior place for that relationship to be founded. We can develop a faithful relationship with God because of our inheritance in Christ and our partnership with the Holy Spirit. Christ in me, the confident expectation of glory!

Our love of grace is a delight to the Lord

Only death and resurrection can lead to newness of life. God's saving work is brought about by Christ and the Holy Spirit. Jesus affects our salvation and the Holy Spirit works it into our lives. He appropriates it to us. Together, they have ended the law (performance) (Galatians 5:13-25). If we are led by the Spirit, we are not under law (Galatians 5:8). Those who belong to Christ have crucified the flesh with its passions and desires (Galatians 5:24). The passions and desires involve the taste, feel, memory, mindset, and longing for sin that make up the flesh; the bad habits of our old man. If we live by the Spirit in our new man, we must also walk by the Spirit (Galatians 5:25), which brings us to Romans 7:7-25 and our so called struggle with sin. This passage explains the former relationship of Torah (law of performance) and sin, while Romans 8:1-17 explains the latter relationship of the Spirit to Torah and flesh as in 8:6: *"the mind set on the flesh is death, but the mind set on the spirit is life and peace."*

When we were in the flesh (past tense) the sinful passions were at work in us, but **now** we have been released so that we serve in the newness of the Spirit. We no longer have a way of life that is in opposition to God as we live in the Spirit.

This does not mean that sin itself is past or that the desires (habits) of the flesh are not still around in the world; but it does mean that we no longer live in that sphere of activity. *"We are crucified to the world and the world to us"* (Galatians 6:4). The words *"but now"* in Romans 7:6 signify that we have moved on from our Jewish or Gentile past to a new life in Christ. A significant part of Romans 7 would appear to be focused mainly on Jewish involvement with the law. *"For do you not know, brethren (**for I am speaking to those that know the law**), that the law has jurisdiction over a person as long as he lives?"* (Romans 7:1)

Romans 7 is both present–past and present–future in its application to the human condition. All religious systems (including mainstream and charismatic Christianity) have a performance orientation based around rules, codes of conduct, and behavior control. The oldness of the letter is past and ended. The newness of the Spirit is present and therefore formational in our experience. Romans 7 is a before and after account of life under Torah and not under Christ. Romans 7:7-25 is Paul's defense of Torah, the law. The law began as a prophecy in the time of Moses; it was an oral outpouring from God to this patriarch and is therefore spiritual (7:14).

This passage describes life before and outside of Christ from the perspective of one who is now in Christ! Life under Torah is like this! It is not describing life in Christ. Sin was everywhere and rampant before Moses. Sin indwelled everyone. People did what was right in their own eyes. They could make their own version of God who would excuse their behavior. People did not class it as sin, but as normal behavior. When the law came, sin was exposed for what it was, hence: *"I would not have known sin except through the (introduction of) law"* (Romans 7:7). Sin was dormant until the Law came and aroused it in the conscience of man.

> *There is no struggle; only freedom not apprehended*

Law can only expose sin, it cannot deal with it. God created atonement, the sacrifice of blood, to cleanse and forgive. The new people (creation) of God are no longer under Torah; they have died to it, and are released from its imprisonment and service. We now know God in newness of life.

This passage (Romans 7:15-25) does not describe a struggle within the believer, between his flesh and the Spirit. It describes what it is like to be under law while in the clutches of sin and the flesh. For the believer in Christ, that situation is in the past. Thanks be to God through Jesus Christ our Lord. He has delivered us from the body of sin. There is no struggle. He that is dead is free! We are learning to stay free! Abiding in Christ is the key discipline of the New Covenant.

The absence of the Presence of the Spirit in this passage (Romans 7:7-25) confirms that Paul is not describing life under the New Covenant. The only struggle here is for the person living under two laws — the law of God and the law of sin. We are now no longer subject to those two laws. We are instead subject to a single dictate, which is the law of the spirit of life in Christ Jesus (Romans 8:2). This wonderful law guarantees no condemnation to believers in Christ as we learn how to put on Christ.

Will we make mistakes as we grow up into all things in Christ? Of course! But as we learn to live in the Spirit and put on Christ, our newness of life propels us into places of relationship that the Old Covenant could not take us. There is no struggle for one who is in Christ. Christ within is our guaranteed goodness from God. The good thing we do comes from Christ personified in our hearts. We are free from the law and sin. He that is dead is free (Romans 6:7).

It is no longer I who live but Christ who lives in me and the life I now live in Him overcomes my flesh. I live by faith in His love and overcoming power (Galatians 2:20). We now have an inheritance in Christ that must occupy our thinking and lifestyle. Far from enduring a struggle, the Father is elevating our walk in the Spirit to include an overcoming identity, an empowering destiny and a place and position of being a joint-heir with the Lord Jesus Christ!

> *The entrance of a positive does violence to any negative*

We do not receive our inheritance when we die. We receive it when someone else dies! What is true in the natural is true in the Spirit. Many Christians believe they must be worthy of their inheritance. That it is in some way tragically linked to their performance as Christians. Our inheritance came when Christ died. It comes from Him and who He is in Heaven for us. It is revealed and made accessible to us because He is in us and we are in Him.

Our inheritance is not given when we go to Heaven in the afterlife. Eternal life is now; therefore we receive our inheritance when Heaven comes to us in the person of the Holy Spirit. His role is to elevate our inner man to a state of conscious fellowship with the Lord. We are not eternal the moment we die. We are eternal the moment we believe. We are seated with Christ in Heavenly places (Ephesians 2:6). In His presence there is fullness of joy and pleasure forever (Psalm 16:11). We have a present–future relationship with God that empowers us in the here and now with an ongoing provision for all time.

Prophecy adores freedom. The Holy Spirit has an intense love and admiration for Jesus. The Truth that sets us free is written in Scripture and echoed in prophecy. He whom the Son sets free is free indeed! There is no struggle. Scripture reveals it and prophecy confirms it.

There is a mindset based on the flesh. As we are learning and establishing our freedom in the Lord Jesus, we must contend with the residue of our illegal past. Our mind must be renewed. Our language must change (from victim to overcomer: from blame shifting to taking personal responsibility) so that we practice agreement with God. The desire to succumb to sin must leave us as we set aside the old nature. We practice the art of being dead to self and alive to God. The best way to do that is always to focus on Jesus — who He is for us and crucially what He has done for us at the Cross.

We do not replace a negative with a positive. That would mean that we are in control of our development. Rather, the Holy Spirit develops the positive to such an extent that the negative is eliminated. The role of the Holy Spirit is always focused on the place of Jesus in the life of the believer. The gift of prophecy must follow the same purpose or be deemed illegal in its ministry and effect. Paul's language regarding the old nature is always in the past tense, whereas our partnership with the Holy Spirit is present.

The mindset that partners with the Spirit creates light life, and focuses on who we are in Christ and what we are becoming in our present circumstances. Life and peace flow from the source of revelation. The gift of prophecy illuminates for us a way to reestablish our standing in Jesus and our walk in the Spirit.

There is no struggle, only an uncompromising desire of the Holy Spirit to edify, exhort and comfort us into our rightful place in Christ. He uses prophecy to upgrade, inspire and joyfully influence us to discover the fullness of all that Jesus died to give us and lives to empower in us.

The Vital Nature of Admonition

I love the sound of the Father's voice in my heart; the firm, melodic intonation of His words that resonate so deeply within. I have heard the thunder of His words like a lion roaring in the same room. It makes one vibrate. The body becomes a tuning fork as the sound of the Creator causes every organ to pulsate with life. He made everything with His word, including man. It is perhaps no wonder that the power of His word could affect us physically, mentally and emotionally, as well as in our spirit.

> A prophet is a heart with a voice

I adore the way that Jesus communes with me. I love the softness of His voice; a whisper, a caress with words. Underneath every utterance one can hear the strength and the power of His heart. The very way that He speaks to us is a revelation in itself. I have been bathed in love, immersed in joy and overwhelmed by peace, just in the intonation of His voice. It is His voice that creates life. The very sound of Him brings forth life in a multitude of ways.

The voice of the Holy Spirit makes me smile, laugh, and stand up on the inside. It is infectious with glory. It is an "everything is possible" voice, full of a wonderful certainty that creates confidence and releases trust. His voice is joyful proclamation. He has a musical quality in His laughter. His smile would keep a small city warm on the coldest day. He radiates certainty. He is contagious with faith. He carries the personality of Heaven and reveals the nature of God within the Truth.

Truth is a person called Jesus. Revelation of God must also reveal His personality. All truth discloses the nature of the Trinity. See God joyfully proclaiming Himself to Moses on the mountain, showing His back and declaring His personality: "I AM is compassionate, gracious, slow to anger, abounding in loving kindness and truth. I AM keeps loving kindness for thousands. I forgive iniquity, transgression and sin. The guilty will not go unpunished and iniquity can be visited on successive generations." (Exodus 34:6-7, author's paraphrase)

He pauses as Moses responds and then resumes:

"Behold, I am going to make a covenant. Before all your people, I will perform miracles which have not been created in all the earth, nor among the nations. All the people in your midst will see the working of the Lord, for it is a terrible (astonishing and amazing) thing I AM going to perform with you." (Exodus 34:10, author's paraphrase)

The Hebrews word for "terrible" is *yârê*. In the context of Moses' dialogue with God, it means to revere and to stand in awe. It is used to describe someone standing in an exalted position where a person or people recognize the power and position of the One who is revered and renders proper respect, such as the twenty-four elders constantly falling down before Him perpetually casting their crowns before the Father in adoration and reverential worship (Revelation 4:9-11).

This covenant was so terrible (powerful) in its application of unity and favor that it became a source of dread to all nations and those in opposition to Israel (Deuteronomy 2:25; 11:25; Exodus 15:14-16; Joshua 2:9).

The Old Covenant constantly supplies us with these amazing pictures of majesty, sovereignty and glory. We see strong images of power, wealth, prosperity, and the glory of Presence among the faithful of God. It all speaks of a relational intentionality emanating from the heart of the Lord. His people represent His Kingdom, His throne, His passion, His purpose and above all, His nature.

The New Covenant constantly supplies us with the language of love, kindness, grace, mercy and GOOD NEWS. Jesus came saying, *"You have heard it said, but now I say to you."* His Sermon on the Mount (Matthew 5) illustrates a new language, perception and approach to spirituality through the Gospel.

This is vital for all prophetic people to understand. Unless our prophetic gift is compatible with the Good News of the Gospel we will become a liability in the Kingdom. We will not be able to differentiate between flesh and spirit and we will damage people rather than develop them.

A prophet is not just a mouthpiece. They are a heart with a voice. They are the intention of God. Imbued with His purpose in the Good News, they are a redemptive voice representing the personality of the One, who is Himself, the Truth. Speaking the Truth in love is a prerequisite for prophecy. There is a difference between what is true and what is truth. Truth is a Person — Jesus Christ (John 14:6). Truth therefore must be about Jesus. It may be true that a person can be fearful but the Truth is that the perfect love of God casts out fear. The one who fears needs to be made mature in love (1 John 4:18). The Truth sets us free (John 8:32). The Truth must become true for us in our experience.

> *God did not write a book then lose his voice!*

Speaking the Truth in love (Ephesians 4:15) is not concerned with speaking out what we find wrong about people and trying to do it in a loving way. We see no one after the flesh (2 Corinthians 5:16). We are looking at people in terms of their potential to become Christ-like. What has the Father provided and set aside for us in Christ? We speak the truth of our new nature in order to inspire people to grow up in Jesus. We do not speak what is true of the old nature that God has already declared dead in Christ! A fountain cannot pour out sweet water and bitter (James 3:11).

If prophetic people cannot use normal speech in a way that glorifies God, then their prophetic utterance will hit a ceiling and level off.

"Let your speech always be with grace, as though seasoned with salt, so that you will know how you should respond to each person." (Colossians 4:6)

"Let no unwholesome word proceed from your mouth, but only such a word as is good for edification according to the need of the moment, so that it will give grace to those who hear." (Ephesians 4:29)

"But now you also, put them all aside: anger, wrath, malice, slander, and abusive speech from your mouth." (Colossians 3:8)

"So then we pursue the things which make for peace and the building up of one another." (Romans 14:19)

"Finally, brethren, whatever is true, whatever is honorable, whatever is right, whatever is pure, whatever is lovely, whatever is of good repute, if there is any excellence and if anything worthy of praise, dwell on these things." (Philippians 4:8)

Ordinary, everyday conversations are a serious part of our training. How we handle confidences before people is of huge importance. Keeping our word, letting our "yes" be yes and our "no" remain no is of high significance. How we navigate loving confrontation, disagreements, and adversarial circumstances are vital. How we respond to accusation, criticism and the party politics of people who are against us will determine if we are to be trusted with the deep sayings of God and the intimate, hidden conversations of His heart. He is not available to a casual seeker (Psalm 119:2).

Our speech is vital to God. Prophecy is not just concerned with content but also with presentation. A good word can be ruined simply by the way it is spoken. A lack of inflection, poor intonation and an absence of emphasis can all conspire to rob a prophecy of its creative spark. Speech is about learning to articulate in a way that envisions and inspires people to see and do. We must see what we hear and be moved by it.

As we pay attention to the method of delivery the content itself becomes more pronounced and therefore more powerful. If a great song can be ruined by a poor singer then prophecy can be similarly abused. A prophetic word should reveal the heart of the One who is behind the message. It will also reveal the heart of the messenger. If the prophet is not in alignment with the heart of God then their lifestyle will detract from the Word.

An upgraded, up-to-date relationship with the Lord is essential if we are to fulfill the prophetic calling. There are lots of prophets whose ability to hear God is greater than their capacity to be changed by Him. Our sensitivity to people is directly linked to our conscious awareness of the nature of God. The further we are from the affections of God, the more damage we will inflict on the people around us. The more cognizant of God's goodness, loving-kindness and mercy, the more easily we will set captives free.

Prophets cannot rely on their carnal insights about people. When we focus on the negatives about people we are exposing our own lack of relationship with the Lord. Every time a prophetic person opens their mouth it is possible to discern the quality of their walk with God. Real prophets build people up in their relationship with the Lord. Prophecy relates people to God's heart for them.

Prophecy is for edification, exhortation and comfort. It reveals the nature of God in the content and the presentation of the spoken word. Jesus introduced in Himself a New Covenant revelation of the prophetic voice of God that resonates with the Good News of the Cross. A price has been paid and judgment suspended in life until the Day of Judgment. The wrath of God has been set aside in Christ until the time of judgment has been set. We are to wait until the Lord comes (1 Corinthians 4:5).

Jesus encouraged His followers to be in relationship with a God who spoke to them personally. The Father did not write a book then lose His voice! He invites people into the Spirit so they can hear the Word, not just read it. The Spirit is of more significance than the letter, which is vital. It is not a case of one in place of another, but one above the other.

The people we read of in Scripture show us all what it is like to hear the voice of God. We read what they heard. We cannot substitute our reading for their hearing, which is immature behavior. God did not behave as a mute. He did not hand Samuel a note so that he could read out a prophecy. People heard God. We are a people who read well, but listen badly.

When we search the Scriptures, we discover that most of the time when we read of "the Word of God" it is verbal, not visual. The Word of God is a voice that must be experienced. People quoted Scripture to Jesus (including the devil). Jesus was not at all impressed but reminded people of the need to hear His voice for themselves. *"My sheep hear my voice"* (John 10:27) and *"He who belongs to God, hears what God says"* (John 8:47).

When our heart is tuned to God every day we will hear Him constantly in all His voices. The deep internal voice arising out of our inner man as we meditate, the cheerful surface voice of God in our renewed mind as we rejoice and give thanks, the intimate whisper of God as we pray and the still, quiet voice as we read Scripture, that, as we pause to reflect, resonates with forceful intimacy in our heart. The audible voice of God is like thunder, like a lion roaring, a happy voice singing, a still small voice intimating, a carefree voice inviting fellowship, a purposeful voice instructing in warfare, a measured voice leading, a provocative voice joyfully proclaiming over us.

> *Our lives are a letter written without ink*

Scripture does not replace the Holy Spirit. Neither is it an additional member of the Godhead. We cannot make it equal with God in status. We do not worship Scripture, but the One the Bible reveals. It is easier for some traditions to revere Scripture more than the One who spoke it into being. The Bible reports what was spoken to encourage us to listen. When we hear God, we have an encounter that releases us into ongoing experience. When our preference for reading overrules our capacity for listening, then we make ourselves redundant in terms of a powerful testimony. Jesus said, *"You diligently study the scriptures because you think that by them you possess eternal life. These are the scriptures that testify about Me, yet you refuse to come to Me to have life"* (John 5:39-40, author's paraphrase). He invites us to read His face as we hear His voice. He never promised us solely a written document. He promised us someone far more wonderful. *"But the Helper, the Holy Spirit, whom the Father will send in*

My name, He will teach you all things" (John 14:26). When we deny the Holy Spirit's place in our lives, we deny the very voice of God in our midst.

Prophecy must produce an encounter with God in the word spoken. Far too many prophets are only interested in the effect the word has on people in the present. They prophesy for a result in terms of agreement or witness to the outcome that the word specifies.

Primarily prophecy is relational. It captures our heart with God. It will connect people to God's affection, not just His intention. Low level prophets do not see themselves as part of God's community of relationship that constantly seeks to connect people with God's passion for them.

We ourselves are a letter written without ink but with the Spirit of the Living God on our hearts (2 Corinthians 3:3-6). God is the great I AM, not the benign I WAS. Maybe our problem is that it is far easier to trust the Scriptures we can control than the God we cannot.

When we hear His voice we receive His personality. We become aware of His nature. We discover that His words unite us with His heart. He is full of Good News because He is wonderfully satisfied with the sacrifice of Jesus. We are learning to put off our old man and put on the new. The way that God speaks to us is intrinsic to that purpose.

Prophecy gives us the opportunity to recalibrate people in the Spirit. We have a grace to break through when we represent God's nature. Of course if we are representing our own nature then admonition is simply not possible. Without God's personality, admonition will become condemnation or worse, judgment. In Christ, mercy has triumphed over judgment which is now suspended (not cancelled) until the end of the age.

Any real prophet is concerned with God's true nature. Has mercy triumphed over judgment in our personality? Do we represent the judge or the redeemer in our ministry? We have to walk in the ministry of displacement.

When we are struggling, failing, and being defeated by life and circumstances, His intention is still to form Christ in us. When our failures are more deliberate and intentional, His heart never changes toward us. He remains the same yesterday, today, and forever. The Good News is not shunted aside in favor of denunciation.

God's heart never changes

Christ was punished for our freedom; therefore the proclamation of freedom is paramount in all that we say. For a prophet, freedom and the nature of God are our prerogative. We cannot help but speak of what we have seen and heard (Acts 4:20).

When people are struggling with sin, they need correction, instruction and training. When they are deliberately not walking in Christ, they will need reproof, rebuke and loving confrontation. The question before us then is this: How do we handle correction, discipline, rebuke, reproof and conviction, while using the correct voice that truly represents God's nature and that does not impugn the Good News of the Lord Jesus Christ?!

The solution to that conundrum lies in our relationship, experience and involvement with the Holy Spirit in His pleasure and willingness to admonish people into transformation. To admonish means to reprimand firmly, but kindly; to urge earnestly by warning. It is a paradox of loving-kindness and undeviating righteousness. It does not take place in a paradigm, which often spiritually, can mean a one dimensional way of looking and dealing with particular issues. All spirituality is paradoxical — two apparently conflicting ideals contained in the same truth. For example, we must give to receive, die to live, be last to be first, humble ourselves to be exalted. The Church is a building and a body, a family and an army. Apostolic ministry is based on agriculture and construction. (1 Corinthians 3:9)

The Old Testament was a paradigm in spiritual terms. It was very black and white in regard to rigid observance of the Law that God gave Moses. The Law was reinforced by the Prophets who would judge and denounce people for sin and would also restore a nation to personal sacrifice and righteousness using the blood of animals. The language was, "Because you have done this, I will do this," says the Lord. The accent was always on performance.

The New Testament is a spiritual paradox of grace and truth. We can be blessed fully as we are learning to grow up in Christ. Grace empowers us to live in the truth and become changed by the goodness and kindness of God. His language is, "Because I have done this (given Jesus as a sacrifice for sin), you may receive this!" The accent is no longer on performance, but acceptance. Jesus fulfilled the Law and the prophets at Calvary (Matthew 5:17). He does that by His sacrifice.

Therefore, any admonition that is focused on only dealing with sin is false. The purpose of admonition is to establish the righteousness of Christ and to develop the identity of the believer in terms of their Sonship. We are accepted in the Beloved (Ephesians 1:6). Admonition must be compatible with the GOOD NEWS of the Gospel or it is fake.

It is false because it carries an Old Testament model, not a New Covenant upgrade. The paradigm of the Old Testament was that people had to earn or deserve their blessing. The paradox of the New Covenant is that everything is "yes" and "Amen" in Christ. We receive fullness while we are making mistakes, learning, and growing because in Christ, we are fully acceptable to the Father. It is Jesus who provides us with our confident place before the throne. In Him we live and move and have our being (Acts 17:28; Galatians 2:20). Real prophets speak to the person in Christ. Poor prophets speak to the flesh in people. The outcome of admonition is to establish Christ and His righteousness through the reception of grace with truth. It is the goodness and kindness of God that leads people to repentance (Romans 2:4).

The Vital Nature of Admonition

The typical example (paradigm) of admonition in the Church is often based on a worldly approach and not a Kingdom value. We have a world-view of admonition that is based around blaming, shaming and punishment. When we try to force change in this manner, it is our own flesh that is dictating the process. We must essentially disapprove of behavior that is against the righteousness of Christ. However, in dealing with that very issue we often step over the same line and behave in a way that is not representative of the goodness and kindness of God. We become what we are against. This is fairly typical Pharisaical behavior. We try to represent God using our old nature, not His nature. We are more focused on the sin than the person involved. Preoccupation with sin makes us more likely to behave in a sinful manner.

Admonition means to help someone check themselves out before God, to urge them to do better, to counsel lovingly but firmly, to draw the line in terms of flesh and spirit, to exhort with grace, to rebuke in love, to reprove so as to make good and to supply cautionary advice. These are all Kingdom expressions that represent the nature of God and the values of Heaven. God is loving and He is holy. He is kind and He is righteous. He is good and He abhors sin. The last thing He would want is for someone to represent His holiness in an unrighteous manner. He detests hypocrisy too!

A pharisee is a Christian who behaves like the world when representing God. There is a self-righteous zeal at work that loves to correct but not empower. A pharisee is one whose legalistic interpretation of Scripture leads to an obsessive concern over rules about everyday life rather than the Spirit of God's essential nature. They are governed by performance, not acceptance.

People who are hypocritical usually have defective judgment that produces fault-finding and censure of others. Hypo (defective, inadequate) critical (judgment). We cannot want the Good News experience for ourselves but deny it to others. The prime parts of prophecy are firstly, the Spirit behind the communication and secondly, the content of the message itself.

Worldly admonition involves the following behaviors: berating people for their behavior, censuring them in some manner, criticizing instead of supporting change, blaming them for their choices, making them feel ashamed directly, coming down hard on people, castigating them, using condemnation to change thinking, lecturing instead of listening, punishing instead of resorting, invalidating their life and ministry because of their mistakes, being more intent on refuting, negating and proving false their calling rather than upgrading their identity. Accusing, defaming and discrediting people to others, thinking that we are serving God's holiness by putting a stain and a stigma on the life of another.

Be schooled in the nature of God

These are all forms of worldly counseling that demonstrate an unconscious contempt for the love, grace, kindness, mercy and goodness of God. Our problem in church is not untrained counselors, but people who are not schooled in the nature of the Father. Admonition can only be successful when it is earthed in a paradox. We handle our disapproval of their behavior by accepting who they are in Christ. We are firm, but non-judgmental.

"Brethren, even if anyone is caught in any trespass, you who are spiritual, restore such a one in a spirit of gentleness; each one looking to yourself, so that you too will not be tempted. Bear one another's burdens, and thereby fulfill the law of Christ. For if anyone thinks he is something when he is nothing, he deceives himself." (Galatians 6:1-3)

Only a hypocrite would violate the principle of being in Christ. Only a humble heart can use admonition well. The issue here is not about how we handle disapproval and show acceptance at the same time. The question is: do we see their trespass as a burden we can share with them and therefore fulfill the Law of Christ, which is to love others as we would want to be loved ourselves?

Admonition is about involvement in the issue and therefore providing the required relational input to provoke breakthrough. Admonition is not a function of ministry; it is the relationship of God-to-man and person-to-person. Discipline without development equals punishment.

Admonition is distinguished from condemnation by the spirit that is seen behind the words. If restoration is not at the very heart of admonition, our gentleness isn't going to be genuine. We may initially cloak our words in gentleness and even humility, but the more we interact with people's issues, the more the real spirit is going to emerge. What drives us cannot be hidden. What motivates us will be revealed. When our walk with God is solely about pleasing Him, His nature cannot be denied.

The law of Christ is love for God and love for one another. The love of God constrains us (2 Corinthians 5:14) and holds us together. It is our joy to be compelled by love; to be preoccupied by the height, depth, length and breadth of God's love for us, and then to secure other people in that same revelatory experience.

In the face of outrageous sin, from so-called Christians who have no desire to change, and whose very behavior acts as a contaminant within the Church, we have little choice. The Corinthian church lived in a society that was rife with sexual sin. No woman was safe. Indeed the only way in that culture to distinguish between Christian women and temple prostitutes was for church-going women to wear something on their head. Sexual license was the order of the day. It would, of course, be a societal issue in that city.

Within the church, a man claiming to be a believer was engaged in sexual activity with his father's wife (probably a stepmother). He was arrogant, even boastful about it (1 Corinthians chapter 5). It is possible that the Corinthian church was trying to practice tolerance or they had a limited view of grace. Real grace does not make excuse for sin, but instead provides a place where people can be empowered to repent, receive restoration and become like Jesus. Grace is limitless; freedom outside of Christ is not. Grace does not allow sin because sin is bondage and death. Freedom outside of Jesus will take people into captivity. Freedom in Christ maintains its power by restraining and crucifying the flesh. The congregation as a whole would be off-limits for the man but he would still have involvement with some people who were helping him with his problems. People do not change in a vacuum. Discipline without development is punishment. Admonition is concerned with restoration.

> There is no freedom without restraint

The individual concerned was already serving the enemy more than Christ. He needed to be separated from the protection of Christ so that he could feel the consequences of his actions. The destruction of the flesh (ungodly habits, mindsets, choices and behaviors) is a valuable part of our growing up into all things in Christ. We cannot see liberty as a cloak for vice (1 Peter 2:16). It cannot be used as a reason to allow sin, nor can it be used to cover up sin that has been committed. Liberty must be concerned with morality or we are all in danger.

The intentionally wicked among us, who have no desire for change, but who are arrogant about their lifestyle, cannot be tolerated. Leaven is a substance that has a huge impact on whatever it is in. The church was tolerating sexual sin. This leaven could affect the whole community. In a sexually permissive culture, the Church must maintain its purity of behavior. Unchallenged sin will dominate the community and contaminate its spirituality.

The man was guilty of sin. The church was guilty of tolerance. In failing to hold him accountable they had become culpable. Any new believer would have cause to commit immorality because the example had been set. Existing Christians would have been driven to step away from holiness or from involvement in the church.

Where there is no repentance, a person cannot be wholly transformed. Arrogant sin is costly. To their credit, the church followed Paul's advice. The man was put out of fellowship. He was faced with his lifestyle and the church set an important criterion for their spiritual community. Without the protection of grace and gracious friendships, he came to his senses and was empowered to repent and put away this lifestyle.

In his next letter to this community, Paul commented that this treatment of the man was sufficient to cause him real godly sorrow so that change could occur in his heart. We must be appalled at our own sin and make no provision for works of the flesh. Paul urged them to forgive, comfort and restore the man (2 Corinthians 2:3-11). The church reaffirmed their love for the individual and he was restored to community. Love was the motivating factor for the church throughout the process.

Paul's heart in this matter was clean and firm. Admonition must cost us first. We need to examine ourselves and our own morality. Do we have areas in our own lives that are in the shadows (Galatians 6:1)? In writing to Corinth, Paul had been in tears over the issue. He wrote out of affliction for the church and the individual. In subjecting this man to church discipline, Paul was thinking of both parties. The purpose of corporate discipline is repentance and restoration. The whole exercise for Paul was that *"You might know the love which I have so abundantly for you."* (2 Corinthians 2:4)

Incidentally, Paul wrote to Corinth on the prior occasion to urge them not to have internal fellowship with certain types of behaviors that would seriously affect the ongoing spiritual, moral health of the community. We are all familiar with the avoiding in our congregation of anyone involved with sexual immorality, covetous behavior, idolatry, drunkenness or extortion. However, Paul also names a reviler (1 Corinthians 5:11) as one of those whose behavior is deemed to be toxic. This is someone who is continually abusive to people, is spiteful, rails at people, and makes mischief. A reviler is one who criticizes abusively. A religious reviler is one who talks against people using the Name of Jesus as a cloak. Not speaking the truth in love would fall into this category. How we speak about people to others is vital. How we represent another individual or group must be truthful, honorable and humble, if it cannot also be loving, kind and generous. Revilers are less likely to be noticed and their toxic nature more easily tolerated, but they do as much, if not more harm, than anything or anyone else.

When Paul used the word "judge" (1 Corinthians 5:3) in his first injunction, he used the word *krino*, which in this particular context means to assess, to distinguish between one thing and another. He was pronouncing an opinion between right and wrong; the reception of which would support the church in making a determination and showing a resolve in order to decree a proper course of action. His heart in the matter is a great example of paradox; wonderfully loving, and yet completely firm.

Admonition must be distinguished from condemnation by the spirit that is behind the words. To admonish means to rebuke with the truth in such a way that it releases people to a better confession of Jesus. All Scripture is inspired by God (2 Timothy 3:16) and is profitable for teaching, reproof, correction and training in righteousness. It is fascinating that reproof and correction are firmly placed in connection to teaching and training. Also that the chief element used in this context is inspiration.

> *Admonition must cost us first*

In our counseling of people, before we tackle any issue, we must ask the question, Who do you want to become in this situation? Not, what do you need to do? Who do you want to become? The most critical part of discipling someone lies in establishing their identity.

When Jesus was preparing to go up to Jerusalem to die, He made arrangements for the journey. People who did not understand His purpose refused to receive Him. James and John were indignant on His behalf and wanted to call down fire from Heaven to consume these people. Jesus quietly rebuked them by saying, *"You do not know what kind of spirit you are of, for the Son of Man did not come to destroy men's lives, but to save them"* (Luke 9:51-56). They did not grasp their identity. Most of our problems are a matter of identity. When we allow people and circumstances to overwhelm us, our identity in Christ is revealed and we must apply for an upgrade. When we react angrily or negatively to situations, the same applies.

All pastoring and mentoring is concerned with identity. People who judge or condemn do not know who they really are in Christ. They are missing a vital piece of themselves. Lack of the right spirit motivates the flesh. What we abide in is what we become.

Again, in his mentoring of Timothy, Paul reinforces the concept of reproof and rebuke being part of a preaching and instruction context (2 Timothy 4:2). Admonition is centered on edifying, not pulling people down. To exhort

> *People who revile others are toxic to themselves*

with great patience is wonderful language, full of love and encouragement. Identity takes time to develop. Mistakes, errors of judgment, misconceptions and poor choices are all a feature of our lives until the life of Christ takes hold of us effectively. People need loving challenge about their identity. They need to be told who they are, not condemned for not being what they have yet to attain.

Children need instruction and loving-kindness. There is no point in parents shouting at or berating children. They do not develop confidence or a love of learning that way. I have two brilliant granddaughters. Evelyn Rose is three and Annabelle Heather is one. I love watching my daughter,

> *The key to transformation is identity*

Sophie, and son-in-law, Mark, teaching them about life, sharing, obedience, and being part of a family. The training and instruction is firm, loving, gentle and kind, often with a touch of humor and lots of affection.

Everyone needs encouragement. I am constantly astounded at the Father's deep affection for me. I love the warm, patient, kind disposition of Jesus. I am always surprised at the humor and enthusiasm that the Holy Spirit demonstrates toward me in my own learning. They help me to understand and receive my identity in them!

All things become visible when they are exposed to the light because everything that becomes visible is light (Ephesians 5:13). The Holy Spirit sheds light on who we are. He makes our identity visible in Christ. He exposes us in such a way that as we comprehend and receive it, we become what we see and desire. Sin has been dealt with in Jesus. The Holy Spirit is promoting who we are in Christ and who He is in us. He is always pointing to Christ within, showing us both our identity and our destiny. Prophecy exposes us to the light. It tells us who we are and what we can become. The result of exposure to the light is that we move toward it. It is not enough simply to pull people away from darkness; we must instill a desire for the light. To walk in the light is everything.

When we practice the truth we come into the light. We are bringing people up in the nature of God. Their deeds reveal their exposure. The wrath of man cannot achieve the righteousness of God (James 1:20). We must encourage people into a love of being in the light. In using admonition, we are creating a hunger and a thirst for righteousness. We are seeking to establish relationships of openness and honesty.

People must be advantaged by the Presence of the Holy Spirit (John 16:7), who is our constant source of help and personal support. He convicts the world about sin, righteousness and judgment (John 16:9-11). He develops us according to the nature of Christ, not the nature of man. He provides positive instruction and training in righteousness according to our identity in Christ.

I love Paul's language in Romans 15:14: *"And concerning you, my brethren, I myself also am convinced that you yourselves are full of goodness, filled with all knowledge and able to also admonish one another."* What a context for admonishing! Goodness and knowledge of all that Christ is for us are two of the major requirements for supporting the learning of other people! Admonish here is *noutheteo*, which means to call to mind. It is designed to help people remember who they are in Jesus. It can come in the form of a mild rebuke, but mostly it represents training by the word.

It is a kind of "Don't forget, this is who you really are in Christ" approach to life. Occasionally it may manifest itself in a warning based on instruction. The conviction behind it is based on who Jesus is for us, and what He is capable of releasing and upgrading. Admonition does not denigrate people; it calls them up to a higher level of spirituality. That fits right in with the prophetic, which is to edify, exhort and comfort.

Admonition is a relational activity that empowers us into new dimensions of spiritual experience with the Lord. It is founded on establishing our identity and developing our personality in Christ. Paul's request of people was that they should value and appreciate people who are diligent in our development; especially those who instruct (admonish) us in the Lord. Those who help us pay attention to our true self are to be highly esteemed and much loved (1 Thessalonians 5:12-13). If admonition was focused only on a negative in bringing a rebuke that was a put-down, I seriously doubt that Paul's request would have been received with any enthusiasm.

Our deeds reveal our exposure

It is a wonderful experience to encounter the love that the Holy Spirit has for the Word of God. He has such uninhibited joy about every word spoken from Heaven. He loves the Living Word — Jesus. He loves the written word — Scripture. He loves the spoken word — prophecy. He loves the taught word and the words that flow in worship. He is a great hymn and songwriter. He is wonderfully poetic. Words are His thing. He has a feel

The Vital Nature of Admonition

for exactly the right word and the best way to say it. Many times I have been broken by His kind words and totally energized by His word of faith. Words are His business. Words are the biggest part of the expression of Heaven on earth. They express intentionality and promise. They provoke trust and faith, creating confidence. They inspire, overcome, upgrade and increase in line with a God who loves abundance and fullness.

Admonition is a part of that context. We become good at encouraging, training, warning and instructing because the Holy Spirit enthusiastically directs our heart into a place of confidence and delight in the Lord Jesus. As we are being made into the likeness of Christ, our heart becomes more gentle and attuned to grace, mercy and truth. We learn from the Holy Spirit how to speak so that people are inspired to press into Jesus.

We are developing a capacity to be rich in the Word. Not in terms of memorization techniques, but more in line with becoming the Word in actual lifestyle experience. We have all met people who can quote large chunks of Scripture, but we wouldn't buy a used Bible off them. When we set out to live the Word, we are opening ourselves up to the wisdom of how to walk with God. Wisdom is the experiential knowledge of how God thinks, how He perceives, and how He likes to do things. We learn the ways of being with God. We become rich in revelation and encounter. We know how to wait on God, how to move with Him, how to hear His voice, and how to position ourselves properly to take advantage of what even the enemy is doing. Prophets find the joy in releasing people from captivity. The Good News of the Gospel is the word that was prophesied concerning Christ by Isaiah:

> "The Spirit of the Lord is upon me, because the LORD has anointed me to bring good news to the afflicted; He has sent me to bind up the brokenhearted, to proclaim liberty to captives and freedom to prisoners; to proclaim the favorable year of the LORD and the day of vengeance of our God; to comfort all who mourn, to grant those who mourn in Zion, giving them a garland instead of ashes, the oil of gladness instead of mourning, the mantle of praise instead of a spirit of fainting. So they will be called oaks of righteousness, the planting of the LORD, that He may be glorified. Then they will rebuild the ancient ruins, they will raise up the former devastations; and they will repair the ruined cities, the desolations of many generations. Strangers will stand and pasture your flocks, and foreigners will be your farmers and your vinedressers. But you will be called the priests of the LORD; you will be spoken of as ministers of our God. You will eat the wealth of nations, and in their riches you will boast. Instead of your shame you will have a double portion, and instead of humiliation they will shout for joy over their portion. Therefore they will possess a double portion in their land, everlasting joy will be theirs." (Isaiah 61:1-7)

Prophecy Eliminates Negativity

The identity statement of Jesus is the mission mandate for all prophetic people. Good news to those afflicted by life and bound up in their pain. The proclamation of liberty and the creation of freedom to captives are at the very heart of the prophetic. Favor in God, vengeance against the evil one, and the bringing of comfort to those who are distressed are key components of the prophetic. Admonition must fit in with the identity of Jesus.

The prophetic is concerned with divine displacement, giving people a sense of beauty about themselves over the ashes of their own self-loathing and bitterness. Prophecy adds to the joy of people by supplanting any negative that causes grief. A real prophet is a cause for celebration. Prophets bring hope and faith that releases a mantle of praise that destroys depression and hopelessness. Prophets rebuild, raise up and repair every damaging thing that has brought degradation and ruin. Admonition fits into that ministry.

Prophecy blots out our disgrace, humiliation and shame. It releases joy into the parts of our life where we have come into disrepute, scandal and the contempt of others.

In this context we become adept at training others, especially in the powerful instructions of how to stay in fellowship and remain abiding in Jesus. We learn that admonition is a prophetic art form that empowers people to live within the language and values of Heaven. We become so good at admonishing people that we could even set it to music. Colossians 3:16 is a fascinating insight into the generous nature of admonition. How can we not love instructing, warning, mildly reproving and encouraging another in this great life we have been given?

Bringing people up in the nurture and discipline of the Lord is as satisfying as parenting. Indeed, if we adapt the role and heart of a good loving parent, we are most likely to experience the Father ourselves. Admonition for the most part is a joyful transaction. As long as we imitate the Holy Spirit and walk after the example of Christ, even the difficult

> Admonition is a prophetic art form

scenarios of admonishing others can provide us with opportunities to enhance our own growth and development. I have faced hard circumstances with some very intransigent people. It helps to know that it is not our responsibility to change people, but to demonstrate the nature of God and desire the good of the one we are connecting with for blessing. When we are solely present to get results, we completely miss the point of the interaction. We can provoke people into a defensive or offended mindset (Ephesians 6:4). Not listening or failing to hear one another is a breach of fellowship. We are present to win someone's heart toward Jesus (Matthew 18:15).

Difficult people must, out of necessity, crop up in our life since they are one of our biggest aids to growth, particularly in the fruit of the Spirit. Patience, kindness and long-suffering are vital characteristics to acquire. We must never avoid difficult circumstances or people. We must use the opportunities for what they are — a potential accelerant into a better spiritual experience that carries with it a relational upgrade.

Sometimes our learning is retrospective. If we cannot learn in the situation itself, then we must learn retroactively. We can retrace the steps we took in a situation to learn what we could have done better or gather the learning that we overlooked. Feedback is the lost art of discipleship. Paul uses a brilliant piece of Israel's history retrospectively in order to introduce to the Corinthian church some positive instruction concerning how to admonish one another (1 Corinthians 10:1-13). He uses Israel as an example of how to blow it when you are on the journey toward a place of incredible promise. Israel craved evil, was idolatrous, played around, was immoral, grumbled, and tested God. All these things are examples of what not to do and how not to behave when your whole future prosperity is on the line. Paul says they were written "For our instruction" — literally to admonish us in the present and to empower us to call this example to mind so that we can avoid the same result.

Admonition is extremely helpful in our self-examination. Are we on track? How do we get back on track? Taking heed that we are not deceived is the point of true admonition. It restores us to the nature of God, the plans of God and the faithfulness of God to walk this road with us in fellowship. Admonition enables us to endure hardness and conflict so that we remain in a position to inherit what the Father has promised.

How will you partner with people in admonition? What has to change in your heart that enables you to play a part in a series of actions that achieve the outcomes that the Father desires? Admonition is a learning process designed to advance people's growth in the Spirit. Define the spirit of breakthrough that is upon your prophetic gift. What is your particular passion regarding displacement? Write your own identity statement regarding your role in the prophetic.

> Connect with people for their blessing

True Shame and the Power of Potential

To admonish someone is to seek their highest good. It means we may have a desire for them that is at least as great as their own, but hopefully in line with God's intentionality toward them. This brings us to potentially the hardest part of true admonition.

How do we handle people who refuse to obey the instructions of God and are careless of their behavior and its effect and impact on other people? How do we relate to people who are a continual source of aggravation and annoyance? How do we connect with people who are abusive, blame shifting, refuse responsibility and are uncaring of the needs of others? How do we respond to people who delete their own worst behavior, distort the actions or words of another out of all proportion and who generalize about their personal accountability?

Often they exhibit no conscience and are not remotely embarrassed at the situation in which they find themselves. Clearly in these cases, admonition must go to a deeper level of instruction.

Paul was always on guard for any wolves in sheep's clothing. He knew that a major part of the enemy's strategy revolves around penetration, demoralization, and subversion. Infiltration is always one of the enemy's best tactics. Christians who abuse Christians are more powerful than the demonic because they are harder to dispel. We can take authority over the devil. The enemy cannot disillusion us nor betray us because we know his character and demeanor. We are not surprised or hurt.

Other believers get under our guard. We can become hugely dispirited, discouraged, and undermined by people whom we expect more from in terms of behavior. All my biggest disappointments have been relational, which is why I want to be the best friend possible. I love relationships. I have many great friendships, loads of good friends, and some fabulous relationships. I am not in any way jaundiced about past relational disappointments.

Paul hears of people who are undisciplined, don't work, and act as busybodies (2 Thessalonians 3:11-15). In the context of their behavior he instructs people to do the opposite and not become weary in developing goodness as a lifestyle. Goodness in our lives is the living proof that we are walking with God. It is a goodness far greater than the world can imagine or produce. It does not take into account its own needs, but seeks the blessing and benefit of another. We do not consume goodness; we receive it so that we can become a contribution to people around us. We embrace goodness and take it deep within so that our perceptions, mindsets, choices and behaviors become radically different.

There is no value to the Kingdom if we live according to the dictates of the society around us. We must be aware of the type of community we wish to create in our village, town or city. It must be noticeably different from the world around us. It requires more than a vision about the work. It involves developing a set of values that determine how we will relate to one another, regardless of circumstances. The Lord is unchanging because Heaven has values that govern outlook and conduct. He is forever the same. He is not capricious, He is constant. Whether we do well or badly, He is consistent toward us in love, grace, kindness and goodness. His love is kind and firm. His heart is fixed toward us. It is His goodness and kindness that leads us to repentance. He does not withdraw love from us when we are not doing well. He demonstrated love toward us initially in that while we were still sinners, Christ died for us. Now that we are redeemed, we are saved by His life in us (Romans 5:8-11). The major part of our praise, worship, rejoicing, and giving thanks emanates from the exultation we feel because of His manifest Presence within our spirit!

> *Goodness is the living proof of Godly relationship*

True Shame and the Power of Potential

Goodness is a by-product of the life within. How we perceive people, how we handle relationships and deal with discrepancies is all motivated by love, kindness, and goodness. We help people find the grace they need so they can be transformed. We never leave people friendless. We do not treat people as enemies. Our community is founded on restoration and renewal. This is the context for what comes next in Paul's letter to the church at Thessalonica:

"If anyone does not obey our instruction in this letter, take special note of that person and do not associate with him, so that he will be put to shame. Yet do not regard him as an enemy, but admonish him as a brother." (2 Thessalonians 3:14-15)

On the surface there appears to be a contradiction regarding Paul's injunction concerning the disobedient. Firstly, the believers are told not to associate with these people, then in the next breath they are instructed to treat them as brothers and keep on admonishing them. This obviously involves continuous contact and connection.

These people are not involved in sexual immorality, idolatry, drunkenness, covetousness, reviling or extortion. Mostly they are lazy and good for nothing, telling tales, spreading stories and freeloading off others. They are takers who do not make any useful contribution to the community.

These people need some personal discipline regarding work. They need admonishing, which is to be reminded of who they are in Christ. They need instruction from the community on how to live and conduct themselves. We treat them as brothers, not enemies. We cannot have a relationship with an enemy. An enemy is someone who is actively opposed or hostile to us.

Help people to find the grace they need!

A brother is both a relative in our family and an associate or fellow member of an organization. Clearly Paul is not saying to sever the relationship. I believe he is saying *be careful what type of fellowship you have with these people.* He is instructing people on the one hand not to keep company with the way they are behaving. The Greek word here is *sunanamignumi,* which means "mix together with."

On the other hand, Paul is saying they need instruction and exposure to the light. The key part of this "relate but don't mix" dynamic, is the introduction of shame into the context of restoration.

We are to take special note of how each of these people is behaving. We do not keep company with them **in this behavior**. For example, if a person is lazy and not working but shows up at dinner — no food. *"If anyone will not work, neither let him eat"* (2 Thessalonians 3:10). If his heart does not get the message, his stomach will.

If they are telling tales about others or spreading gossip, we must be emphatically clear about our own position. For me personally, that would involve picking up the phone in their presence and calling the person who is the focus of the gossip. "Hey Pete, this is Graham. Listen, I have John here who is telling me some things about you that are not good. Has he spoken to you directly about these things? He hasn't? Okay, I'll put him on so he can tell you himself." I would then hand the phone over. Is that embarrassing for them? You bet it is.

One guy was shocked and enraged. When he had calmed down enough for a decent conversation, I shared my observations with him. "When you were relaying the gossip to me, you were animated, lively and energized. When I put you on the phone you were embarrassed, flustered and mortified. Why the difference in behavior? That difference was shame. You knew that you were doing something wrong when you were talking to me. You are always welcome in my home and in my life, but that behavior is not who you really are in Christ. When you hear something about someone, check it out. Call the person and ask them. It may be malicious gossip from which they need our protection and support. It may be true in which case they will need a good friend. You are better than this. I believe you can be a good man and a good friend."

It eventually led into a conversation that provoked some change. He never did the gossip thing with me again. It is important for us to be clear about who we are and who we want to become. That makes us consistent with Christ on our journey.

Shame is valuable, but it must be godly. It must come to us fresh from the Kingdom. Worldly shame is sick and despicable. It humiliates another. It brings dishonor, contempt and degradation. Worldly shame detaches people from grace, which is what we call disgrace. They feel unclean, unworthy and wretched.

Shame is too valuable to use unwisely

Godly shame is best generated indirectly. I did not directly confront my friend with his gossip behavior. I put him in contact with the individual so that he could explain himself. Paul does not say, "You put him to shame" directly. He intimates that by closing ranks against this type of behavior, the individual will be embarrassed enough to look at what they are doing. The Greek word for shame is *entrepo* which signifies: to invert, to turn people inward to contemplate their behavior, and to teach people a reverence for truth and goodness.

It is a wholesome shame which involved a change of conduct. It creates a turning point within oneself that produces recoil from what is wrong. If we apply shame directly we will lose the person from the restoration process. We need to be as wise as a serpent and harmless as a dove. Nathan the prophet understood the value of true shame and applied it in his friendship with David the King:

> "Then the LORD sent Nathan to David. And he came to him and said, 'There were two men in one city, the one rich and the other poor. The rich man had a great many flocks and herds. But the poor man had nothing

except one little ewe lamb which he bought and nourished; and it grew up together with him and his children. It would eat of his bread and drink of his cup and lie in his bosom and was like a daughter to him. Now a traveler came to the rich man, and he was unwilling to take from his own flock or his own herd to prepare for the wayfarer who had come to him; rather he took the poor man's ewe lamb and prepared it for the man who had come to him.'

Then David's anger burned greatly against the man, and he said to Nathan, 'As the LORD lives, surely the man who has done this deserves to die. He must make restitution for the lamb fourfold, because he did this thing and had no compassion.' Nathan then said to David, 'You are the man! Thus says the LORD God of Israel, "It is I who anointed you king over Israel and it is I who delivered you from the hand of Saul. I also gave you your master's house and your master's wives into your care, and I gave you the house of Israel and Judah; and if that had been too little, I would have added to you many more things like these! Why have you despised the word of the LORD by doing evil in His sight? You have struck down Uriah the Hittite with the sword, have taken his wife to be your wife, and have killed him with the sword of the sons of Ammon. Now therefore, the sword shall never depart from your house, because you have despised Me and have taken the wife of Uriah the Hittite to be your wife." Thus says the LORD, "Behold, I will raise up evil against you from your own household; I will even take your wives before your eyes and give them to your companion, and he will lie with your wives in broad daylight. Indeed you did it secretly, but I will do this thing before all Israel, and under the sun."'

Then David said to Nathan, 'I have sinned against the LORD.' And Nathan said to David, 'The LORD also has taken away your sin; you shall not die. However, because by this deed you have given occasion to the enemies of the LORD to blaspheme, the child also that is born to you shall surely die.' So Nathan went to his house." (2 Samuel 12:1-15)

> The root cause of sin is disrespect for God

Nathan knows that David is a man after God's heart. He is essentially a fair man who has completely lost his way. He is using his position to steal, kill and destroy — just like the enemy. He has stolen Uriah's wife, killed him, and destroyed his family. In telling the story, Nathan gets in touch with that essential decency and justice in David that has been overwhelmed by his lust for Bathsheba. David responds to the injustice in the story and declares what needs to happen. This is indirect counseling at its best. At this point Nathan says, "You are this man!"

Prophecy Eliminates Negativity

Shame shocks us into realignment. It opens us up to our own behavior. It throws back the curtains, rolls up the blinds and floods the room of our conscious heart with light. There is no escape. At this point the word of the Lord needs to enter. People need to see that primarily our poor behavior is against God. As believers we sin because we do not value our relationship with the Lord.

David's response is, *"I have sinned against the Lord."* He has also sinned against Bathsheba, Uriah and their family. He has sinned against the throne of Israel as well as the people of Israel and Judah. This is important. We must not just deal with sin and its impact on other people. The root cause of sin is a disrespect of God. Unless that is dealt with first, then the person will reoffend later. They will be more careful not to get caught by people. They will not be transformed because their inner self has not conformed to the image of Jesus.

In grace we must be emphatic. "You have sinned against the Lord and that must be put right first. Then we can deal with the impact and fallout on others." If we rush into restitution and reconciliation with others too quickly, we will not cure the problem. We will simply drive it underground. If we do not take time to deal with the level of personal disrespect that they have for Christ, they cannot be transformed. They may change behavior initially but will fall back eventually into their old ways.

The foundation of transformation is the restoration of first love. We cannot realize our true identity outside of the affection of God.

True shame is vital to this process. A wholesome shame creates contrition, self-reproof and real self-examination. This is necessary because people have chosen their old nature above their new creation. They have chosen flesh over spirit. We do not shame people; we allow them to feel shame by their own internal introspection. We invert them so that they contemplate not just their behavior but also their identity.

What is it that they believe about themselves that makes them behave in this way? That perception has become their deception. That negativity empowers people to behave badly and feel justified. Shame is a vital shock to the system but only if it is godly. It must be put there by the Holy Spirit. If we put it there, the reaction may be that people become offended and withdraw, they become defensive and put up a wall, or they can become victimized because of how you made them feel (smokescreen). The shame that we engender will enliven the flesh. True shame elevates the inner man of the spirit back to its rightful position.

> Perception is either our inspiration or our deception

We cannot properly exhort, encourage or admonish people if we only express our disapproval. We need to declare our commitment to them as people. They must see our willingness for engagement and support of their true identity in Christ. Do not treat people as enemies, but as brothers. We have a relationship and we want to safeguard our fellowship. Our relationship is not under attack; that should be safe and inviolate in Jesus. It is our fellowship that is under huge threat. Fellowship is the external outworking of an internal relationship.

To my shame, I have brought shame directly into people's lives. I made them feel bad because they were bad. I offended some and wounded many. When we accuse we do the work of the accuser (Revelation 12:10). Mostly I saw people withdraw or drive their behavior underground. I have reaped what I sowed. I have been on the receiving end of other people's direct shame input into my own life. It's a horrid experience. There is a more excellent way. To repent is to take the inward journey of transformation. Worldly shame often prevents that from happening.

True shame liberates people to find God and discover His Father's heart. God has no feelings of shame in His heart toward us. He is joyfully part of our sanctification process. For this reason He is not ashamed to call us brothers (Hebrews 2:11). He is not ashamed to be called our God (Hebrews 11:16). Our relation with the Father is built on such a profound confidence in His Name and Nature that we are never allowed to be destroyed by shame at His involvement in our lives. Hope does not make us ashamed (Romans 5:5; 10:11). The word used in these two scriptures is *kataischuno*, which translated means disgraced, confounded. To have such feelings of fear or shame that it prevents a person from doing something or receiving something from God. Godly shame reveals His love and our actions at the same time. Desire for God converts our shame into confidence that we can boldly approach the throne of grace in order to receive mercy and find grace to help us in our time of need (Hebrews 4:16).

There are two kinds of shame. The first is from the Kingdom which empowers us to develop a reverence for the truth. It is a wholesome change that allows us to examine where we are and rediscover the goodness of God. It is transformational.

The second type of shame is worldly. It humiliates without empowering. It causes disgrace rather than an opportunity to change. It contains dishonor, contempt, and degradation. It detaches people from the goodness of God and allows people to feel unworthy and wretched. It prevents the discovery of God's nature and creates inertia at a time when we need momentum.

The prophetic must edify, exhort and comfort people. Therefore it must confront what is attacking them without denigrating the individual or the group. We must have a passion for what Jesus loves and we need a hatred of the devil and all his works. Prophets set people free. We do not imprison them or add to their burden. We are able to do that because we have compassion for people.

People get into a bad place with God and humanity because they have been abused and degraded, are uncaring and irresponsible, are self-centered and selfish, are arrogant and hard-hearted, and love the dark more than the light. These traits are what make us traitorous. We become two-faced, faithless, double-crossing people who betray the ones that care for them. Worldly shame will encase all those characteristics and not bring release from the bondage of the enemy.

At a meeting on the East Coast of America, I gave an altar call and watched people coming down to the front of the building to receive prayer. I saw a tall, young guy standing off to one side, head bowed. My heart was drawn to him as I prayed over the group. I saw two of the ministry team approach him at different times and pray with him. He visibly flinched each time and stood like a rock, hardened and impervious. Yet he remained standing at the front. I asked the Lord what was going on with him. I could feel the Lord's smile of affection as He said, "he is into lust and pornography and he thinks I don't love him. He hates himself and is full of self-loathing, and he thinks that I feel the same way about him."

We have all done that at one time or another. Put our own feelings about ourselves onto God. Later, I discovered that this young man had been sexually abused as a child by an older brother. His father and brother were extremely close and when the young boy attempted to ask for help and support, he became the one that was outcast. His father was livid with rage and so the abuse continued until he became strong enough to fight off the attentions of his brother. As so often can happen, the abused becomes an abuser. He had scores of deviant and perverted sexual relationships with women. He was addicted to hard core pornography. Miraculously he had met Jesus and loved Him. His inability to change his habits had left him in the shadows, standing at the edge of the light. Wanting freedom, feeling trapped. He told me later that he had received ministry a number of times and either absolutely nothing happened or he left feeling more ashamed, more self hatred, and more distant from God's love. He was caught, snared in the performance trap, trying to earn God's love and favor. Twice, he had been given prophetic ministry. Both times people had received a word of knowledge about his problems. On each occasion he had been exposed in his sin but not helped. Relationships around him deteriorated and he was forced to move on. Yet here he was, presenting himself to God!

As I looked at him, I could feel God's heart for him. It was a tangible affection. Sin has been dealt with in Christ so there are no obstacles to love except what is in our own hearts. There is no enmity, anger, or displeasure in God's heart toward sinners. He is well pleased with the sacrifice of Jesus. The Advocate has paid the price and people are free to be loved regardless of their character, bad habits and stupidity. The Father did not see the sin; He saw the pain. Sin has been taken away and nailed to a tree (Colossians 2:13-14). The sin nature is dead and the sin habit can now be overcome by love, grace, and truth.

As I approached the young man, I could feel the Father's affection and compassion for him. I could see in the man's eyes the despair of separation from God; the self-loathing and the helplessness. He flinched as I put my arms around him. Steel shutters came down all around him. Sensible boy. We must protect ourselves in a hostile world, but not when the King of love is present. Grace is a fabulous lock-picker. God can undo us with mercy and kindness. This man, more than anything, wanted to be clean. He felt filthy and was full of shame about his immorality and impurity. He was contaminated, polluted and defiled. It came off him in waves.

Prophecy moves in the opposite spirit. The Father showed me the man's condition so that I would understand the depth of his personal dilemma. As I understood his pain, my heart was flooded with compassion. I prophesied to him about a cleansing period of refining and restoration. The joy of being clean now! A history expunged, a mindset expurgated and a lifestyle erased. Grace picked the lock of his heart and all the defenses crumbled. He held onto me and wept. The meeting closed down around us as a disgraced human being discovered the esteem of being in Christ and the feeling of being beloved by God.

We went for supper. His joy was tangible. He was elated. That's the work of Jesus within, partnered with the Holy Spirit. Instead of shame we receive a double portion of happiness. Instead of humiliation we can shout for joy over our allocation of favor and blessing. Joy is the evidence of the outworking of the Holy Spirit. A tangible feeling that now, suddenly, incredibly, we are doubly blessed (Isaiah 61:7). Prophecy destroys worldly shame.

Shame is an assault on our true identity. Therefore, the prophetic must open up and establish our identity in Christ. How does God see this person? Prophecy changes perception. It gives us something to take hold of as we process this current part of our story and journey. We do not need to shame people in order to convict them of sin. They are already convicted and trapped by their own shame into personal disgust and self reproach. They need the conviction of who God is for them and the confidence of their identity in Jesus. When people are convinced about who they are in Jesus that conviction provides a confidence in God that overcomes all prior behavior.

Kingdom shame works because we point to who they are in Jesus. We convince them of what the Father has set aside for them. They become fully persuaded of the truth of their identity in Christ. That inner exposure to the glorious light of the truth clashes with their lifestyle, memory and current behavior. Shame about what they are not comes into conflict with their longing to be different. Kingdom shame is transformational because it inverts people. It turns them inward to compare and contrast their current lifestyle with their true identity in Christ. It allows people space to contemplate their behavior and reach for something more profound. Shame at what they had allowed themselves to become is mixed with the joy of discovering all that God intends them to be in Jesus. Kingdom shame produces joy.

Joy undergirds our heart, bringing confidence and conviction of God's goodness and favor. It's called conversion in Scripture. The word *epistrepho* means to make to turn toward. It indicates an encounter with God that produces an immediate and decisive change. Like Saul on the road to Damascus (Acts 9). Conversion is a positive, voluntary response to the presentation of the truth of God's intention for people. Literally when we reveal God's nature to people they become arrested by the prospect of knowing God. As we see God's heart turned toward us, so our heart turns toward him.

The enemy has blinded people so that they cannot see God's nature and do not perceive His heart toward them. When the GOOD NEWS is made known people can repent and return. Sin is wiped away and times of refreshing may come from the Presence of the Lord (Acts 3:19-20). Prophecy is compatible with the Gospel.

Jesus gave Simon a prophetic word in Luke 22:31-34:

> *"Simon, Simon, behold, Satan has demanded permission to sift you like wheat; but I have prayed for you, that your faith may not fail; and you, when once you have turned again, strengthen your brothers." But he said to Him, "Lord, with You I am ready to go both to prison and to death!" And He said, "I say to you, Peter, the rooster will not crow today until you have denied three times that you know Me."*

"When once you have turned again." This is *epistrepho*. Simon's heart would be turned back toward God in a moment when shame would fill his heart (John 18:15-27) as he denied Jesus three times. Conviction and conversion bring us to the place where we are fully persuaded about who God is for us. Prophecy is a part of that process. It opens the eyes of our heart and brings enlightenment concerning God's provision and our identity.

Prophecy accelerates us toward God. It elevates us into a higher place of anointing and Presence. Admonition when used properly compels people to look up, stand up and grow up. Prophecy upgrades identity and empowers us into the next dimension of God's purpose. Also, it can prevent us from going down a poor road and get us back on track. The best prophecy always invites a conversation with the Father. It opens a doorway into Heaven. It enables us to fashion prayers that are full of faith and promise.

Prophecy takes us out of the clutches of the enemy and puts us squarely in the hands of a loving Father who never gets tired of us. It is part of our redemption, sanctification and the gaining of wisdom which is available to all believers.

Prophets who understand the true value of admonition are a thorn in the side of the religious, a threat to the enemy and a Godsend to the Church.

Witness of the Spirit

Prophecy communicates heart-to-heart and spirit-to-spirit. We need to recognize God's voice through a process called the "witness of the Spirit." This occurs when we recognize not just the voice of a prophet, but that God Himself is present and speaking through their voice. When someone speaks prophetically to us, our spirit witnesses to it and something inside us keys into the Holy Spirit. As we learn to hear God's voice, we allow our spirit to interact with the Spirit of God, going beyond mere understanding, and awakening recognition within us. We then become aware of when God is speaking, not just when it is the voice of man. It's all part of our response, our receiving of the Word of God.

When prophecy has been spoken, we must evaluate the spirit behind it. Is it good words from a respectable person who has a good heart for us? We can receive that on the level that it has been given. Is it a general word of encouragement and good advice that carries a decent level of blessing? This is relationally important. The Church is a community of good friends who know how to relate in the loving-kindness of God.

Generally, as we follow such words, our lives are made better and we receive valuable input that is helpful to us in the development of our story with the Lord Jesus. Our walk is improved and we journey with confidence.

When we discover a wrong spirit at work behind the prophecy, then we must protect ourselves from the effects of that intrusion. It is not my intention to go into that subject matter in this segment because it has been thoroughly dealt with in one of my previous books, *Prophecy and Responsibility*. In chapter two, "Evaluating the Prophetic Word," there is a defined account of what to avoid and how to respond in this type of situation.

> *God speaks into our past to deliver us from it!*

When we discern that the Spirit is of God, then we must become wholehearted in our response to what God is speaking and planning. We need to formally take receipt of the prophetic words given to us. When a parcel or a vital letter is received, we are used to signing for it and sending a receipt back to show that we have taken possession of the message. Likewise, God loves to see people formally accept and acknowledge their prophetic words in the relational process. We need to say "yes and amen," or as Mary put it, *"may it be to me according to your word"* (Luke 1:38). The people around us need to hear our confession: "This is the voice of God to me."

Then we must study the word and the particular language that is employed. What is being described to us? Prophecy has a very pictorial element to it that allows us to see what we are hearing. What descriptive words and phrases are being used toward us? It may be describing us in the past, present or future, or any various combinations of those elements. Each nuance will be important for us to understand so that we can partner with the Holy Spirit as He generates the momentum required for this new time or season.

If a word is describing only our **past**, it would illustrate that all is not well with us. It could indicate that something is holding us down in our identity or holding us back in our spiritual development. We may need to be cut off from the enemy or from our history with certain types of people. A victim mindset

> *Progressive transition is rooted in our identity*

cannot make decisions in the present because it is stuck somewhere further back at a point in the history of the individual. We need the freedom of the Cross to be applied so we can recognize that we are dead to the past and need to become alive to God in the present. Preoccupation with the past can only be interrupted by a mindset change rooted in repentance; for example, the art of thinking again and the empowerment that comes from a renewed mindset (Romans 12:2).

If the prophecy is focused on the **present–past**, it will be concerned with making a fresh determination between the old and new in our lives. It will signify a progressive transition that will empower us to find fresh relationship with God in a new identity rooted in Christ. It heralds the start of a new beginning and opens us up to the claims of Christ in the here and now. It means that a time of vital transition is available **now**. The Father is serious about our setting aside the old and establishing the new. Our mindset change must be: "Who is God for me now?" People want new, but think old. We are learning to move in the opposite spirit and cultivate living in the opposite experience to what is coming against us!

When a prophecy is rooted only in the **present**, it is signifying the need for an upgrade in our walk with the Lord. We must move on and continue to grow up in Christ. It is easy to stand still when we are preoccupied with externals rather than fixed on the nature of God in Christ. God Himself is unchanging but we are always adapting, adjusting and becoming more of who He is in us. It may mean that we require more revelation and encounter with the Holy Spirit, who is establishing Christ within. This can be very true of people who got saved but have not developed their relationship much beyond that first encounter. It signals a time for an upgrade. The mindset change begins by asking relevant questions that enable us to explore a new dimension of spiritual reality in Christ. One such question would be: "What experiences must I receive from the Holy Spirit to ensure that I am empowered to become more like Jesus?"

"Now" prophecy produces an upgrade in the Spirit

A **present–future** prophecy is purely about the need for progressive transition that leads us to acceleration in our spiritual development. The roots of this change may already be present and we need to understand the signs. It may be that we are experiencing a divine dissatisfaction — a longing for more of the Father, a hunger for the Presence of Jesus, and a greater desire for the person of the Holy Spirit. It is vital that our dissatisfaction does not become disillusionment. Witnessing to the Spirit means that we are able to interpret the word correctly in the light of current events. Enlightened by the Lord, we can plot our way forward by the guidance He provides. We can update our identity to have more to aim for in the future. We receive goals and outcomes that shape our future as God envisions it. Our mindset change is in line with the major biblical transition of Pentecost that thrusts people into a whole new era of experience and activity. The questions asked on that day were: "What does this mean?" and "What must we do?" (Acts 2:12; 37).

Finally, if a prophetic word is only for the **future** it may signify that We must reengage more forcefully with God's plans so we can build a stronger sense of expectancy (biblical hope) for our future (Jeremiah 29:11). It will be meant as an encouragement to press on into bigger things in the Lord Jesus. We are not meant to stand still. Constant change is here to stay. Forgetting what lies behind we need to press on for the prize of the upward call of God in Christ (Philippians 3:12-14). Our mindset change will be concerned with cultivating thoughts that provide us with God's intentional vision regarding our calling in the Kingdom.

> *Present–future words carry acceleration into our experience of God*

When we study the language used within the prophetic words we receive, the descriptive components provide us with a visual presentation of what we are moving into next. Witnessing to what the Spirit is revealing allows us to form vital confessions that will empower our behavior in the current season. The witness of the Spirit is the first part of major transformation.

Every time we say "yes" to the Lord we must say "no" somewhere else. Any gifted person, whether an actor, athlete, or musician understands the vital importance of saying "no" to distractions. Sportsmen know that medals are won on the training ground, not the track or field of play. If we let our bodies down in training, we will run out of steam in the vital areas of competition. Our "yes" to the Lord must be accompanied by a "no" elsewhere.

Witnessing to the Spirit will empower us to enter into the covenant that God requires for our continued growth. The old anointing must give way to the new. Our relationship with the Father always involves the deepest expression of covenantal love that Heaven allows. The witness of the Spirit allows us to discover and embrace the fullness of God's promises to us in Jesus. When we witness to the work of the Spirit, we enter into a partnership

> *Future words facilitate a greater expectancy!*

through our confession that provides tangible power and anointing to come our way.

Provision and promise come to those who affirm and attest to the intentionality of the Father. Our testimony announces God's intent as a fact of life. We become aligned to certainty. Our perceptions become altered, our thinking more focused and our faith more evident. We trust easily and are ready, positioned for what the Father will work out in us.

From this place of preparation we become ready for the work of God. We take the necessary steps to believe and become the person God envisions for us. Our alliance with goodness makes us tangibly expectant of its appearance and power in the ongoing story of our journey into the land of promise, which is habitation with Jesus.

We form a cartel with the Trinity that develops a spiritual community far greater than we can imagine. It is in this place of communion that we draw in the relationships God has put around us. These friendships are designed to do two things: first, to keep negativity at bay, and secondly, to empower the development of our upgraded identity in Christ.

In the first we want protection; a true safeguard from slipping back into bad habits regarding our identity. There is a difference between defaulting and defining. Under negative pressure we can default to prior behavior that is rooted in low self-esteem or bad habits. Alternatively we can use the situation to define who we are in Christ and establish that as a fact of our lifestyle and new habit.

When we come under pressure in that area again, we do not default to the sin habit but we press the reset button that defines our new identity. Our reset position must be our childlike simplicity in Jesus. We cannot afford to revert to a type rooted in trauma or an unsuccessful past. Our friends need permission to stop the rot and enable us to disempower our disappointment. We neither want nor need the enemy to pull the wool over our eyes. Real friends put us straight when our path becomes crooked.

In the second we need assurance of who we are becoming. The key to everything is identity. We simply must have people around us who can see, understand and help cultivate who we are becoming next in relation to the ongoing life of experiencing Christ in us, the hope of glory (Colossians 1:27). My friends know who I am and are aware of the promises of God upon my life. I am part of a relational community within The Mission in Vacaville, CA, known as the Tribe. We practice a relational community that is present–future. We know who we are now and who we are becoming, and we are committed to one another's development and growth.

Relationships of this magnitude ensure that our confession of identity is upheld and that we are necessarily challenged in terms of loving accountability to one another. By itself, mental assent may yield very little when prophecy is spoken. All prophecy involves a process; a series of steps that take us from where we are now to the place where God's revealed intention may be realized.

Impartation and Process

The Father uses two ways to develop our spirituality, and prophecy will fit exactly into Heaven's methodology. He moves in both impartation and process. If impartation is first, it will be followed by process later, and vice versa. All spirituality is paradoxical. It means that God will always use both in every circumstance. Impartation is always on God's agenda because He loves encounter. Process is always His will for us because He adores establishing our encounters into lifelong experiences.

When the prophecy is spoken, an immediate impartation is released. This is an encounter with God that launches us into a whole new place of favor, permission and authority. We must explore that space, not just enjoy the experience. We must seize the opportunity being presented to move joyfully into the place where we are unrestrained in the joy and love of God.

It is important to keep pushing and continue pressing in until God is satisfied with our place and position in Christ. It is important that we enjoy the euphoria of what is happening, but we must make sure that we take some ground in our relationship with God. Impartation enables us to redeem time and get back on track with where we should be in the purposes of God. It is vital that we press in during encounter to the place where we are ahead of our time.

Sadly, most people just enjoy the party but do not take ground in their relationship with God. We can go through renewal at a surface level or allow it to take us into a deep place in the heart and affections of God. We always turn our impartation loose on our hang-ups and issues. We make sure that any negative place in us is completely killed off by Presence. Take time to grow in the affections of God. Allow God to indulge Himself in His loving-kindness. He is the original territorial Spirit who mapped out the boundaries of the land that He wanted Israel to occupy (Joshua 15-21). In impartation God wants to map out our territory in the Spirit. He has laid out new ground in His heart and affections for us to both enjoy and embrace. Stepping into that new relational territory and occupying it is as important for our ongoing relationship with Jesus as holding the promised land was to Israel. Jesus is our Canaan.

In impartation we let worship increase so that we can get a breakthrough in rejoicing. Allowing God to turn our internal world upside down is vital. It guarantees ownership, partnership and leadership of this next season in the Spirit. Impartation is beholding the Lord and conforming to His purpose.

Eventually the impartation will seem to be reduced to nothing. Actually, it is still present, but the emotional connection has been turned off. The power is still available. The relationship is intact. God has not taken it away. It is safe and available, but must now be accessed in a different way. The Truth that we have encountered and joyfully experienced must now be established in our daily obedience. This is where the process is absolutely vital to our growth in Jesus.

Manifestation and hiddenness are the ways that God uses to reveal and establish truth. In manifestation we have the impartation and encounter that propels us into a whole new place, which must be both enjoyed and occupied. Hiddenness is the process whereby we learn to occupy and rule over the internal territory we have taken. We rule through our obedience and faith. The ground taken must be established in reality. Process is absolutely central to our gaining the inheritance that the Father has set aside for us in Christ. There will be a fight involved. The enemy seeks reentry to the ground he has lost and we must establish ownership. When God gives us new territory and possessions, we must establish our ownership of them against the enemy. Then we must move in stewardship of them toward the Lord and His people. It is a paradox — to successfully combat the evil one we must own and occupy our inner territory in the name of Jesus. Then, in the purposes of God for the earth, we steward His giftings to serve His will. For a deeper look at this issue, read *Hiddenness and Manifestation,* which is available online.

Once the impartation has worn off, we must engage with the process. Everything God gave us in impartation is still present, but the lack of emotion makes it invisible for a time. Process allows us to establish the truth by our trust, faith and obedience. Put simply, we live in the same way as though we were still in the impartation, however, now we use trust and faith where before we used emotion and feelings. God is still the same, only the access points have changed. We are learning to live by faith and by every word that proceeds out of God's mouth. In impartation, our feelings and emotions are a beautiful part of the experience. In process these are hidden from us so that trust, faith and obedience can make manifest the same experiences.

Impartation and process are the two ways that God develops our spirituality. Impartation works **from** an experience into the process, which is the truth. Process works with the truth toward a place of encounter, which is impartation. In prophecy we are either helping people process their impartation into a lifestyle or we are developing an encounter with God through the process of establishing the lifestyle. Impartation and process go together. They are two sides of the same coin — a paradox. We cannot have one without the other.

Secondly, when prophecy is spoken and no immediate impartation is released, it means that the Lord has chosen process first, which will later lead to an impartation of encounter. We do not choose what happens. One is not better than the other. Both are hugely enjoyable. We need both to become the mature people of God that He envisions when He looks at us in Christ.

When prophecy is spoken and no impartation is released, then the process kicks in immediately. Process is a series of steps that take us from where we are now to where God wants us to be. Process is about learning simple trust in God's integrity. "God said it. I believe it. That settles it!"

Look at the prophetic word and ask the first of a series of questions: What does this mean? What must I do? These are the questions asked at Pentecost and are important points that allow us to engage in transforming dialogue with the Holy Spirit. Process is about meditation, which is the art of thinking deeply about who we are now and who we are becoming. It also involves a healthy dialogue in prayer with the Lord Jesus as we determine who we are in Him and how to make that a reality. Finally, transformation through process involves action, which is obedience and wise choices.

All process is primarily relational. We are learning about our own identity and how to align ourselves with the purposes of God. Also, we need to discover who the Father is for us in this growth season. What is He going to declare to us of Himself and how will we respond to His specific invitation to become more Christ-like in those areas? In process God has a very specific agenda with us in terms of relationship and identity.

Process is therefore about learning the relational joy that exists between the Father and the Son, to which we are so obviously included. Process is designed to lead us into simple abiding, and from there into divine acceleration. We engage fully with the Holy Spirit, who is a genius at doing life. It is His role that will be pivotal for us. He is given to us to empower us to become like Jesus. He loves all the angles of process that develop through the initial thinking into the place of heart change and lifestyle adjustment.

When we look at the prophetic word, we must get a vision for the new self that it reveals. The whole idea of process is that we become what we behold. The new vision is also our agreed outcome with the Lord. We then get to experience some momentum as an act of trust. When we enter process without the accompaniment of emotional engagement, it is more than just a mental exercise. It is a walk of faith that begins with the development of a simple trust in God's goodness to get us to where He wants us to live. Relational process is about the joy of walking through life with the Lord at the center. It is about the sheer pleasure in our cooperating with the Holy Spirit in the dialogue and the actions that follow. Process is the delight we have in partnership with Jesus as we become like Him. Process is concerned with agreement, alignment and activation of our Christ-like identity. We can do all that without any necessary over-reliance on emotion. I love emotion. I love the way God made us. To have feelings is wonderful, but there are times when the Father pulls back our emotions in order to grow trust, faith and obedience.

Process is where we establish the truth to specific areas of our life. It establishes obedience and choice as an important part of our relationship with God. Jesus said, *"You are My friends if you do what I command you"* (John 15:14). This is spoken in the context of loving friendship and being fruitful in the way we live. Process guarantees fruitfulness as we focus on the partnership that is emerging.

Examine the prophecy/promise. What specifically is God's promise to us at this time? Enter into a dialogue about what this looks like and develop some expectations of the Father's heart. Start a journal so that your progress can be tracked effectively. When we ask the question *What does God want to be for me now?* we are engaging with His passion for us first. This is vital, because without Him taking the lead with us, we can get embroiled in a self-help program that will be doomed to failure. Process is not primarily about our performance, though obviously we will be expected to act. Process is about the discovery of who God is for us and the part He wants to play in our transformation. Initially then, process is about sensitivity to the heart and nature of God for us. It will focus on His intentionality and purpose.

Prophecy Eliminates Negativity

We are always in the business of conforming ourselves to Him. He initiates, we respond. Therefore, the overtures of God are most important because they will liberate us into His faithfulness toward us. We need to know His heart toward us at the start of the process. It is His intention that will become one of the central planks of our experience as we walk out the truth with Him.

Process enables us to rely on God's goodness toward us. We are going to make mistakes and stumble in the process of transformation. Knowing God's heart of loving-kindness toward us will encourage us immensely on our off days. Process will not be plain sailing. It is usually turbulent, gut-wrenching, and vomit-inducing; but mostly it is joyful, serene and astonishing. The whole point of process is that we focus on what we are gaining and becoming.

As the process picks up some traction in our life, the next question becomes vital: Who am I now and who am I becoming? This is the start of a present–future relationship with the Father that allows us to move toward the agreed outcome. We can deal with the here and now when we have an understanding of who we are becoming and the identity to which we are to conform. We have to look at our present state even as we are getting a vision for our future standing in the Lord Jesus Christ. State and standing are important components in our liberation and our development. We need to be released from what we are not as part of the process of becoming who we already are in Jesus.

State is how we live outside of any reality in Christ. We can be victims, feeling useless and hopeless. We can be abusers with hair-trigger tempers and a mean heart. We can be procrastinators who lead a passive lifestyle. We can be cynical, pessimistic and negative. There are a thousand wrong things to be in terms of attitude, outlook, lifestyle and identity. Part of process is coming clean regarding the things in our life that require change. Other people's honest opinion will be decisive for us in stepping out into the discovery process of who we can become. We do not want our new identity being superimposed over the old. That's like building a house over a swamp. At some point in the future something is going to subside!

Standing is who we are in Jesus. It looks at our identity in Him. As a new creation we are set aside by God for His own possession. All grace abounds toward us and we experience His sufficiency in everything. We are ambassadors of Christ because we are the Beloved of God, His Bride, precious to Him and blessed. We have a bold, confident access to the throne of God where we stand in the grace that Jesus won for us. We are chosen by Him and He indwells us with His Presence and Fullness. We are His co-heirs, blessed with all blessings, fruitful, and gifted. We are disciples, declared holy and free as we revel in being a habitation of God. We are highly favored and inseparable from the love of God in Christ. We are more than conquerors because of His righteousness and sanctification. We are powerful with a joyful strength that emanates from our being seated with Christ in Heavenly places.

Over time, process makes our standing a tangible reality in our experience. Process leads to abiding and acceleration in our relationship with the Holy Spirit. It is the way that we get to turn our experience of truth into an encounter with God in power. Process is where we learn relational joy and the sheer pleasure of daily walking out our salvation in God's goodness. We get to abide in the encounter and learn the values and principles of walking it out. Process is about becoming what we behold.

The combination of impartation and process allows us to be captivated by our identity as we overcome any negativity that gets in the way of our development. Prophecy gives us an outcome that we can use to overcome anything negative. Therefore, the negation of what the enemy is attempting to put on us is made more powerful because we start with an outcome already in view!

The danger of impartation without process is that we enjoy the encounter but do not go deep into an experiential lifestyle. We feel disillusioned when the experience/feelings dry up and we have not gone to the next place of involvement with the Father.

Process without impartation means we do a lot of work but fail to produce the encounter that the Father wants to give us. We can fall down in sight of the winners tape! We do not enjoy the journey of obedience and trust, so we fail the test of maturity.

Impartation and process are two sides of the same intention of God — to make us more like Jesus. When we prophesy over people and it is accompanied by encounter, we can encourage people to enjoy the experience, but also be aware of the process that will follow. Similarly, when we prophesy and there is no immediate impartation, we must make people aware of the need to use the prophecy differently. Impartation will come when we have established our identity. Encounters are always the goal of God in His relationship with us.

When the Opposite Occurs

In the Parable of the Sower (Matthew 13:1-23), Jesus said that persecution and tribulation can come because of a word we have received. This is as true about prophecy as it is about the reception of revealed truth. The enemy always contests the word of the Lord. "Has God said?" — way back in Genesis 3:1 — is the first recorded act of temptation and warfare against a word from God.

We see this contesting vividly portrayed in the book of Exodus. When Moses met the elders of Israel and prophesied that the nation would be delivered from Egypt, he was supported by a number of signs and wonders, including a staff becoming a snake, and a hand turning leprous. This demonstration was so powerful that the people of Israel believed and worshipped the Lord (Exodus 4:29-31).

But when Moses spoke to Pharaoh, the exact opposite of the prophetic word happened. The king ordered the Israelite slaves to produce the same number of bricks without being given the straw necessary to make them. Now, the people had to gather straw as well as make bricks (Exodus 5).

When Moses came to prophesy again in Exodus 6:6-8, the people's reaction was one of disbelief and discouragement. The latter prophetic word was fulfilled in part to that generation; however, only two adults, Joshua and Caleb, received the total fulfillment (Numbers 14). Everyone else over the age of twenty died before inheriting the completion of the prophecy.

We see exactly the same scenario at work in the life of Joseph. He shared his prophetic dream about ruling over his brothers only to later find himself staring up at them from the bottom of a pit! Far from ruling over them, Joseph found himself being sold into slavery, then made to serve as a criminal (Genesis 37 and 39). He received the fulfillment of his prophetic word as he held onto the Lord in his circumstances. He did not allow his situation to determine his response to the prophecy. In fact, the prophetic word about ruling was in part fulfilled in the slave home and the prison as Joseph held onto the Lord.

Receiving prophecy brings us into the orbit and attention of the enemy. I must confess that this brings me a real sense of excitement. Prophecy puts us on the cutting edge between the clash of two kingdoms. I would rather be attacked by the enemy than be left alone by God.

I once prophesied over a man that he was moving into a time of unparalleled prosperity where God would bless him with financial abundance. Less than a week later, the same man called to inform me I was a "false prophet." Clearly upset and angry, he told me he had just lost his job — for the first time in his life. He was now unemployed in a region with a twenty-five percent unemployment rate. Rude and adamant, he declared that I was a false prophet. After hearing him out, I told him that I felt there were three possibilities to consider in this situation.

First, I could have missed the heart of God. If this was the case, then I would have to return to his church to speak to him and his leaders. I spoke the word publicly; at the very least I would have to make a formal, public apology. Not only that, but I would invite him to sit on a panel of his leaders and mine to discuss the appropriate action for my ministry. If I had indeed missed it, I could need help and counsel to put me right. I would certainly want him to feel safe and covered from my mistake.

The second possibility was that the enemy was trying to snatch the word away. Jesus said in Matthew 13:19 that this was possible. Personally, I am not sure of exactly how much power the enemy has in this matter. After all, there were several hundred prophetic words about Jesus, His birth, life, and eventual death. If the enemy had really understood the power of His death on a cross, he would have chopped down every tree in Israel. Stealing the word is a possibility, but probably not all the time. However, it needs to be considered.

When the Opposite Occurs

The final possibility was that God knew beforehand that the man would lose his job, and wanted to give him a word of encouragement for this difficult time. I asked him to talk those three possibilities over with his leadership and get back to me. When he returned the call, it was to apologize for calling me a false prophet and to agree that the third possibility had received a genuine witness with himself and his leadership. At that point, we prayed together over the telephone.

The man told me that he had a meeting scheduled a few days later to discuss his severance package. Apparently, everyone in the company was being given five thousand dollars. As we prayed, I felt the Lord impress on me that he was to ask for ten thousand and the company car. This took some convincing; the man was reluctant to ask for more because everyone was getting the same amount. But there wasn't any harm in asking as the company couldn't fire him twice. He finally agreed and we prayed together for God's blessing.

When he arrived at the meeting, he discovered that the finance manager, who usually handled such details, was ill. A stressed-out finance director was supposed to meet in his place, but he asked for the meeting to be rescheduled as he was extremely busy trying to sell off parts of the company. My new friend refused to reschedule; he wanted to get the meeting over with.

"How much do you want?" the director asked, point blank.

"I want ten thousand and the company car," he answered.

"Done," said the director, who shook his hand and filled out a contract release form. The man was the only person in the company to receive such a payout; then again, he was the only person in the company with a prophetic word about prosperity.

We talked several times over the next few months as he sought new employment. Eventually, after a temporary contract, he found a job with nearly three times the salary he earned at the old company.

This man made the common mistake of allowing the circumstances to challenge the prophecy, rather than using the prophecy to attack the circumstances. God knows everything that is happening in our lives. He sees the end from the beginning.

My friend was about to lose his job anyway. The Lord, in His kindness, gave him a word about financial blessing before the lay-off so that he would have a promise to hold onto during the tough times. When God speaks, He reveals the absolute intention of His heart toward us. He does not speak for novelty's sake. He speaks to challenge our circumstances. The prophetic word turns everything upside down.

The Lord is moving us into things that are impossible for us to accomplish on our own. Every church will take on projects that are impossible; many of these efforts will have their roots in the prophetic community of their local body. God wants to deliver His Church from a "safety-first" Christianity, and lead us into risk-taking. In church life, there are times when we need to step out of the boat and do the impossible. Faith is a walk in the unseen realm; prophecy opens the door to that world.

The nation of Israel was delivered from Egypt according to the prophetic word given to Moses. There is always a contending against the intentions of God. Prophecy gives us a declared outcome. Time and again Israel had the opportunity to trust the outcome of the prophetic declaration regarding their entry into the promised land. When we use prophecy to challenge the circumstances, the outcome is totally guaranteed.

However, when we allow the circumstances to be more real to us than the spoken word of God, then we align ourselves with negativity. Ten times Israel failed to pass the test of faith in God's promise. Eventually their unbelief talked them out of the blessing of prophetic fulfillment.

Joseph went through all of his tests and held onto the words and dreams of God that foretold his prophetic destiny. When initially sold into slavery, then in Potiphar's house and finally when put in prison, he rose each time to a place of prominence in line with his destiny. There were fulfillments of the word at every level, culminating in his final position as the most important person in Egypt after Pharaoh.

When the opposite of your prophecy occurs, take a fresh grip on what God has promised, and rejoice that you have a guaranteed outcome as you use the Word of the Lord to challenge your circumstances.

The Prophetic Word is a Great Weapon

A contesting happens on two fronts: spiritual and circumstantial. The spiritual battle will occur when prophecy puts us at the flash point between the Kingdom of Heaven and the kingdom of darkness. When God speaks a directional prophetic word into our lives, His intention is to draw us further into a Kingdom perspective, and to involve us in expanding His domain. Whenever we allow ourselves to respond to that challenge, we become an object of interest and attention to the enemy.

The enemy doesn't have the time or manpower to afflict every Christian personally, so he mainly uses the flesh and the world to keep us out of God's will. Whenever we resist those two areas by living in the Spirit, we usually come into personal confrontation with the enemy.

In these situations we have to learn appropriate responses and behavior. Everything that challenges me is a direct challenge to the Lordship of Christ. Why? Because I am in Christ! God has put me into the one place, the person of His Son, where the enemy finds it the hardest to overcome my life. That is why the great need today is to develop men and women who will stand in Christ. In warfare, we do what we know how to do: pray, believe, be clean, have an expectation of God — and we stand, not allowing ourselves to be moved one inch away from the unchanging God of the Gospel.

The enemy prefers us to be apathetic and passive; that way he can control our lives. When the prophetic spirit comes upon us, God stirs us into action. At this point, a different kind of warfare takes place. *"This charge I commit to you, son Timothy, according to the prophecies previously made concerning you, that by them you may wage the good warfare,"* Paul instructed in 1 Timothy 1:18.

Paul wanted Timothy to examine the substance of his prophecies and to clothe himself in them. Literally, he wanted Timothy to put those words on and wear them as armor in a battle against the enemy. The prophecies in his life could be used as weapons to shatter the lies of the kingdom of darkness. It is difficult to believe you're worthless when Heaven itself has clothed you in purpose. As the enemy contests the ground of our lives, we can use the prophecy against him.

Prophecy establishes our upgrade in the Lord Jesus. It will stir us up in faith to take hold of our identity and destiny, which is the present–future of our ongoing experience with God. Identity is who we are now in the present, and destiny is who we are becoming by God's grace and partnership with the Holy Spirit. Prophecy provides the opportunity to examine the present and the future in the same space, and make decisions that define our purpose in the will of God.

The prophetic empowers us to stir up the gifts that are within us. We live by every word that proceeds from God's mouth. This is why prophecy is so vital in our development. It gives us both strength and impetus for the journey ahead. Prophecy can pinpoint where the provision is when problems show up on our radar. Prophecy provides faith because it reveals the outcome that God has declared will be present for us.

The proceeding word is always proclamatory; therefore our response must be to declare the word is true, regardless of what the opposition is doing to nullify it. What God proclaims, we must declare! With prophecy we can fight a good fight. We can fight back because the outcome is a sword in our hand. We know whom we have believed and we have the prophecy to prove it! It is a personal weapon for our current set of circumstances.

Such prophecy carries a cutting edge that allows us to trim the fat off our negativity. With prophecy we can resist the devil and he will have to run from our engagement with God. We are capable of battling through any resistance because prophecy provides the open door into a whole place of provision in the Spirit. It gives us a position on the battlefield of life that enables us to overcome and be more than a conqueror. We overcome when the enemy contends against us and we are more than conquerors when he fails to show up for the fight. Sometimes he doesn't like the odds as he looks at our maturity in Christ.

A prophetic word turns everything upside down and right side up. The contesting will also be circumstantial, because every prophecy that has a directional context will have a physical and practical outworking. God is intensely practical; He made clothes for Adam and Eve and He made sure the Egyptians paid the Israelites enough to launch their economy in their new homeland. He even had breakfast flown in every day on their journey through the wilderness. In the midst of stressful and challenging situations, God's attention to detail is awesome.

The introduction of prophecy will probably herald a change in our circumstances. Sometimes when things look bad, they actually aren't; it's simply God wanting to change our circumstances. By examining the content of the prophecy, we can gain clues as to how we are supposed to hang onto the Lord.

We must not allow ourselves to get drawn into a debate with the devil regarding our current circumstances. We need to challenge those issues with the prophetic word or the opposite will happen by default. We will find ourselves standing in our circumstances, taking issue with the prophecy.

Prayer is vital to the process of holding on to a prophetic word. We need to draw close to Him and say, "Lord, You spoke this word. It looks like everything is going in the opposite direction of what You have said. I'm under attack from the enemy, but by Your grace and strength, I'm going to walk in the light of Your word. By Your anointing and the power of the Spirit, I will see the word fulfilled."

We contest the same ground in prayer, and we learn how to stand firm in the Lord and the power of His might.

Prophecy Eliminates Negativity

<u>Prophecy Eliminates Negativity</u>

Reflections, Exercises and Assignments

The following exercises are designed with this particular chapter in mind. Please work through them carefully before going on to the next chapter. Take time to reflect on your life journey as well as your prophetic development. Learn to work well with the Holy Spirit and people that God has put around you so that you will grow in grace, humility and wisdom in the ways of God.

Graham Cooke.

What Constitutes Maturity?

- Understanding how lovely we are to the Lord in failure
- Being empowered to overcome failure
- Becoming an Ambassador of Reconciliation
- Judging the enemy, not people
- Proclaiming liberty and freedom
- Moving in compassion to comfort people with prophecy
- Living from God, not toward Him
- Life in the Spirit is always about displacement
- Owning your freedom in Christ
- Accelerating your freedom from religious performance
- Learning the different voices God uses in relationship
- Seeing the Kingdom value of admonishment and shame
- Knowing and practicing the law of Christ
- Maintaining freedom through practicing restraint
- Knowing the affection God has for you
- Viewing people in the Spirit, not the flesh
- Helping people to find the grace they need
- Working in alignment with God's revealed intention
- Promoting relationships that guarantee your upgrade
- The value of responding to impartation and process in developing your spiritual experience
- Knowing how to challenge circumstances with the prophetic

What Constitutes Immaturity?

- Thinking that our failure demeans God
- Allowing failure to distance us from God
- Representing God with negatives
- Not valuing reconciliation as part of the Gospel
- Using prophecy to bring people down
- Moving in anger and judgment
- Being preoccupied with the bad things in life
- Disconnecting people from God's goodness by misusing the prophetic
- Living in ignorance of the completed work of Christ on the Cross
- Owning the struggle with the flesh rather than the freedom of the Spirit
- Reading the Word, but not hearing it
- Living and operating apart from the Good News
- Moving in worldly admonition and shame
- Representing God's holiness in an unrighteous manner
- Lecturing instead of listening
- Using freedom and grace to cover up sin
- Not being fully aware of God's affection for you
- When your "yes" to God is not followed by a "no" elsewhere
- Failing to witness to the Spirit in your prophecy
- Not allowing impartation and process to overcome your inherent negativity

ASSIGNMENT ONE

It is vital that we know what the Lord has called us to, so that we can upgrade our anointing to match His intentionality. The promises of God over us are always personal, never just functional. He does not only give us a call and a vocation in ministry, He also gives us personal assurances of His Presence.

Righteousness to the Father is not about living in a way that is circumspect and proper, wonderful as that is in the Spirit. It also means that He commits us to a place where He will always do what is right for us. A Holy God moving in righteousness means that He can be fully trusted at all times to do what is right in every situation we find ourselves. He backs that revelation up with a personal assurance that He watches over us and holds our hand in the tricky places of our journey.

We all are a part of His covenant to the earth in Jesus. He will commit resources to us as we seek to play our part in the establishing of the Good News. It's really good to know that in our normal lifestyle, we get to be a visual aid for the world to find Jesus. I have always enjoyed gossiping the Gospel. Every moment of every day, someone is getting out of prison, being healed, being set free and growing up in Christ. We are unstoppable in the goodness and kindness of God.

It is a good time for us to think about glory; specifically, to think about the glory that the Father can receive from our actions and words. The Father receives the most glory when the impossible happens—then everyone knows that it must have been God. Safe, conservative lifestyles never seem to get on the edge, out of the boat, or into risky situations. When we choose to walk by faith, we take risks that are beyond us.

In this new season the prophetic is awakening in a more profound manner. There are upgrades available where everyone may go to another level in terms of hearing the voice of God. Wouldn't you want to know what comes next in your life and that of your family and friends? Your capacity to hear the Lord will increase in this next season and you will learn to be present–future in your relationship with the Lord.

1. a)What is the most difficult situation in your life at this time?
   b)Put yourself inside God's heart. What would He want to be for you now?

2. If you are struggling with a particular sin habit, what element of righteousness do you need to displace it?

3. a)In what specific way are you a part of God's covenant to the world?
   b)If you were a gift to humanity from God, what would you be?

4. What is the specific glory that you can bring to the Lord through your life and ministry?

5. In what areas of your life are you playing it safe when you need to believe God and risk something? What is the next level of faith that you need to exhibit?

6. What would you attempt next in your life if you knew it could not fail?

7. What new doors are opening for you in a) your life? b) your relationship with God? c) your work/ministry?

8. What do you see happening next in your spiritual community?

9. What upgrades are stacked up over your own life at this time? What needs to happen to bring them down?

10. What new thing would you like to be involved with in this next season?

11. Regarding your relationship and walk with the Lord, what would you like the Holy Spirit to proclaim over you?

Reflections, Exercises and Assignments

Goodness—Fruit Of The Spirit

I am always saddened to see the Church stand in judgment against the world. We are here to give a blessing, not a sentence. Christendom is called to give the earth a taste of what Heaven will be like. If more Christians would stand up in the goodness of God, acting it out in every facet of their lives, society would be changed overnight.

Why won't we let His goodness affect our hearts? God wants to bless us again and again and see that blessing spill over from us onto other people. When He blesses us, He is actually blessing many people around us, for our friends and family can't help but share our lives and excitement. That's how good God is—His blessings flow to everyone around us!

What if having a sense of wonder was as easy as being awed by what God is doing in our life? Shouldn't His goodness and grace lift our hearts? Shouldn't our spirit be vibrating with excitement at the thought of how God is working in and around us? What if we let go of the cynicism of the world? God has so much for each of us, that even if we lived to be one hundred and twenty years old, we wouldn't scratch the surface of His goodness.

God's goodness should inspire us to see the world with vibrancy and joy. A heightened sense of wonder is absolutely vital to a renewed relationship with God; after all, the power of God should constantly fascinate us. Here are some suggestions of ways to further develop your own sense of wonder.

1. Spend the day with a child. See things through their eyes. Take them to a playground or a toy store. Buy them some candy. Watch how they love new things.

2. Connect with nature. Find a park or beach and let the rhythm of God's creation wash over you. Ask Him to walk the trails with you.

3. Go to a book or music store and try some new products. Listen to music you wouldn't normally listen to. Read excerpts of books on topics you find inspiring. Spend the day there, asking God to show you more of Himself through other people's creativity.

4. Enjoy the company of good friends. Remember, where two or three are gathered, Jesus is there in the midst of them. (Matthew 18:20)

5. Throw a feast. Celebrate a rite of passage in your life by inviting people to a party. Treat them with the same joy with which God treats you.

6. Find an old castle or cathedral and sit in it for a while. Enjoy the architecture and the history.

7. Do what you love. If you love to golf, go golfing. If you love to paint, buy a new canvas and begin a new work of art. If you love to write, start scribbling. Meditate on the greatness of God.

8. Secretly bless someone. Pay attention to the needs and desires of those close to you. Become a kind-of secret admirer, filling that want. Enjoy their reaction.

9. Visit your church. Sit on the edge of the stage and look around the empty room. Breathe it in. Thank God for the blessings He's poured out. Envision it with your friends in it—and speak blessing over them.

Reflections, Exercises and Assignments

CASE STUDY

Matching Prophetic Delivery With Content

The delivery of a prophetic word must match its content. One cannot grab someone by the throat and prophesy love and peace. Likewise, a prophecy about warrior strength cannot be properly prophesied in an airy whisper. The context must match the content.

The following is a prophetic word I gave to an individual (name changed) at one of my prophetic schools. In this exercise, read the prophetic word and answer the following questions.

> *Simon, I see a picture of a group of people crowding around a door, trying to get on a train. There is a train guard in uniform pushing them forward, attempting to squeeze them onto the train. The train is the next move of God. The doorway speaks of new opportunities. The people represent both individuals and small groups. The train guard is you, Simon. The uniform represents authority and power.*
>
> *There is an anointing on you to create forward movement in the lives of people. Prophetically, you know when it is time to push people on in the Spirit. You have a passion for people to be included in what God is doing. You have the necessary concern and compassion to see that no one misses their opportunity to move on in the things of God. There is a new strength of encouragement in you and an authority in the Spirit being given to you at this time. You will affect all manner of people, groups and organizations with your prophetic capacity to see what God is doing and inspiring people to get on board.*

1. What is the focal point of this prophetic word for Simon?

2. What would be the best way to speak the word (giving necessary attention to your tone of voice and body language)?

3. What gifting is being upgraded for Simon and why?

4. What spiritual impartation can be released?

5. What would you pray over Simon to seal this prophecy into his heart?

LECTIO DIVINA

Lectio Divina (Latin for *divine reading*) is an ancient way of reading the Bible—allowing a quiet and contemplative way of coming to God's Word. *Lectio Divina* opens the pulse of Scripture, helping readers dig far deeper into the Word than what would normally happen in a quick glance-over.

In this exercise we will look at a portion of Scripture and use a modified *Lectio Divina* technique to engage it. This technique can be used on any piece of Scripture. I highly recommend using it for key Bible passages the Lord has highlighted for you, and for anything you think might be an inheritance word for your life (see the *Crafted Prayer* Interactive Journal for more on inheritance words).

Read the Scripture:

"So all the congregation lifted up their voices and cried, and the people wept that night. And all the children of Israel complained against Moses and Aaron, and the whole congregation said to them, 'If only we had died in the land of Egypt! Or if only we had died in this wilderness! Why has the LORD *brought us to this land to fall by the sword, that our wives and children should become victims? Would it not be better for us to return to Egypt?' So they said to one another, 'Let us select a leader and return to Egypt.' Then Moses and Aaron fell on their faces before all the assembly of the congregation of the children of Israel. But Joshua the son of Nun and Caleb the son of Jephunneh, who were among those who had spied out the land, tore their clothes; and they spoke to all the congregation of the children of Israel, saying: 'The land we passed through to spy out is an exceedingly good land. If the* LORD *delights in us, then He will bring us into this land and give it to us, 'a land which flows with milk and honey.' Only do not rebel against the* LORD, *nor fear the people of the land, for they are our bread; their protection has departed from them, and the* LORD *is with us. Do not fear them.' And all the congregation said to stone them with stones. Now the glory of the* LORD *appeared in the tabernacle of meeting before all the children of Israel." (Numbers 14:1-10)*

1. Find a place of stillness before God. Embrace His peace. Chase the nattering thoughts out of your mind. Calm your body. Breathe slowly. Inhale. Exhale. Inhale. Exhale. Clear yourself of the distractions of life. Whisper the word, "Stillness." Take your time. When you find that rest in the Lord, enjoy it. Worship Him in it. Be there with Him.

2. Reread the passage twice. Allow its words to become familiar to you. Investigate Joshua and Caleb's words in this story. What images does it bring to your spirit? What do you see? Become a part of it. What phrases or words especially resonate with you? Meditate especially on those shreds of revelation. Write those pieces down in your journal.

3. Read the passage two more times. Like waves crashing onto a shore, let the words of Scripture crash onto your spirit. What excites you? What scares you? What exhilarates you about this revelation of the nature of God? What are you discerning? What are you feeling? What are you hearing? Again, write it all down in your journal.

4. Write the theme of this passage in your journal.

5. Does this passage rekindle any memories or experiences? Does it remind you of any prophetic words you have given or received? Write those down as well.

6. What is the Holy Spirit saying to you through this Scripture? Investigate it with Him—picture the two of you walking through it together. Write those words in your journal.

7. Read the passage two final times. Meditate on it. Is there something God wants you to do? Is there something He is calling you to? Write it down.

8. Pray silently. Tell God what this passage is saying to you. Tell Him what you are thinking about. Write down your conversation together. Picture yourself and the Holy Spirit as two old friends in a coffee shop, chatting about what God is doing.

9. Finally, pray and thank God for His relationship with you. Come back to the passage once a week for the next three months. Read it and let more revelation flow into you. If you feel compelled to, craft a prayer based on this passage for yourself, your family, friends, or church. Pray that prayer until you feel God has birthed it in you.

Reflections, Exercises and Assignments

Notes

Prophecy Eliminates Negativity

Notes

MODULE FOUR

WORKSHOP & CASE STUDY

Workshop & Case Study

THIS WORKSHOP IS A CHURCH assignment meant to be undertaken with someone from the leadership team of your church who can act as an advisor and assessor.
This assignment is in two parts:

1. Receiving and delivering a prophetic word to your church.

2. Writing out a *Case Study* for each step you take. Answer the questions where you see this *Case Study* symbol: Cs We need to be able to see your progress throughout the assignment and be able to comprehend your thinking and understanding.

THE WORKSHOP

Step One
Cs How would you describe the current phase the church is going through?

Step Two
Cs How would you define the spirit/state and the mind/mood of the church at this present time?

Spirit/State   Mind/Mood

Step Three
Cs What do you believe the Lord wants to say to your church? What is the overall concept?

Step Four
4a) Write down key words and phrases, while also using Scriptures and pictures if you have them. Pray over them.

C₅ 4b) Try to determine a pattern or an order for them to flow into. Think in terms of a beginning, the key points and any promises from God? What response is required, if any?

Step Five

What type of word is it?

a) Inspirational and encouraging?
b) Directional and stimulating?
c) Correctional and challenging?
d) Any mixture of the above a–c?

Explain the purpose of the word and give your choice of a–c above.

Step Six

C₅ 6a) What part of the prophecy is diagnostic (negative overtones or God simply telling you what is happening), and what part is actually prophetic? Separate the two!

C₅ 6b) Is God trying to change your heart for this church to come more in tune with His? If so, how?

C₅ 6c) Are the negative overtones a true picture of events? Or have they been colored by your perceptions and those of others, or even by enemy activity?

C₅ 6d) Demonstrate how you overcame your own frustrations and opinions in order to receive a pure prophetic word.

Step Seven

C₅ 7a)Write the prophecy down and share it with leaders. If it is *b* or *c* from step 5, allow the word to be judged and weighed. Take appropriate advice from your leaders.

C₅ 7b)If the prophecy fits into step 5c, wait for a confirmation from the leadership.

C₅ 7c)What advice/counsel/feedback did your leaders provide?

Step Eight

8a) If given the release to deliver the word, think about how you will do that. What method will you use?

C₅ ☐ Written Word ☐ Symbolic Act ☐ Drama
☐ Spoken Word ☐ Visual Object ☐ Song

C₅ 8b) Explain on paper the method you will use and why.

Step Nine

Before you deliver the word of prophecy, talk privately with the leadership about what needs to happen in the church and how the prophetic can be released to effect real change. You may need to answer one or all of the following:

9a) Does the morale of the church need to be lifted? If so, how would you use the prophecy to achieve the breakthrough?

9b) Is God calling for a positive faith response in warfare, praise, or prayer? How does your word fit into that?

9c) Is God calling the church to a solemn assembly, a period of fasting and intercession, a time of feasting and celebration, a period of sacrificial giving, or a time of submission and putting away bondages while giving up unhelpful pursuits? How can your prophetic word stimulate the right response?

N.B. In attempting to answer steps 9a–c, you will need obvious dialogue with your leadership. You will also need their approval and support so that if your prophecy is relevant to the current health/dynamic of the church, then the leaders can follow up the word with their own stimulus and response.

Step Ten

10a) Choose the time and deliver the word. Make sure there is a leader or designated person present.

10b) Give yourself marks out of ten (ten being the highest mark) for your actual delivery of the prophecy.

Marks out of 10	Your Mark	Leader's Mark
1. Your understanding of the current situation in the church (mood, morale, and phase)		
2. Your observable level of increase in prayerfulness over the church		
3. Your ability to overcome the negatives (frustrations, opinions, etc.)		
4. Content of the prophetic word		
5. Your growth in prophetic maturity		
6. The delivery of the prophecy; presentation		
7. Your ability to work with the leaders		
8. Your level of grace and humility		
9. Your growth as a positive spiritual influence		
10. Effectiveness of the prophetic word in the immediate life of the church		

N.B. 10C) LEADERS ONLY: Please give your marks out of ten and answer step 11b.

Step Eleven

11a) Looking at 10b, describe what (if anything) you would change.
ᒐ How would you improve things and what would you do differently in the whole assignment?

11b) LEADERS ONLY: Do you agree with the perceptions expressed in 11a? If not, please explain why.

ᒐ 11c) If there are any discrepancies between your marks out of ten and comments, and those of your leadership, explain the difference.

Step Twelve

How was the word received in church? Describe the outcomes, both positive and negative.

Step Thirteen

Describe how the assignment has affected your:

a) View of the church
b) Perception of the power of prophecy to create change
c) Working relationships with your leaders
d) Ability to de-program the negatives in yourself and be a positive spiritual influence in the church
e) Capacity to overcome the enemy and be a catalyst for spiritual breakthrough among the people

This must be an individual assignment where possible, unless you are attending the same class working through this book or a School of Prophecy run by Graham Cooke.

You may need to confer together if you are getting *a)* similar words, or *b)* words that fit together.

Try to complete the assignment in a three-to-four-month period at the discretion and availability of your leadership.

You will have learned how to:

1. Understand the current state of your church.

2. Determine the spiritual phase the church is going through.

3. Receive prophetic input regarding the work, and put it into order.

4. Understand and explain the type of prophecy and method of delivery you should use.

5. Tell the difference between diagnostic words and actual prophecy.

6. Work with your local leaders to develop and shape the prophecy.

7. Receive and submit to advice and counsel regarding methodology, timing, etc. of the word.

8. Eliminate negativity from your own heart and refuse ungodly human perspectives.

9. Positively affect the morale of the church and release spiritual breakthrough.

10. Honestly examine your practice of delivery and any adjustments you might make.

11. Understand and express how this prophetic assignment has affected you personally.

12. Exercise self-control and discernment in order to confront the enemy and win a positive response over the church.

13. Master your own frustrations/opinions in order to deliver a true word from the Lord.

Notes

Notes

FINAL
APPLICATIONS

MODULE FOUR
Final Applications
WHAT YOU WILL FIND IN THIS SEGMENT:

- A meditation explanation and exercise

- A relational value and its application regarding non-negotiable love

- A life principle for prophetic ministry and its application regarding the nature of God

- A checklist for dialogue, discussion and relationship building in partnership with leaders

- Development issues to safeguard the prophetic gift in the church in seeking help and support from leaders

- A prophetic word to be read, studied and acted upon

- A recommended reading list

A MEDITATION AND EXPLANATION EXERCISE

To MEDITATE MEANS TO THINK deeply about something or someone. It means to explore with mind and heart, allowing what you think to touch your innermost being.

Meditation is creative thought which leads us to the higher realm of revelation and wisdom. It takes us beyond the place of reason to where joy is seated and faith is activated.

Meditation allows us to search, both inside and outside the box of our current paradigm. What you see and hear there touches you profoundly. It adds a ring around the core truth of Christ, which is God within, the certainty of freedom.

Therefore, fruitful meditation is not a casual seeking for revelatory insight. Initial creative thoughts are merely the "X" that marks the spot. There is treasure in meditation and a guarantee of wealth in the pursuit of God.

Many are satisfied with collecting random truth on the surface of their consciousness. It is good wholesome stuff, but it does not satisfy and it cannot challenge the complexities of life in a warfare context.

Deep truth has to be mined over days and weeks. It takes joy and patience to take truth down to its deepest level. This is beyond meeting our current needs, beyond the depth of understanding the power it releases to us against our adversary, and down to the depth where God lives in the highest places of Heaven. For all meditation must ultimately come before the throne of His majesty, sovereignty and supremacy. He fills all things with Himself.

Our current situation requires wisdom, but even more it yearns for Presence. Meditation allows us to experience both through the word coming alive in our spirit. Meditation leads us to God and the permission of His heart. Learn to be in the question peacefully with God. Let the Holy Spirit teach you how to abide. Turn inwardly and rest, wait patiently... He will come. When your heart gets restless, turn to worship. When the interior atmosphere settles, return to listening.

Write down initial thoughts, but do not pursue them just yet. Do not be distracted initially by what you hear. Set it aside and come back to it later.

When first entering a lifestyle of meditation, take care to ease into it slowly. It is good to begin with an hour at first, then longer until you can do it for half a day and so on.

Always have a focus; do not try to wait in a vacuum. This next exercise is a particular statement followed by a series of questions. This is both to give you practice in meditation and to bring you into the revelation of God through the focus statement.

Use the questions as the Spirit leads. This exercise is not prescriptive, but merely a guide to enable your contemplation. No doubt you will discover better questions as the Holy Spirit tutors you. Enjoy!

Meditation Exercise

Disempower Your Disappointments

Whatever we focus on, we give power to. *"Set your mind on things above, not on things that are on earth."* (Colossians 3:2)

We have all had experiences of being hurt, wounded, betrayed and let down. As sure as the sun rises and sets, we will have similar experiences in the future. Life is not about avoiding unpleasant situations; it is about making a profit from them.

What if every potentially damaging situation was really a shortcut to a brilliant experience of Jesus? Instead of being wounded, we would become Christ-like! Through His blood and sacrifice, we do not have a right to be wounded; we have a right to be healed.

Take your eyes off the negative and you will disempower it. If you are wounded and offended, it proves that your old nature is still alive. The best way to keep it dead is to live in the new nature of: *"Christ in you, the hope of glory."* (Colossians 1:27)

Do not treat disappointments as house guests. In the Kingdom we attack the negative and drive it out. It has neither possession nor inheritance with us.

- What are you focusing on now that is bringing you heartache and pain?

- What is the opposite of those mindsets?

- Write down the opposite and determine how you will disengage from the negative and develop the mind of Christ.

- If you are overly passive (feel hopeless and helpless), take this exercise to a pastor, home group leader or some friends to ask for help.

- How can you make a profit from your negativity? Discuss with friends and family.

- Give up your right to be offended and take up your right to be healed. What does that look like for you?

- What inheritance is being held up because of your negative thinking and lifestyle?

- Determine the opposite blessings that God wants you to enjoy!

A Relational Value

- Do not merely treat this value as an exercise, but as an opportunity to develop Christ-like intent for yourself.

- Develop this value into a prophetic word in order to demonstrate the importance of your ministry arising out of your relationship with the Lord.

- Read the Scriptures out loud several times.

- Think through the introductory paragraph and the main points.

- Work through Action Points 1-8.

- Improve the Value Statement and make it your own.

N.B. This exercise can be done by individuals or groups of two to four, working together using dialogue. This guide is understated deliberately to allow for wide range thinking or discussion.

A group should be able to take the concept further in dialogue.

Follow up the action points with each other and get personal feedback from everyone regarding their progress.

Believing the Best

Scriptures:

- 1 Corinthians 13:7-8

- Romans 12:10-12

- Philippians 4:8

- Titus 1:15

- Colossians 3:11-17

- Luke 6:31

How we see people is often a mirror image of how we see ourselves. How we accept others is a significant indicator of our own self-acceptance in Christ. We believe the best about others because we believe the truth about ourselves in Jesus.

Giving others the benefit of the doubt will lessen the doubts we have about ourselves. This enables us to express an incredible depth of love and freedom to people. We are bestowing the gift of acceptance and receiving it afresh in each human transaction.

- Be patient with your defects, and those of others.

- Treat others how you would love to be treated.

- Love is the perfect bond of unity.

- Be devoted to one another in love and prefer one another in honor.

- Do not be wise in your own estimation, be humble.

- Respect what is right, cover what is wrong in grace.

- Practice Philippians 4:8!

- Relational breakdowns are really opportunities for a breakthrough—cunningly disguised!

Action

Ask the Holy Spirit to enable you to see people as He does. Think of how you would speak to them with this newfound understanding. Be aware that tense moments in relationships give you special opportunities to practice loving acceptance by believing the best.

Value Statement

It is impossible to grow relationships when living in an atmosphere of disapproval. Believing the best about people is not about ignoring their faults, but about recognizing that everyone wants to change and become like Jesus. We are always a work in progress and therefore deserving of mercy, grace and love.

Whenever we see Christ in one another, He is present!!

Action

1. Think of the times when people have not believed the best about you. How did you feel about their behavior?
2. What would have to change in you to make you more accepting of others?
3. How would you make the loving distinction between a behavior that you disapprove of and a person who still needs love and acceptance in order to change?
4. In the current relationship around your life, describe the opportunities that you see through your upgraded loving-kindness.

N.B. If a person consistently demonstrates their unfaithfulness, lack of trust and commitment, it is impossible to believe the best about their **actual** behavior. However, we can believe that they have the **potential** to become better.

- What is the difference between actual and potential behavior?

- If you were to believe that a person had the potential to become better, how would you express that in words to them and how would you demonstrate that in actions?

Final Applications

A Life Principle For Prophetic Ministry

We must pursue our calling within a working structure of intentional relationships. On days, this process will inevitably revolve around being purified, moving in loving confrontation, and the discipleship necessary to enable each one of us to grow up into all things in Christ. Cultivating values and principles in how we use our gifting will enable us to be proactive in our own development into a place of freedom and maturity.

We are all responsible for our own behavior. We are answerable to the Lord and to one another in the improvement and expansion of our gift and calling.

This life principle, if followed, will enable us to understand and experience the personality and character of the Lord Jesus as it relates to moving in the gift of prophecy.

All of Life is Spiritual

Scriptures:

- Acts 17:26

- Romans 8:14

Distinctively, we have asked the eternal God to dwell in our spirit; this is only made possible by the sacrifice of His Son, Jesus. We are now continuously led by Him through the Holy Spirit.

The blueprint for our existence was conceived and birthed in the Kingdom, which is a realm that is spiritual. We are currently experiencing a portion of that blueprint of DNA connected to a specific purpose in human history. Explicit in every person's DNA is a hunger for significance, which can only be fulfilled in the spiritual dimension. Given that the Kingdom is eternal and all encompassing, while the natural realm is finite and limited, spiritual principles and consequences are interwoven into all of life.

The tendency to compartmentalize and disregard the spiritual significance of all areas of life will limit our success and prevent the realization of true destiny. Conversely, if we are attentive and receptive, we can hear in our spirit what is being spoken to us of our eternal significance wherever the journey leads, from the broadest vision to the most minute detail.

- Destiny can only be achieved by accessing the spiritual realm.

- We are spirit beings, who temporarily live in a body—the connection with the spiritual world of the Kingdom is Spirit to spirit.

- Our spiritual response leads us to deeper levels of character development.

- The Father wants to reveal His essential nature and purpose to us in every circumstance of life, and actively encourages us to seek that revelation.

- The Spirit is never wrong. Your natural mind can only receive logic and information. Your spirit receives wisdom from the Holy Spirit that is pure, distinct and never wrong.

- Learn to live in our spirit. *"Those who are **continuously** led by the Spirit, they are the sons of God"* (Romans 8:14, author's paraphrase). Grow from being a child of God to being a son.

Action

A developing spiritual experience (**child** of God) enables us to access resources beyond ourselves in Christ. How would we develop a mature relationship with God to move toward **Sonship** — where we seek to establish spirituality as a way of life?

What are the areas of life that you have compartmentalized? If you viewed all of life as spiritual, document what might change.

Value Statement

Since all of life is spiritual and our destiny can only be achieved through embracing a spiritual paradox, we give the Holy Spirit access to all areas of our lives through our spirits. This spiritual paradox of life gives meaning to our past, helps us prioritize our present, and provides a compass to discern our future.

Exercise

1. Explain why there is no sacred and secular divide in the Kingdom of Heaven.
2. Explain the damage that having such a divide can have on relationships all around you.
3. What does it mean for you to be "continuously led by the Spirit" across all areas of life?
4. If it is true that maintaining this divide leads to a form of religious mindset and behavior, how could that affect the ministry of the believer in the world?

What Kind of Partnership With Leaders?

1. Leaders want to see prophetic people overcoming failure in themselves, and being a voice of encouragement to inspire others to do the same.
2. A teachable spirit when loving feedback is given regarding methodology and presentation of prophecy.
3. Leaders actively working with prophetic people to determine what kind of negativity is affecting the congregation, and how to overcome it using teaching and prophetic impartation.
4. That prophetic people can be utilized on the front line of ridding the church of negative mindsets and behaviors.

Final Applications

5. Learning how to use proclamation as a tool to bring freedom and ongoing liberty.

6. Developing a spirit of compassion that carries with it the power to create momentum in the lives of people.

7. Learning to view people in the Spirit, not in the flesh.

8. To see prophetic people in a viable partnership with pastoral ministry.

9. That prophetic people understood and practiced both Impartation and Process in their own lives!

10. Develop the right attitude of heart and mind in order to use admonition positively in a prophetic context.

11. How to develop the identity of others and to seek their highest good.

12. Knowing how to challenge circumstances with the correct use of a prophetic word.

What Kind of Help and Support From Leaders?

1. Prophetic people need help and support to empower them to develop new mindsets.

2. Leaders can be very inspirational to people who are developing their prophetic gift. Conversations about content and delivery of prophecy are always helpful.

3. Use a small group setting to enable prophetic people to develop their skills of encouragement and inspiration in the battle against negativity.

4. Provide a dialogue forum where the poor practice of prophecy can be redeveloped, changed, and upgraded.

5. Connect prophetic people to a greater understanding, experience, and practice of the goodness of God.

6. Develop their prophetic gift to make it compatible with the Good News of Jesus.

7. Ensuring that pharisaical behavior is adjusted so that people can represent God's holiness in a righteous manner.

8. Liberate gifted people into a deep experience of the affections of God.

9. That gifted people understand the difference between worldly and Kingdom shame, and work on helping people to find the grace they need to be transformed.

10. That an action plan be developed so that prophetic people can eliminate their own negativity and become a voice of encouragement to the Church and beyond.

A Prophecy—Inheritance and Glory

BELOVED, PERMISSION IS GRANTED BECAUSE of who I Am, not because of what you see about yourself. The Kingdom is about Me; about who I am, what I see, and how I like to order things in the world of My heart.

It is My perception of you that must govern your heart; My appraisal of you that must make your heart glad and your mind renewed. So I say to you, rest in the fullness of My heart toward you.

I have a huge heart for you; a mighty, all encompassing compassion for you. I understand your struggles and your weaknesses. In My great love for you, I have set aside an ocean of grace and peace for you personally—more grace and peace than you will ever need for yourself. Understand this, Beloved: I make the fullness of My grace and peace available in such huge proportions that each of My people could influence and affect thousands of people through this abundance.

Be overwhelmed, Beloved; it is the only way you can understand Me. I always give more than what is needed. I adore abundance. I love outrageous grace. I am the peace that passes all understanding. I love being who I Am. I love Myself dearly. It is because I dwell in the magnificence of love that I Am able to love so amazingly well.

As My Beloved, it is your duty, your joy and your delight to be overwhelmed by love. You are My Beloved. You are dear to Me. You are dear to Me. You are dear to Me. I want you. I have pursued you. I have captured your heart and now I seek to captivate you.

The law of life in Christ Jesus is *"Give and it shall be given to you, pressed down, shaken together, and running over."* This is My word, Beloved. My word is who I Am. I AM THE LIVING WORD. That means that I live by the same word that I bestow on you.

I do not seek your adoration, I seek your blessing. Adoration is a consequence of a life, Beloved, seeking to love in return. I seek to love and love and love. I seek to love for the sake of loving, for I AM Love. As My love is poured out and received, it comes back to Me.

The more extravagantly you allow yourself to receive love, the more you will become Beloved and the stronger your passion for Me will become. I give extravagantly, therefore, I receive extravagantly. It is a law of the Spirit of life and I love it!

Final Applications

Permission has already been granted for you to explore, discover, and own extravagant living in My Spirit. As promises are revealed, permission is released and provision unfolds.

There is not a single blessing in Heaven that you cannot have. It is your inheritance. I Am your inheritance and you are Mine. Every blessing is yours. Your ability to receive can only be limited by your identity.

As you grow up in all things in Me, blessings become available to My Presence in you. I attract blessing, and when you open yourself to all that I Am and want to be for you, blessing becomes attracted to you.

This is another law of life in the Spirit, Beloved. Live in Me and I will live in you. Abide in me, let My words abide in you, and you may ask what you will.

I wish that all My people would live extravagant lives in love; that they would receive me wonderfully, so that I may give to them outrageously.

What spiritual blessing do you need at this time? By this I do not mean love, joy or peace; they are yours always, for all times and all circumstances. They are freely available in absolute fullness, forever. Enjoy! They belong to the nature of God in the Holy Spirit and you are already a partaker of these things as you abide in Me.

Beloved, it is your time of manifest destiny to be revealed. You have been chosen with all foreknowledge and zeal on My part, that you should occupy a high place in My affections and live a blameless life before Me as one who is fully the Beloved.

Always, My intention is that you would be the Beloved of My heart. Do not think of yourself outside of romance and intimacy. The faith that works best is the one that is built upon acceptance in the Beloved. Belief is ignited by romance. I am the Lover of your soul; therefore, you are the Beloved of God.

By My intentionality all of Heaven is opened to you; by your response it is released. Permission is granted for you to assume the best, believe for the outrageous and experience everything My heart permits. Hear me shouting, "YES!!!" Beloved.

You are always with Me and all I have is yours. My Presence reveals all and provides all. I have given My blessing for you to possess your possessions. All you want from where you live in Me. It is done! It is the kind intention of My will that you should fully belong to Me, for Me to enjoy!

You belong to Me for the express purpose of experiencing the riches of My glory. All of your life is about having a divine encounter with My glory that leaves you open-mouthed with astonishment and dancing outrageously in thanksgiving.

It is My intention that the majesty and glory of My grace in your life should lead you into such a dynamic of praise that you would be exposed to what Heaven takes for granted.

A Prophecy — Inheritance and Glory

All of this is readily available, freely bestowed with full permission granted for you to take it, hold it, and enjoy. My grace is so powerful it fully redeems every condition. My grace is My permission. I lavish it upon you. It is inexhaustible. It can never run out.

Grace can never be given in small doses. It can only be lavished. Grace is opulent, extravagant, profuse, exuberant, prolific and sumptuous. It is bountiful, plentiful, generous and openhanded. It is lush, copious and free! Because it cannot be given in small parcels, it cannot fully be received unless your encounter with it fully exposes your life to unparalleled and unprecedented favor.

Grace requires insight and wisdom on a huge scale so that you might fully experience the intentionality of your God. Everything in Heaven and on earth is summed up in the fullness of grace in Jesus.

My grace is so glorious to you, says the Lord, it should become a focal point for a new entry into dynamic worship. Grace elevates you, Beloved. BE LIFTED UP!

Grace is so amazing. It glorifies Me as you live in it and therefore your experience of Me becomes glorious. The riches of My grace make you affluent in the Kingdom. Your life becomes a treasure chest of My goodness and kindness. Grace empowers you to become the Beloved of God.

Redemption, forgiveness, change and empowerment are all a part of the richness of grace that I freely bestow upon you. It is My desire that grace should elevate you above your usual, natural experience of life so that you may see Heaven and taste the powers of the age to come.

I love to lavish grace on you. My grace is exuberant; it is a vibrant enthusiasm toward you from My heart. Grace is vivacious, cheerful, lighthearted and brilliant. It is also strong, powerful, healing, loving, generous and merciful. Grace is full of beauty and laughter. It is full of understanding and compassion. It is the door of entry into continuous new dimensions of ongoing permission.

Be excited about grace, Beloved, even as I am excited about you. It is grace that enables you to have bright, vivid, memorable encounters with My heart. Stand on the ground of grace, dear heart, and ABIDE.

As you learn to value GRACE, it will propel you into experiences with Me that will release WISDOM into your life. Wisdom is the active knowledge of how I think, perceive and act.

Grace will give you insight into how to walk with me, in humility with boldness. Grace must affect you, Beloved, it must affect you gloriously. Grace opens the way for you to become as intentional as I am. I have purposed so much for you in your identity in My Son. Grace helps you realize My plans for you.

My grace is My permission. It's the place where I kiss you, touch you and change you. It is the place where I embrace who you are and empower you to become like Me. My grace is My gift and My blessing to you. It is My permission in your life that creates joy, love and laughter.

Final Applications

It is grace that will position you before Me in order that you may receive. Your inheritance is a fixed thing in My heart. I know who you are and what you will become. On the road of your life I have placed blessings, provisions and authority. They are often situated next to crisis, enemy activity and human opposition, just where you need them to be so that you may always overcome.

I will teach you to be more than a conqueror. In times of distress, a conqueror does more than survive the battle, they prosper in the fight. They do not just keep themselves free; they rescue people around them. They do not just stand and hold their ground; they take ground on behalf of others who are less motivated.

I have predestined your inheritance in My kind intentionality toward you. Provision abounds, Beloved, but your eyes must be on Me to see it. All provision is bound up in worship, thanksgiving and rejoicing. These disciplines keep your heart open, your mind renewed and your eyes bright and watchful.

I have already worked out who you are and what you will become. It is settled in My heart. Enjoy the process of discovery as I will enjoy being lavish and enthusiastic toward you.

Develop a mindset that says, "I cannot fail because I am amazingly loved." Move away from past failures; this is a new day. There is a fresh mindset and a renewed hope that I am bestowing upon you. Do not be subject to old thinking, but allow Me to renew you in the spirit of your mind.

I am **present–future** in My heart toward you. I see who you are now and who you will become in Me. The provisions for your life are tied to the identity that you receive from Me. See yourself therefore as I see you!

I will supply all your needs, but that is simply the baseline of faith. There is a bigger, bolder place than that, which I want to release to you. It is a place which is tied to how you view yourself.

Having your needs met is for the time when you are struggling and not doing well. I will empower you to receive on your worst day. All My children may have their needs met, always. However, I do not want you to remain children. I have sent My Spirit that you may learn how to grow up into all things in Christ. Those led by My Spirit can become sons in the Kingdom.

My true sons live in a place above need. They live in their inheritance! I want you to come to a place in My Spirit where your identity releases your provision. You ask from your inheritance, not from your need.

I want you to know your inheritance. I want you to plan, strategize and budget from that source; that you would have such a confident expectation in Me! That in the place of high praise you would confidently declare your identity in Me and confess your inheritance before My throne. Such prayer will open windows in Heaven. Creative miracles, outrageous provisions and incredible favor will fall upon you. No good thing will I withhold from those who walk uprightly in My Spirit. Beloved, do not be bowed down nor weighed down by

A Prophecy — Inheritance and Glory

your circumstances. Stand up, come up and rise up to the place of your identity, manifest destiny, and gather your inheritance.

Behold, this is the place that I have set aside for you. I do not want you to be earthbound, pleading out of need. I want you to come into Heaven, into My Presence, and worship, and then boldly ask for your inheritance. I gladly gave it to the prodigal son. I gladly gave it to the elder brother. How I will joyfully give it to you!

I want you to inherit because I long to see you living in the praise of My glory. For My glory to fill the earth, I need My Beloved to become more glorious.

I want you to be fully sealed into My Holy Spirit, fully locked into an experience of the Holy Spirit where every promise **must** be fulfilled. THIS IS THE GOSPEL!

I give you a down payment today on that revelation. There is so much more to come. An abundance beyond your imagination to receive—so big, in fact, that the revelation of it can only come to you in the form of a dream that must be interpreted. Ask Me for dreams, dear heart, that you might perceive the fullness of what I have planned.

Your natural eyes and ears cannot receive what I am planning. The imagination of your heart cannot conceive of what is in Mine for you. The place of dreaming will take you outside of your normal experience to access the fullness of My desire for you.

Every time I take you to a deeper level of the Spirit, the purse strings are also opened. Every time I extend your vision and calling, your account gets increased too. Your inheritance is incremental, tied to the ongoing calling and identity that I am showing you! THERE IS MORE!

Permission has been granted for you to have a spirit of wisdom and revelation in the knowledge of Me—so that you may fully know Me. I WANT TO BE KNOWN! KNOW ME! KNOW ME! KNOW ME!

When you perceive Me, you can perceive yourself in Me. As your revelation of Me is upgraded, so your identity grows into a deeper place of Sonship. The eyes of your heart will be enlightened and you will know, even as you are fully known.

It is My intention that you would know My confident expectation in the calling I have given you; that you would know what I want to achieve in and through you; that you would know My full vision for your life and calling.

It is My intention that you would understand and have experiences of Me that are glorious; that you would know glory, be bathed in glory and that you would have a radiant idea of your God; that the God you encounter in your Heavenly experiences would be the God who manifests in you on earth.

It is My intention that you would understand the whole concept of inheritance. My inheritance in you and yours in Me! Inherit Me! Inherit Me! Inherit

Me! You are My heir and you are joint-heirs with Jesus. Partner with Us. Come under the download of what We have set aside for you.

It is My intention that you would live a life overwhelmed; that you would experience what it means to live in the surpassing greatness of My power. I have been drawing you for years, out of mediocrity into a deluge of My Spirit. I want you to be baptized into a vast and stunning power, that you may overthrow the worker of darkness and devastate the enemy wherever you find him.

Beloved, you are coming into the season of My power and My intention. You have latitude to explore and to ask and to seek, knowing that you *will* find, you *will* receive and things *will* open up.

This is the season where I please Myself among you. Do not ask Me for things out of need. Ask in line with the destiny I am showing you. This is the place of My indulgence. I will declare My partiality. I will spoil you. I will spoil you. I will spoil you. I will give you more than you ask for — so ask big! Live large. Become bigger on the inside than your circumstances on the outside.

Act out of your own growth. Do not merely pray for the present things. Ask Me with the future in mind, for you are in a time of acceleration. Ask from the future so that you might build for the future.

I am indulging Myself. I intend to freely yield to the pleasure of blessing you. I will give you the desires of your heart as you delight yourself in Me.

My indulgence is in line with My ability to do more than you can require of Me—to show Myself glorious on your behalf. The Lord of Hosts is in your midst; strong, powerful and overruling the enemy.

Indulgence is the place of My throne in your midst—authority ruling and reigning so that My goodness would reach out to fill the earth. Indulgence is Me bringing all the fullness of Heaven into the earth so that goodness would battle with wickedness and overcome it; that the whole earth be filled with the glory of God and the Beloved Bride would be made ready for her Husband.

A Prophecy—Inheritance and Glory

Recommended Reading

Title	Author	Publisher
Hearing God	Dallas Willard	InterVarsity Press
The Gift of Prophecy	Jack Deere	Vine Books
Surprised by the Voice of God	Jack Deere	Zondervan
Growing in the Prophetic	Mike Bickle	Kingsway
The Seer	James Goll	Destiny Image
Prophetic Etiquette	Micheal Sullivant	Creation House
The Prophets' Notebook	Barry Kissel	Kingsway
User Friendly Prophecy	Larry Randolph	Destiny Image
Prophecy in Practice	Jim Paul	Monarch Books
Can You Hear Me?: Tuning in to the God Who Speaks	Brad Jersak	Trafford Press
When Heaven Invades Earth	Bill Johnson	Treasure House
Knowledge of the Holy	A.W. Tozer	O.M. Publishing
The Pleasures of Loving God	Mike Bickle	Creation House
Manifest Presence	Jack Hayford	Chosen
Living the Spirit-Formed Life	Jack Hayford	Regal
The Agape Road	Bob Mumford	Lifechangers
The Sensitivity of the Spirit	R.T. Kendall	Hodder & Stoughton
Living in the Freedom of the Spirit	Tom Marshall	Sovereign World
Secrets of the Secret Place	Bob Sorge	Oasis House
The Heart of Worship	Matt Redman	Regal
Experiencing the Depths of Jesus Christ	Jeanne Guyon	Seedsowers
The Unsurrendered Soul	Liberty Savard	Bridge-Logos

About the Prophetic Equipping Series

Graham began teaching prophetic schools in 1986. Eight years later he wrote *Developing Your Prophetic Gifting*, a book which has won universal acclaim. Translated into numerous languages, reprinted many times over and published by several companies, it has been a best seller and widely regarded as a classic. Graham has continued to develop new material each year in the Schools of Prophecy. Now after almost twenty years of teaching continuously upgrading material, the School of Prophecy has developed into one of the finest teaching programs on the prophetic gift, ministry and office of a Prophet. This new material effectively makes *Developing Your Prophetic Gifting* redundant.

The Prophetic Equipping Series encompasses six volumes that combine classic teaching with the journal format so popular in the *Being with God Series*. It also embraces a workshop and training manual, with emphasis on producing one of the finest teaching aids on the prophetic gift and ministry. These manuals are appropriate for individual, small group or church-wide use. All Christians can prophesy and would benefit from Graham's wisdom and experience in ministry. The assignments, exercises, workshops, lectio divina and other material are designed to further the understanding of the prophetic gift, ministry and office. If used properly, the process will develop accountability for prophetic people, healthy pasturing of the prophetic, and give relevant questions for leadership and prophetic people to ask one another. The series includes:

Volume 1 – *Approaching the Heart of Prophecy*
Volume 2 – *Prophecy & Responsibility*
Volume 3 – *Prophetic Wisdom*
Volume 4 – *The Prophetic Impact*
Volume 5 – *Prophetic Partnerships*
Volume 6 – *Prophecy and the Ways of God*

To find more information on Graham's training schools and events, please visit www.GrahamCooke.com

About the Author

Graham Cooke is part of The Mission's core leadership team, working with senior team leader, David Crone, in Vacaville, California. Graham's role includes training, consulting, mentoring and being part of a think tank that examines the journey from present to future.

He is married to Theresa, who has a passion for worship and dance. She loves to be involved in intercession, warfare, and setting people free. She cares about injustice and abuse, and has compassion on people who are sick, suffering and disenfranchised.

They have six children and two grandchildren. Ben and Seth both reside and work in the UK. Ben is developing as a writer, is very funny, and probably knows every movie ever made. Seth is a musician, a deep thinker with a caring outlook and an amazing capacity for mischief.

Sophie and her husband Mark live in Vacaville and attend The Mission. Sophie & Mark are the Operations Managers of Brilliant Book House, the publishing company of Graham Cooke. Sophie has played a significant part in Graham's ministry for a number of years, and has helped develop resources, new books and journals, as well as organize events. Mark and Sophie are a warm-hearted, friendly, deeply humorous couple with lots of friends. Mark and Sophie have two daughters. Evelyn (August 2006) is a delight; a happy little soul who likes music, loves to dance and enjoys books. Annabelle (December 2008) is lovely, happy, content and very tiny.

Their other daughters are Alexis, who is loving, kind and gentle, and very intuitive and steadfast toward her friends; and Alyssa, a very focused and determined young woman who is fun-loving with a witty sense of humor.

Also, Graham and Theresa have two beautiful young women, Julianne and Megan, both in Australia, who are a part of their extended family.

Graham is a popular conference speaker and is well known for his training programs on the prophetic, spiritual warfare, intimacy and devotional life, leadership, spirituality and the church in transition. He functions as a consultant and freethinker to businesses, churches, and organizations, enabling them to develop strategically. He has a passion to establish the Kingdom and build prototype churches that can fully reach a post-modern society.

A strong part of Graham's ministry is in producing finances and resources to the poor and disenfranchised in developing countries. He supports many projects specifically for widows, orphans and people in the penal system. He hates abuse of women and works actively against human trafficking and the sex slave trade, including women caught up in prostitution and pornography.

If you would like to invite Graham to minister at an event, please complete the online Ministry Invitation Form at www.GrahamCooke.com.

If you wish to become a financial partner for the sake of missions and compassionate acts across the nations, please contact his office at office@grahamcooke.com, and his administrative assistant will be happy to assist you.

Graham has many prayer partners who play a significant part in supporting his ministry through intercession and sponsorship. Prayer partners have the honor to be Graham's shield. They are his defensive covering that allows him to advance the Kingdom all over the world. The partners are a vital part of Graham's interdependent team.

If you are interested in becoming a prayer partner, please contact his international coordinator, at prayer@grahamcooke.com.

You may contact Graham by writing to:

Graham Cooke
6391 Leisure Town Road
Vacaville, California
95687, USA

www.GrahamCooke.com